RELIGIOUS PLURALISM

A Metaphorical Approach

Chris Arthur

The Davies Group, Publishers   *Aurora, Colorado USA*

Religious Pluralism: A Metaphorical Approach
© 2000, Chris Arthur

The Davies Group, Publishers
Attn: Permissions
PO Box 440140
Aurora CO 80044-0140
USA

Library of Congress Cataloging-in-Publication Data

Arthur, C. J. (Christopher John), 1955-
  Religious Pluralism: a metaphorical approach/Chris Arthur.
    p. cm.
  Includes bibliographical references and index.
  ISBN 1-888570-54-7 (alk. paper)
    1. Religious pluralism. 2. Religion--Philosophy. 3. Metaphor-- Religious aspects. I. Title

BL85 .A78 2000
291.1'72--dc21

99-056327

Cover photo credit FPG International LLC/iSwoop

Printed in the United States of America
January, 2000

0 9 8 7 6 5 4 3 2 1

Metaphor is, for human beings, what instinctual groping is for the rest of the universe—the power of getting from here to there.

Sallie McFague TeSelle

CONTENTS

CHAPTER 1

A REVOLUTION IN RELIGIOUS CONSCIOUSNESS

THIS BOOK is about a revolution in religious consciousness, the impact of which affects us all. We are living at a moment in history in which access to the different religions of humankind is of unparalleled range and depth. There is, of course, considerable variation from individual to individual in terms of how far people delve into the information about the world's faiths which now lies so readily to hand. There remain some cultural enclaves which, either through choice or geographical isolation, are still relatively insulated against outside influences, but the main trends of history, the major currents which pulse through our time and bear us towards the future, are inexorably pluralist in tendency. They promote a multifaceted awareness rather than securing the unchallenged dominance of any one religious way of seeing things. This is not to deny the upsurge in fundamentalism that has been a common reaction to these historical currents. Such fundamentalism is, however, very much a defensive strategy against the revolution I am talking about, rather than evidence that it is not happening. Fundamentalism attempts to make boundaries impermeable, to seal particular faiths into conceptually airtight capsules whose territories are independent of, and uninfluenced by, other traditions. To attempt to retreat into artificial isolation in this way is to swim against the tide of historical reality. As James Wiggins puts it, "the reality of religious diversity has become inescapable in the contemporary world."[1]

Our grandparents (perhaps even our parents) are likely to have been raised in the singularity of one belief system which, for the most part, commanded majority assent in the bounded, national societies of which they were a part (its internal diversities notwithstanding, and whatever their individual stance towards such a belief system may have been).

We, our children and grandchildren, on the other hand, are citizens of a quite different religious world. Unlike our forebears, we have been made aware (through the media, travel, the multi-ethnic nature of modern cities) of a number of different outlooks, none of which enjoy the same level of unified allegiance as those of previous generations. Moreover, beyond the immediate impress of religious pluralism upon us, the resources of modern scholarship now allow anyone with the time and inclination to do so to become immersed in an enormity of detail about the different faiths. Specific exceptions could, obviously, be cited in the face of this raft of generalizations. But utterly dwarfing the significance of these exceptions is the fact that our religious landscape has undergone seismic changes in the course of only two or three generations. This book focuses on what I see as the principal landmark of the contemporary religious scene, namely the fact of our being informed (at whatever level) about Buddhism, Christianity, Hinduism, Islam, Jainism, Judaism, Sikhism, Taoism and so on, rather than knowing about only one religion. In such a situation, how do we decide which, if any, faith to follow? Do any of their teachings speak to our particular situation? Do any offer a lens through which the confusion, complexity and apparent randomness of life might be refracted into some sustainable sense-giving vision, according to which we might live our lives?

It is one thing to be a Buddhist or a Christian or a Muslim or a Sikh and to be faced with the rich plurality of religions which flourish around the globe. One will then have guidance from within one's own faith as to how the others are to be viewed.[2] This is not to say that the encounter of the faithful with the faithful of other traditions is unproblematic. On the contrary, it is something fraught with difficulty and danger, and heavy with the possibility (and reality) of violence. While readers from within particular faith traditions will, I hope, find much of what follows interesting and relevant, the book is not primarily addressed to them. Rather, it is concerned with the situation of the individual who claims allegiance to no particular faith, yet who is aware of a range of different religious outlooks. How is such a person to proceed in terms of evaluating the religious hypotheses which offer such apparently different views of the world? How is one to decide which, if any, of the world's religions offers a formula for what we might call "right living?" In the pages that follow, I attempt to show how someone might move towards answering such important and difficult questions. The book is not written in defense of any particular faith. Instead, it explores religions from the point of view of someone not presently committed to any of them.

The common view of religious pluralism tends to see it (understandably) as something that has enormous potential to wreak havoc on human relationships. It is something associated with the terrible and tragic stories of interdenominational hatred in Northern Ireland, interreligious conflict in the Middle East, the murderous tensions between Hindu and Muslim on the Indian subcontinent, violence between Buddhist and non-Buddhist in Tibet. I accept (as I think everyone must) that differences in religious outlook and allegiance have indeed led to quite dreadful acts of intolerance, cruelty and mayhem. However, I want to suggest that the revolution in religious consciousness which we are experiencing, even though along the way it will undoubtedly lead to further inter-religious conflict, also has a much more positive potential. In fact it holds the promise of a paradigm shift in religious thinking, in that it provides the raw material for enormously enhanced creativity in this realm of human thought.[3] The extent to which this potential and promise will be realized is, of course, highly uncertain. We are only at the very beginning of a new epoch. We can only speculate about what events will be born into actuality as its uncertain duration unfolds into the fabric of lived time.

Let us not under-estimate the seriousness of the situation with which we are attempting to deal. It is not as if someone who was chromatically undecided was faced with a rainbow of colors and had to pick out a favorite. Colors do not offer a view of the world, suggest reasons for living, comment on the nature and purpose of human existence, advance an opinion as to who, ultimately, we are and how we should be spending the moments of our brief and fragile span of sentience here beneath the stars. Colors do not judge us, they do not divide families, neighborhoods, nations, persecute and wage war on each other. Colors do not suggest ethical norms, lay down dietary requirements, establish rituals for birth, marriage and death. Religious pluralism constitutes an arena for choice that is neither trivial nor easy. Ultimate issues, strong passions, deep loyalties are at stake. Decisions made have the potential to be life-changing for individuals. Cumulatively, they may lead to momentous changes in terms of how society and history will be shaped. As we enter the hall of mirrors, constituted by all the different and diverse religions of our kind, we should remember that this is where people seek validation for their deepest aspirations and dreams, this is where they go for solace when they are feeling alone and naked and vulnerable in the face of time and accident and death. This is, for some, the holiest of holies, where what would otherwise be random and senseless existence crystallizes into an altogether different value. This is where people commune with their gods and spirits, hear the haunting notes of the eternal and the infinite echoing mysteriously beneath the babble of their everyday discourse. This is where they think of their souls and seek salvation from the pain and terror of being which might otherwise engulf them. We are entering territory sacred to millions, in which we will be surrounded by ideas which people have been willing to die (and to kill) for.

❧

To move from life and death issues to matters of terminology may seem like a clumsy, grating shift in intellectual gear. But it is important to be as clear-minded as possible when dealing with so emotive and complex an area. So, before proceeding further, I want to explain the sense in which I am using the term "pluralism." This is particularly necessary given that, in a religious context, this word now admits of various specialist meanings that take it well beyond the realms of ordinary usage. Ian Hamnet makes a useful distinction between two now common senses:

the term can refer either to a state of affairs (namely, the co-existence of two or more major religious systems within one society or culture), or to an ideological posture, commonly associated with a "liberal", syncretistic and relativist approach to religious belief as such. In the first sense, only a society or a culture or a state can be described as "plural". In the ideological sense, however, it is possible to describe an individual, or a school, or a theology, or a tradition of thought and practice, as manifesting "religious pluralism."[4]

A good example of an ideological use of pluralism comes in Peter Byrne's *Prolegomena to Religious Pluralism*, in which he states that "by 'pluralism' I refer not to the fact that there is a plurality of religions in the world, but to one intellectual response to that fact."[5] Unlike Byrne, I am not using pluralism in any ideological sense, but simply to describe the key characteristic of the religious revolution in which we are all caught up. It is a characteristic which has, of course, quite enormous ideological significance, given that our attitudes are likely to be very different before and after an encounter with it. However, to use the same term to describe both these changed attitudes, and the factor which gives rise to them, does not strike me as helpful. By pluralism I simply mean the fact of our awareness of many different religions, not the way in which we respond to this situation (though it is a fact whose huge and pressing weight of implication I hope to impress on readers' minds). So, anyone *au fait* with the pluralist stances offered in the work of such scholars as, most prominently, John Hick[6], should try to remove the theological turn given to pluralism there. It is not a turn that I shall employ.

Let me impose on the reader's patience a little longer (I know that fine distinctions in terminology are tiresome, but it is important to pin down this key term). Diana Eck, director of the admirable Harvard Pluralism Project, argues for a distinction between "pluralism" and "plurality":

> plurality is just diversity, plain and simple—splendid, colorful, maybe even threatening. Such diversity does not, however, have to affect me. I can observe diversity. I can even celebrate diversity as the saying goes. But I have to *participate* in pluralism.[7]

While I hope to show how experiencing a situation of religious pluralism does in fact demand engagement, reflection, decision—rather than
just observation—and that it has the potential to lead to new ideas, I'm
afraid I will not follow Eck's distinction. Instead, I will assume that
pluralism and plurality are effectively synonymous. Perhaps unusually
for an academic, I am using the words to mean exactly what a dictionary tells you that they mean (i.e. pluralism = plurality; plurality = the
state or fact of being plural; plural = numbering more than one.)

A final point about terminology. In interesting contrast to Diana
Eck, James Wiggins suggests that "religious diversity" is preferable to
"religious pluralism" because:

> the word diversity emphasizes differences from which some learn-
> ing can occur, whereas pluralism conveys residual confidence in
> some deep underlying commonality that all too often minimizes
> differences or dismisses them as unimportant.[8]

I hope that my common-sense, non-ideological use of pluralism will
prevent me falling foul of Wiggins' criticism. I certainly do not intend
to suggest by this term the existence of any sort of underlying commonality. The question of the existence, or extent, of shared territory between the different faiths remains one of the most difficult (and important) questions in this whole realm of inquiry.

〜〜〜

Since this book requires the reader to engage his or her imagination in order to make the central metaphor come alive, let me reempha-
size what has been said above via a simple imaginative exercise which
will further help to set the scene.

Wherever you happen to be, imagine who would have been here,
in this space that you now occupy, five, ten, twenty, a hundred, two
hundred years ago. Specifically, how would the religious filaments of
time have changed over these periods? As you go step by step back into
history, how would the people who were once warm and alive here, in
this same place where you now draw breath and radiate your own indi-

vidual warmth, have thought about religion? Obviously the exercise will require some deft adjustment for some of the locations occupied by the unmet and unknown community constituted by the readers of this book. If in some mode of transport whose very existence would not survive more than the briefest step back in history, think of how travelers between your destinations five, ten, a hundred years ago would have gone about their journey, what they might have believed, how they are likely to have viewed the world religiously. To be conducted with any degree of subtlety, the exercise would require a considerable grasp of history, an awareness of the way in which all sorts of influences came to bear on religion. The growth of science and technology, Darwin's theory of evolution, the impact of developments in philosophy and history, the rising tide of globalization—a whole slew of complex factors would need to be taken on board to fully map even a single religious filament rooted to one place over, say, two centuries. For my purposes, though, a very rough sketch, rather than a detailed analysis, is all that is necessary.

From this, I think it is clear that one of the most striking trends which this kind of imaginative time-travel will reveal is the way in which our awareness of religious pluralism radically increases as we approach the present. How many books on religions would your library or book shop have held a decade ago, two, three, five decades ago? Would an individual in 1899 have had any real concept of the number or diversity of human religions? Would he or she have routinely encountered representatives of the different world faiths? Imagine travelers between continents before the relative ease of modern aircraft. Would their traveling companions have believed and practiced significantly different faiths? Could they have hoped to find members of every major faith living in virtually every city on earth? Think of the syllabus of subjects covered by a university only fifty years ago. Would students routinely have had on their shelves copies of a selection of the world's scriptures— informed, undogmatic treatments of Hinduism, Sikhism, Taoism, Islam, guides to Zen meditation, Sufi mysticism, New Age philosophy, Christian spirituality? Consider the range of religious reporting in newspapers today and in the 1920s; examine the ways in which television's religious content has changed over a much shorter time span; be amazed at the exuberant growth of diverse religious groups which is evidenced so richly on the Internet. How many of our parents or grandparents would have dreamed of visiting Benares, of having friends, colleagues and neighbors who observe Ramadan and go on hajj, of seeing a new Hindu temple built amidst the glass and concrete of a Western city, of learning how to meditate from a Buddhist teacher? Imagine the surprise of Americans at the beginning of this century had they been able to look ahead and read the following details from a web-site at the end of the century:

> There are Islamic centers and mosques, Hindu and Buddhist temples and meditation centers in virtually every major American city. The encounter between people of very different religious traditions takes place in the proximity of our own cities and neighborhoods. How Americans of all faiths begin to engage with one another in shaping a positive pluralism is one of the most important questions American society faces in the years ahead.[9]

The fact is, we are living very much in the presence of a still evolving revolution in religious consciousness. We enjoy proximity to, and access to information about, a range of religions, in a manner that has never before happened in history. The world has become, in living memory, a religiously plural planet. Of course it has always been so, but the *realization* that it is so is a relatively recent event in the human story (and an event whose implications are likely to be profound and wide-ranging). This is not to say that people in earlier times were entirely unaware that there were "other" faiths. What is special about the twentieth/twenty-first century is that our awareness does not need to be confined to the superficial and dismissive. We are brought into contact with different religions on a day-to-day basis, not as something strange or exotic or threatening, but as part and parcel of who our friends, neighbors, colleagues, and relations are. And we can easily learn a great deal about the histories, philosophies, ethics, rituals, aesthetics of all these different faiths, beyond their immediate impress on us, by turning to the readily available work of scholarship in religious studies.

In today's information society we are made conscious, in a manner that is historically unprecedented, that the religious life of our species is diverse and plural. Of course there are still situations in which singularity and ignorance characterize the religious milieu. The outcome of this revolution in religious consciousness is neither individually nor geographically even. But, as we move towards the millennium, it becomes ever more obvious to ever more of its inhabitants that the Earth is astonishingly rich in the number and variety of religious outlooks it supports. Unless we are prepared to accept the accident of birth as an adequate reason for religious allegiance, such awareness raises some very difficult questions about choice and commitment. The individual is now faced with a perplexing range of often apparently conflicting religious pictures of the world. Which, if any, show things the way they really are? Which, if any, offer a vision of things that the questing individual might adopt as his or her own outlook? Do any of these religious pictures offer a reliable map for living? Should any be discarded as dangerously inaccurate and misleading?

Enormous though the change in our religious milieu has been, it is not always easy to appreciate the truly revolutionary nature of a situation one has grown used to (which is why I am taking such pains to state what may, to some readers, be obvious). Let me underline the matter with a specific example. Today it is very easy for us to forget that for many centuries of their existence Buddhism and Christianity were largely unaware of each other's outlook. The scale of that unawareness is staggering. For a significant stretch of history it almost amounted to two halves of the globe going about their business in virtual ignorance of the existence, let alone the beliefs, of the other. And when Buddhism first began to dawn on the Western consciousness, it appeared as a "monstrous religion," as an "abominable sect" founded by a "very wicked man." It was ridiculed and rejected as "a plague," "a gangrene," "a ridiculous doctrine."[10] This type of easy dismissal, brought about by an almost complete ignorance of the facts, is wholly untenable once serious engagement with the history and thought of Buddhism becomes possible. Prior to the permeability of religious boundaries brought about by globalization (a term I will explain shortly), the Buddhist concept of *sunyata*, or emptiness—to focus on just one idea—was unknown and irrelevant to Christian theologians. Now, as Langdon Gilkey puts it, "a close encounter with the nothingness of Buddhism will effect noteworthy changes in every recognizable form of contemporary discourse about God."[11] Previously, from a non-Buddhist perspective, the sound of *sunyata* was simply unknown. Now it is one among many new notes available in the massively extended repertoire afforded by a situation of multi-religious informedness. Today, Christian thinkers can count Buddhist ideas and practices among the building blocks from which they may construct theologies and spiritual exercises. Not surprisingly, as Stephen Batchelor notes, "today it is hard to grasp that Europeans and Americans had no coherent conception of Buddhism until 150 years ago."[12] We have moved only very recently from the monoglot perspectives allowed by single, unchallenged dialects, to being (at least potentially) religiously multi-lingual. For any individual seriously attempting to grapple with religious issues, this is a hugely significant change. And it is a change which, beyond the individual, has far-reaching implications in terms of ethics, education, politics and law, as societies take steps to ensure that tolerance, rather than extremism, attends the unavoidable inter-religious relationships which now criss-cross our world.

～～

This book offers a metaphorical approach to religious pluralism. The main metaphor, introduced in Chapter 3, is that of the hall of mirrors. I use this as a shorthand symbol for the religiously plural situation in which so many of us find ourselves today. Being in the hall of mirrors means being aware of different religious outlooks. Such awareness poses problems for the individual, in terms of establishing a sense of identity, direction and value. However, the hall of mirrors is by no means the only metaphor which readers will encounter. Most of the chapters are structured around a lead metaphor (the slap and the salamander, same house, different worlds, the skull on the mantel and the burden of goodness, and so on). Again, these act to symbolize key ideas. But why use metaphor to explore an encounter with religious pluralism? Why not just describe it in straightforward literal terms? Let me say at once that I am not going to define metaphor, nor give any extensive analysis of how it functions. Nor do I want to try to demarcate the respective territories of such near relations to it as analogy, symbol, simile, allegory and so on. That there is much overlap between the members of this group seems both obvious and, at least in this context, unproblematic. There is an extensive literature on the nature and importance of metaphor which I am happy to point readers towards,[13] but I do not wish to be drawn into it, beyond noting three brief remarks which help to underscore the very practical reason I am adopting a metaphorical approach: namely, because it works! (The book's epigraph will, I hope, already have alerted readers to the fact that metaphors are a fundamentally important means of advancing our understanding.)

The first remark is from George Steiner, who has bemoaned the fact that although we have histories of massacre, deception and other less admirable human achievements, we have none of metaphor. Yet when, for example, someone saw autumn in a friend's face for the first time, this was surely a cognitive revolution in terms of how the world was conceived. "Such figures," Steiner writes, "are new mappings of the world, they organize our habitation of reality."[14] In other words, they suggest new ways of seeing, fresh perspectives, different angles at which to set our efforts at understanding. The second remark is taken from a fascinating article of Earl MacCormac's entitled, "Religious Metaphors: Mediators between Biological and Cultural Evolution that Generate Transcendent Meaning." MacCormac suggests that new metaphors generate expressions that "disturb the status quo of ordinary language,"[15] a status quo which, if left undisturbed, would be unable to cope with the new. The third remark comes from Lakoff and Johnson's important study, *Metaphors We Live By*, a book in which the enormous conceptual, ethical and political significance of metaphor is repeatedly illustrated. Looking at metaphors that are imaginative and creative (as opposed to those we have become so used to that we no longer see them as metaphorical), they say: "such metaphors are capable of giving us new understandings of our experience."[16]

Given that this book attempts to deal with a revolution in religious consciousness, metaphor seems a highly appropriate tool with which to investigate the new contours of experience which have thus been created. I hope that the hall of mirrors, the skull on the mantel, the slap and the salamander, and all the other metaphors which will soon be met with, will disturb the status quo of language and suggest to readers various fruitful ways of mapping the world of religious pluralism. We are only newly aware of being in such a world. If it is not to leave us feeling dazed and disorientated, we will need to acquire ways of thinking about it, strategies for navigating paths through it, devices for picturing it. Metaphor can, I believe, effectively address such needs.

I am aware, though, that my reliance on metaphor will not be to everyone's liking and that it will severely test the patience of some readers. For I suspect that there is a broad cognitive division running through *Homo sapiens* which separates us into metaphorical and literal thinkers. It is not a hard and fast distinction, more of a continuum, and there are many amphibious intellects who are equally at home in either medium. For those closely adjacent to the literal pole of things, however, this book will not be a congenial reading experience. And, alas, a further test is soon to be heaped upon the already diminished tolerance of this constituency, in the shape of a character called Cipher. Academic books tend to adopt an objective, unpeopled tone, to engage with ideas through impersonal analysis and argument. The appearance of the authorial "I" is frowned on (alas I have offended on this front too!) and the occurrence of characters almost unheard of. They are consigned to the pages of fiction. The snapping noise I can now imagine is the patience of a particular type of reader giving way as it is taken beyond its breaking strain. All I can do is apologize and bid them farewell. The metaphorical approach is the one I am taking. No book can expect to be to everyone's taste.

Cipher is an imaginary character whose birth and attributes will be described in Chapter 3. The exploration of his experience of religious pluralism forms the core of the book. The reason I have focused so much upon him (despite his neutral nature, it would have stretched his already tenuous credibility too far to have left him ungendered) is because I am specifically interested in the problems posed by religious pluralism *for the individual*. The revolution in religious consciousness which I have suggested we are experiencing, a revolution rooted in religious pluralism, has enormous social and political implications. Although these are both interesting and important, I do not want to do more than allude to them here. My chosen point of focus is how religious pluralism impacts on the individual, and Cipher seemed a good device for ensuring that this focus did not get lost through shifting the discussion onto a study of large-scale, impersonal issues.

Since his original invention over a decade ago, I have come to recognize more clearly some of Cipher's shortcomings. But rather than visiting some metamorphosis of Kafka-esque proportions on him, such that he would be entirely re-created, it seemed better to detail some of the most important of his failings here, before readers are properly introduced to him. This advance rehabilitation of an unmet character will, I hope, lessen the chances of his being rejected or condemned on sight. There are seven failings that I want to identify. No doubt there are more, but these strike me as the most significant. They have to do with (1) his representativeness; (2) his neutrality; (3) the narrowness of his understanding of where human religiousness is located; (4) his assumption about making an either/or choice; (5) his lack of awareness of other approaches; (6) his insufficiently stressed preliminary nature; and (7) the text-bias to which he may have succumbed. I want briefly to go through these seven failings in turn. Readers eager to make Cipher's acquaintance instantly may wish to skip to Chapter 3. If they do so, however, I would ask that, should they then be tempted to criticize him, they first come back to these qualifications and give them due consideration.

1. Cipher is not meant to be representative of everyone. From some perspectives his interest in exploring possible religious outlooks may well appear self-indulgent and bizarre. For instance, those millions of others unknown to us beyond the bland intimacy afforded by TV's routine voyeurism, which allows us to eavesdrop on their suffering anonymously and unobserved, would no doubt be left unimpressed with Cipher's set of priorities. The nameless Cambodian street urchin, the starving Sudanese mother, the elderly and infirm Croatian grandfather standing dazed in some bleak transit camp, the itinerant Indonesian worker earning a pittance from stitching designer footwear for wealthy buyers in the West, these and millions like them will have much more immediate concerns than trying to decide which, if any, of the world's religions offer a picture of how things are. Survival imposes its own imperatives which very quickly make anything not directly geared to food, shelter, clothing and security, seem beside the point.

Humanitarian idealists, who consider that the plight of the world's dispossessed ought to inform and direct every action, will find Cipher an easy target for condemnation. After all, his quest in the hall of mirrors does not have the same immediate claim to ethical respectability as, say, the work of someone engaged in famine relief. Beside such endeavors his pre-occupations may seem grotesquely self-centered. It would require too lengthy a digression to defend the morality of Cipher's situation. Three points can, however, very briefly be made. First, there is no reason to suppose that outside that part of his life imagined here, i.e. beyond his dealings with issues of choice and commitment in a religiously plural world, Cipher may not be actively involved in a career or lifestyle that, at least in part, addresses the needs and sufferings of others directly. Second, we have to be very cautious about making superficial moral judgments in terms of first appearances. Amidst the complexities of the contemporary world it is not always clear what constitutes goodness, or how our moral priorities should be ordered. Third, Cipher's quest could, in fact, be seen as a profoundly moral endeavor in that he is engaged in looking for the right way to live. From the perspective of those who are far enough removed from the immediate concerns of survival to think about life, the situation of being aware of several different religious outlooks, and not knowing which (if any) is worth adopting, is not unusual (and it seems certain to become increasingly common). Cipher is intended to speak to *this* situation, not to every situation. Ninian Smart makes much this point in *Choosing a Faith*:

> We live in a world of choice. That is, we who read books like this. Maybe a poor farmer in Bangladesh has few choices and might find the idea of choosing a faith ridiculous. But we who are well beyond subsistence live in a world which is global, plural and consumer-oriented.[17]

Though I have a high regard for Smart's work (he has made an enormous contribution to the modern study of religion), and though his description of the world as global, plural and consumer-oriented can be applied to Cipher's situation, I cannot agree with his assertion, made a few pages after the above quotation, that "this book is, in its own way, more or less unprecedented."[18] Since the original edition of *Religious Pluralism: A Metaphorical Approach* predated Smart's work by almost ten years, Cipher can surely claim to have set an earlier precedent! Moreover, talking about living in a world of choice perhaps strikes the wrong resonance of association. Choice may suggest the luxury of having a range of options, from which one may pick and choose according to one's particular predilections. The "choice" which Cipher is faced with, however, is not some optional or indulgent intellectual luxury. Rather it is a necessity brought about by the parameters which define his situation. He has no choice about the imperative to choose which appears to face him so insistently in the hall of mirrors. It is as much a part of his situation as the imperative to follow a single faith was for earlier generations. So, to summarize this first point, while Cipher is not intended to be some sort of universal exemplar, symbolizing the human situation per se, he is intended to exemplify a not uncommon situation, which is both unwilled and uncomfortable.

2. Cipher's claimed neutrality may, on first reading, sound so improbable that he will be dismissed as not merely fictional, but fantastic.

I appeal to readers not to leap to conclusions on the basis of this one word. Cipher's neutrality is a matter gone into in much greater detail in Chapter 8. To anticipate the most obvious criticism, it does not mean that he occupies some sort of godlike (or robotic) stance of complete objectivity, or that he is not rooted in some specific tradition of values, expectations, ideas, by virtue of birth and upbringing. It simply means that Cipher is not committed to any particular faith. My interest in this book is not in how a Buddhist or a Christian, a Hindu or a Jew, a Muslim or a Sikh may cope with the religious environment constituted by the hall of mirrors (though each of these situations poses an interesting problem), but how someone may do so who considers themselves outside any particular faith.

3. Although his focus on the individual may in fact save him from this point of criticism, one might want to take Cipher to task for a certain narrowness of vision and somewhat pedestrian thinking when it comes to locating where the religious outlooks are which he wishes to examine. Might he not be accused of assuming too readily that religion is confined to the obvious and explicitly religious sites associated with the great world faiths? Of course due notice is taken of the internal diversity of Buddhism, Christianity, Hinduism, Islam, Judaism, and so on, and of the arguments of Wilfred Cantwell Smith and other scholars about the dangers of imposing too neat, monolithic and exclusive an identity on any of the great world faiths. But such awareness notwithstanding, I think an older and wiser Cipher might be more alert to the existence of religion in some rather unexpected places.

In *Gods in the Global Village*, Lester Kurtz offers a useful point of contrast between life long before the revolution of which our awareness of religious pluralism is a part, and life today. According to Kurtz:

> Our ancient ancestors sat around the fire and heard stories about their forebears—about the time when life first emerged in the universe, about lessons for living their lives. When people gather today, the flickering light comes from television rather than a fire, but we still hear stories about the nature of reality as it is perceived in our culture.[19]

Kurtz draws attention to the fact that, prior to modern means of mass communication, most people only encountered one set of stories, but that in the globalized situation in which so many find themselves today, multiple narratives are encountered.[20] This raises again the question of how the different religions relate to each other. Do they tell variations on the same basic story, or do they follow different plot lines, characters, beginnings, endings? And how (to reiterate Cipher's dilemma in the terms suggested by Kurtz) is the individual who hears many stories to cope with this narrative pluralism? Which story, if any, tells the story of his life? Which beginning and ending should he adopt as framings for understanding his own genesis and extinction?

In emphasizing storytelling Kurtz also identifies an important shared concern of media and religion which is highly significant in terms of any definition of where we should locate religion. Such is the role of the media in bringing value-laden stories before us, that some now view the media *themselves* as constituting religious or quasi-religious phenomena,[21] fast taking over many of the traditional functions that religion used to perform in society. This should, perhaps, make us recall Thomas Luckmann's warnings that:

> what are usually taken as symptoms of the decline of traditional Christianity may be symptoms of a more revolutionary change: the replacement of the institutional specialization of religion by a new social form of religion.[22]

Perhaps we are sometimes at risk of mistaking change for decay. Might the jeremiads of media critics like Neil Postman and William Fore be failing to appreciate "symptoms of revolutionary change," reading them as destructive of existing religion rather than as creative of a new form of faith? (Which is not to say that this new faith should be welcomed.) Does it make sense, at this particular point in history, to confine our concept of religion only to its traditional occurrences? May there not be circumstances in which, for example, a television program can be more religious than a church service, in which there is more spiritual import in computers than in chalices, where media, more than meditation, offer a site for deep reflection, where individuals draw their values from films rather than faiths? As Richard Niebuhr once pointed out, "religious currents have often flowed in other than obviously theological or ecclesiastical channels."[23] If Cipher confines his attention only to the obvious theological or ecclesiastical forms of religion, he may miss much of interest. There are more mirrors in his hall of mirrors than those constituted by the great world faiths. There are more sources of life-guiding story than those that belong to traditional religious narratives. This raises the question of how we should define religion in the first place, a question that we might want to recommend for Cipher's closer attention.

4. One might argue that in thinking predominantly about making a decision in the first place, Cipher is manifesting a very particular outlook on the nature of religion and being religious. The looser models of commitment which allow individuals to observe and practice aspects of different religions (in Japan, for example, individuals may turn to Christianity for marriage ceremonies and to Buddhism for death ceremonies), might suggest a different assessment of the hall of mirrors than the one which Cipher makes. Perhaps he needs to think more in terms of both/and, less in terms of either/or. Some such awareness is evidenced in the course of his deliberations, and it is stressed in Chapter 10, but it might usefully be given greater prominence. Is there any reason why Cipher should set out on his quest thinking in terms of accepting some one, single, easily identifiable religion? Does the hall of mirrors not offer the possibility of choosing a range of different reflections (or fragments of reflections) from different sources?

5. As I said earlier, to have left Cipher ungendered would have threatened whatever small amount of credibility he may have. The fact that he is presented as male is not, obviously, a shortcoming in itself.[24] However, since his dilemma has been created by the fact that there are different outlooks on the world, it might have been appropriate for Cipher to have explicitly acknowledged that other men, other women, people of other ages, different ethnic backgrounds and so on, read and respond to things in a different way. His is one way through the hall of

mirrors; there are many others. Cipher would, for instance, do well to take note of June O'Connor's comments about seeing:

> The most powerful ideas are those we think with. They are the ideas that lie "behind" our eyes, enabling us to see: what we do see is shaped by them. A Chinese proverb makes this point baldly: "Two-thirds of what we see is behind our eyes"—a sobering and disillusioning insight for those of us working to see reality as it is. And yet the proverb resonates a truth. Much of what we see, we see because we have been trained, educated and socialized to see in certain ways. This means that there are also things we do not see, questions and insights to which we are blind, paths not taken, whole areas that are concealed to us, as others are revealed.[25]

Cipher needs to recognize more clearly that his is only one way of seeing the hall of mirrors. Different people will read the same reflections differently. Putting it more generally than in the feminist terms which O'Connor favors, and linking this point to the high valuation which is given throughout this book to metaphor, Cipher might take to heart a point made by George Lakoff and Mark Johnson at the end of their study of this form:

> We continually find it important to realise that the way we have been brought up to perceive our world is not the only way and that it is possible to see beyond the "truths" of our culture.[26]

Cipher's situation is one in which a sensitivity to different ways of seeing will be an essential skill.

6. The sixth failing I want to identify is, of course, like the others, more a criticism of Cipher's creator than of Cipher himself. One of the things which I think should have been stressed more clearly at the outset of his quest in the hall of mirrors was that it is only concerned with the essential preliminaries of the journey he intends to make. *Religious Pluralism: a Metaphorical Approach* is an attempt to map the course he is going to take. It is not an account of the journey itself. The focus of concern is on how Cipher will proceed, what are the best routes to take, how he can overcome initial problems and so on. Readers looking for Cipher's specific explorations of the images of Buddhism, Christianity,

Islam and so on will be disappointed. This book does not record such endeavors; it seeks instead to show how Cipher may focus and direct such inquiries.

7.   The final shortcoming that may be worth mentioning is certainly one from which the academic study of religion has suffered. So, to the extent that he derives his information and ideas from this disciplinary area, it may be supposed that Cipher too would fall under similar criticism. This has to do with a tendency to be text-biased, to assume that religion is located in written texts, and to ignore or undervalue religious expression in other media. If we over-emphasize any one medium of expression we are likely to skew the picture we have of religion. Cipher needs to be alert to the importance of religious art, dance, architecture, music, ritual, and so on, rather than just to focus on the written word alone.[27] This point is very much connected to the third of Cipher's failings identified above, namely the tendency to assume that religion occurs only within the neat confines of what is easily and explicitly identifiable as being religious. Cipher needs to be aware of the huge range of human religiousness and the many forms in which it can find expression.

Despite these seven shortcomings, however (and no doubt there are others), I think Cipher has much to recommend him as a device for exploring the revolution in religious consciousness in which issues of religious pluralism figure so prominently. Indeed, he has stood the test of time rather better than initial indications might have suggested (being rendered almost instantly extinct by a voracious publisher is not an auspicious beginning for anyone). I was worried in the first edition of this book about claiming too much for him, of putting him forward as a representative figure. In fact, I think that millions of people now fall roughly into the category which he is meant to represent. This is a situation that many of us have to cope with; it has become commonplace (if still largely unacknowledged). It looks set to become even more widespread as we move into the new century. Cipher shows some of the ways in which the problematic nature of this situation may be approached and perhaps resolved. As such, I hope readers will forgive his failings.

❧

My hope is that the dilemma addressed in the pages that follow is one with which any thoughtful individual living on the brink of the twenty-first century will be able to identify. Regardless of what our own particular outlook may be, we are all faced, to some extent at least, with the same situation as that symbolized by Cipher and the hall of mirrors. Like most authors, then, I like to think that my book will appeal to a wide cross-section of readers. However, I am also aware that, the claimed universality of the problem it explores notwithstanding, *Religious Pluralism: A Metaphorical Approach* presupposes a particular mind-set. It will appear wholly unattractive and uninteresting to that large constituency of people who do not happen to be in this particular intellectual gear. The difference between the two constituencies is perhaps worth spelling out very briefly, not to try to convert the uninterested (in the unlikely event of their having picked up the book at all), but to further clarify the nature of Cipher's explorations.

Consider the following haiku:

> Midway through my list,
> Baked beans, bread, potato crisps,
> I remember death.[28]

This book will be of no interest to a "baked beans, bread, potato crisps" perspective. It is addressed to those who have "remembered death." But this is not to say that it is some sort of funereal excursion into the shadows. On the contrary, the last line of this haiku could be altered to read, "I remember life," and it would still serve to identify in general terms the overarching focus of what follows. To put this more literally, in our day to day existence we write shopping lists, take our children to school, go to work, watch TV, plan holidays, conduct love affairs, talk to friends and just get on with the business of living, but with little reflection on life itself. Sometimes, though, what I suppose could be called the meta-physical dimensions of being break through the mundane and we are left confronted with stark and difficult questions about how we ought to live, what values we should accord to self, others, the world, what meaning, ultimately, our lives may have (if indeed they have any meaning at all). It is with this kind of mind-set (which I designate in Chapter 3 as a sense of lostness and a lack of "world certainty") that Cipher explores the hall of mirrors. It is a mind-set which may be occasioned by thinking about time, fate, accident, or death. Or it may occur spontaneously for no obvious reason, midway through doing our shopping or some other routine chore. Such a mind-set is unlikely to stay with us all the time. This book focuses on Cipher's response to it, but we should not suppose, if he were real rather than an educative fiction, that he would "remember death/life" all the time. No doubt, like everyone else, he would often tire of thinking about such serious matters, switch back with relief to the "baked beans, bread, potato crisps" perspective and just watch TV or go out drinking with friends, or play computer games, or gossip on the telephone, or go mountaineering, or indulge in whatever else might take his fancy.

I would argue that there are areas of human experience which provoke questions of ultimate meaning, that there are moments in anyone's existence when the perspective alluded to in the last line of the haiku is inescapable, such that we wonder about who we are, where we came from and what, ultimately, our fate, and the fate of humanity, will be. Such wondering is an integral part of being human and has been with us since our species first emerged into sentience, its horizons of desire pushed to the distant skyline of self-reflection, far beyond the immediate up-close concerns of physical survival. One important response to such wondering has always been religion (which often provides the stimulus for it as well). In fact, religion might be regarded as one of the social arenas which seek to structure and symbolize our quest for over-arching meanings and values beyond the baked beans, bread, potato crisp perspective (science and art are others). Once, human beings who "remembered death," who pondered life's course and reason beyond the topography afforded by any shopping list, did so in the context of a particular religious tradition (albeit one in which there might be an range of local dialects). Even if they did not accept the answers it proposed, their wondering was sited within the singular discourse of one dominant faith tradition that provided the vocabulary in which their speculations about life's ultimate nature and meaning were termed. That situation has changed dramatically (and is still in the process of changing). As I hope I have made clear, a religious revolution has transformed the whole context in which this side of life is set. It is on that transformed context that the following chapters focus.

This book first appeared in 1986, under the title *In the Hall of Mirrors: Some Problems of Commitment in a Religiously Plural World.*[29] It went out of print almost immediately, one of the unnoticed casualties when a traditional publishing house was swallowed up by a much larger company. It was irritating at the time to have one's first book disappear from public view so swiftly. However, had it remained in print, it is unlikely I would have contemplated a new edition. This would have meant missing what has turned out to be a fascinating intellectual experience—going back to an earlier phase of one's thinking, assessing the extent to which it is still valid, and attempting to provide some appropriate points of update and more considered reflection. I was both pleased and surprised to discover the extent to which the book had not been overtaken by history. Indeed, if anything, its central concerns have become of more pressing importance as the fact of religious pluralism becomes ever more unavoidably stamped on our consciousness. This edition contains substantial new material. Three chapters have been added (Chapters 1, 2 and 10) and the entire text has been revised, though I have tried not to destroy the integrity of the original (this is, after all, intended as a new and enlarged edition, not a completely new book). Since *In the Hall of Mirrors* had its genesis in the first of two series of lectures which I had the honor of giving at the University of St Andrews under the auspices of the Gifford Bequest, and since that Bequest has had, and continues to have, so profound an impact on work in this subject area, it also seemed appropriate to add a brief appendix on Lord Gifford himself and the program he established.

Authors who are interested in reader-response now have at their disposal a marvelous form of communication, unknown at the time this book first appeared, namely e-mail. I have always regarded such responses as an invaluable source of insight and correction. Accordingly, I invite you, the unmet reader, to comment on the ideas contained in this book, should you feel inclined to do so. I can be reached at:

arthurc@lampeter.ac.uk

and would welcome any feedback.

Notes

1. James B. Wiggins, *In Praise of Religious Diversity.* New York & London, 1996, Routledge, p. ix. For an excellent analysis of contemporary fundamentalism, see the extensive work of the Fundamentalism Project. Details are given in Martin E. Marty & R. Scott Appleby (eds), *Fundamentalisms Observed,* Chicago, 1991, University of Chicago Press (the first of the project's multi-volume study). For an assessment of the Fundamentalism Project's work, see my "Intolerance Explained," *Times Higher Education Supplement,* June 12 1992.
2. For instance, Christians will find such guidance in a work like Jacques Dupuis' *Toward a Christian Theology of Religious Pluralism,* New York, 1997, Orbis. I give a few further suggestions about work of this type in Chapter 2 note 31. However, for a comprehensive bibliography, readers should consult Dupuis. Harold G. Coward's *Pluralism: a Challenge to World Religions* (New York, 1985, Orbis) looks at the way in which pluralism has been responded to from within a variety of faiths. *The*

Experience of Religious Diversity, edited by John Hick and Hasan Askari (Aldershot, 1985, Gower), provides an interesting collection of essays on pluralism from Buddhist, Christian, Hindu, Muslim and Jewish stances.

3. In *The Structure of Scientific Revolutions* (Chicago, 1970, University of Chicago Press: second [enlarged] edition), Thomas S. Kuhn has famously drawn attention to the way in which scientists view the world according to socially sanctioned "paradigms." Anything which does not fall into line with a paradigm which happens to be dominant at any particular time tends simply to be assimilated into the familiar picture, whether it really fits there or not. Extending Kuhn's schema, old paradigms of religious thinking tended to be exclusive, intolerant and dismissive of any religion other than themselves. This paradigm is far from extinct. However, I would argue that the revolution in religious consciousness described above brings with it, and has been born from, a paradigm shift associated with the growing awareness of pluralism. This new paradigm involves seeing that no particular faith has any clear *a priori* claim to preference or priority; that we are faced with a number of options or hypotheses, rather than a single position that can automatically assume normative authority. The experiment of the "anomalous" cards, which provides a good illustration of how paradigms work, is discussed briefly in Chapter 4.

4. Ian Hamnet, "Religious Pluralism," in Hamnet (ed), *Religious Pluralism and Unbelief: Studies Critical and Comparative,* London, 1990, Routledge, pp. 6-7.

5. Peter Byrne, *Prolegomena to Religious Pluralism: Reference and Realism in Religion,* London, 1995, Macmillan, p. vii.

6. Hick provides a further useful point of terminological reference in his article on religious pluralism in the *Encyclopedia of Religion* (Editor-in-Chief Mircea Eliade, New York/London, 1987, Macmillan/Collier Macmillan, Vol. 12 pp. 331-333): "Phenomenologically, the term 'religious pluralism' refers simply to the fact that the history of religions shows a plurality of traditions and a plurality of variations within each. Philosophically, however, the term refers to a particular theory of the relation between these traditions, with their different and competing claims. This is the theory that the great world religions constitute variant conceptions and perceptions of, and responses to, the one ultimate, mysterious divine reality" (p. 331). I am using "religious pluralism" in a phenomenological, not philosophical, sense. Although I take a different perspective on pluralism to that of John Hick, this is not to

question the significance of his work in this area. Hick's extensive and insightful writings on pluralism are of considerable interest. In *The Rainbow of Faiths* (London, 1995, SCM, p. 18), Hick credits Alan Race with the first use of the "exclusivist," "inclusivist" and "pluralist" typology which has since attained such currency (see Race's *Christians and Religious Pluralism* London/New York, 1983, SCM/Maryknoll, [2nd edition 1994]). Hick's writings on pluralism, which show a pleasing feature not always evident in theological writing, namely a readiness to change as the author's thinking develops, can be found in several of his books. The most important are: *An Interpretation of Religion* (London/New Haven, 1989, Macmillan/Princeton University Press), an expanded version of Hick's Gifford Lectures, delivered in Edinburgh in 1986-7; *Problems of Religious Pluralism* (London/New York, 1985, Macmillan/St. Martin's Press), a collection of previously published papers; and *God Has Many Names* (London, 1980, Macmillan,).

7. Diana L. Eck, "Challenge of Pluralism," *Niemann Reports*, Vol. XLVII no.2, Summer 1997. I am quoting from the version which appears at:
    http://www.fas.harvard.edu/pluralism/html/article-cop.html

8. Jame B. Wiggins, *op.cit.*, p. ix.

9. From the Harvard Pluralism Project's web-site, at:
    http://www.fas.harvard.edu/~pluralism/html/about.html

10. These dismissive and insulting terms are taken from Henri de Lubac's summary of early Western attitudes to Buddhism (in his *La Recontre du bouddhisme et de l'occident*), as quoted by Guy Richard Welbon in his *The Buddhist Idea of Nirvana and its Western Interpreters,* Chicago, 1968, University of Chicago Press, p. 20.

11. Langdon Gilkey, "God," in Peter Hodgson & Robert King (eds.), *Christian Theology: an Introduction to its Traditions and Tasks,* London, 1983, SPCK, p. 86.

12. Stephen Batchelor, *The Awakening of the West: the Encounter of Buddhism and Western Culture,* London, 1994 Aquarian, p. xi.

13. See, for example, George Lakoff and Mark Johnson, *Metaphors We Live By,* Chicago, 1980, Chicago University Press; Andrew Ortony (Ed), *Metaphor and Thought,* Cambridge, 1979, Cambridge University Press; Sheldon Sacks (Ed), *On Metaphor,* Chicago, 1978, University of Chicago Press; Janet Martin Soskice, *Metaphor and Religious Language,* Oxford, 1985, Clarendon Press. Many pointers for further inquiry are contained in Warren A. Shibles, *Metaphor: an Annotated Bibliography and History,* Wisconsin, 1971, The Language Press. Though somewhat dated, Shibles suggests some interesting perspectives.

14. George Steiner, *After Babel: Aspects of Language and Translation,* London, 1975, Oxford University Press, p. 23. There may be no account of the sort Steiner has in mind, which pinpoints the genesis of metaphor in our cognitive repertoire, but William Golding has offered a brilliant imaginative substitute. At one point in his novel *The Inheritors* (London, 1970 [1955], Faber, pp. 194-195) he describes how Lok, the Neanderthal protagonist, is trying to comprehend the "new people" (i.e. *Homo sapiens*), who have suddenly and disruptively appeared as a perplexing unknown in his accustomed environment: "Lok discovered 'like.' He had used likeness all his life without being aware of it. Fungi on a tree were ears, the word was the same but acquired a distinction by circumstances that could never apply to the sensitive things on the side of his head. Now in a convulsion of the understanding Lok found himself using likeness as a tool as surely as ever he had used a stone to hack at sticks or meat. Likeness could grasp the white faced hunters with a hand, could put them into a world where they were thinkable and not a random unrelated irruption. He was picturing the hunters who went out with burnt sticks in skill and malice. 'The new people are like a famished wolf in the hollow of a tree.'"

15. Earl R. MacCormac, "Religious Metaphors: Mediators Between Biological and Cultural Evolution that Generate Transcendent Meaning," *Zygon* Vol 18 (1983), p. 58.

16. George Lakoff and Mark Johnson, *Metaphors We Live By,* Chicago, 1980, University of Chicago Press, p. 139.

17. Ninian Smart, *Choosing a Faith,* London, 1995, Boyars, p. 1.

18. Ibid., p. 4.

19. Lester R. Kurtz, *Gods in the Global Village: the World's Religions in Sociological Perspective,* Thousand Oaks, CA, 1995, Sage, p. 3.

20. Ibid.

21. See, for example, William Fore, *Television and Religion: the Shaping of Faith, Values and Culture,* Minneapolis, 1987, Augsburg; Gregor Goethals, *The Electronic Golden Calf: Images, Religion and the Making of Meaning,* Cambridge, 1990, Cowley; Quentin J. Schultz, "Secular Television as Popular Religion," in R. Abelman & S. Hoover, (eds.), *Religious Television: Controversies and Conclusions,* Norwood, 1990, Ablex, pp. 239-248.

22. Thomas Luckmann, *The Invisible Religion: the Problem of Religion in Modern Society,* New York, 1967, Macmillan, pp. 90-91.

23. H. Richard Niebuhr, *The Kingdom of God in America,* New York, 1959, Harper, p. ix. Film provides one example of a non-theological, non-

ecclesiastical channel in which religious currents seem to be flowing with particular richness and force. I am not referring here to explicitly religious films, but rather to the way in which religious themes find implicit expression across a whole range of popular films, as they also do in TV programs. This is something that has been explored in a cluster of recent publications. See, for example, Joel W. Martin & Conrad E. Ostwalt, (eds.), *Screening the Sacred: Religion, Myth and Ideology in Popular American Film,* Boulder, 1995, Westview Press; John R. May, (ed.), *Image and Likeness: Religious Visions in American Film Classics,* New York, 1992, Paulist Press; John R. May, (ed.), *New Image of Religious Film,* Kansas City, 1997, Sheed & Ward; Clive Marsh & Gaye Ortiz, (eds.), *Explorations in Theology and Film,* Oxford, 1997, Blackwell; Margaret Miles, *Seeing and Believing: Religion and Values in the Movies,* Boston, 1996, Beacon Press.

24. Nor, I hope, will it be considered a shortcoming that I have allowed the no doubt unintentionally sexist language in many of the quotations to stand unchanged.

25. June O'Connor, "The Epistemological Significance of Feminist Research in Religion," in Ursula King, (ed.), *Religion and Gender,* Oxford, 1995, Blackwell, p. 47.

26. George Lakoff and Mark Johnson *Metaphors We Live By,* Chicago, 1980, Chicago University Press, p. 239.

27. For more on how religious studies is affected by this failing, see my "Media, Meaning and Method in the Study of Religion," *British Association for the Study of Religion, 1996, Occasional Paper no. 16 .*

28. Taken from "Snares," a collection of haiku which appeared in *The Antigonish Review,* Vol. 106, 1996, p. 28. The enormous growth of interest, internationally, in the haiku form, provides an interesting example of the way in which the permeability of boundaries has led to a once purely Japanese phenomenon occurring all across the globe, with national influences feeding back into the country of its origin. Readers interested in the range of haiku writing today should look at issues of *Blyth Spirit,* or *Frogpond,* the magazines of the British Haiku Society and the Haiku Society of America respectively. Information on the latter organization can also be found at:

http://www.octet.com/~hsa

29. C. J. Arthur, *In the Hall of Mirrors: Some Problems of Commitment in a Religiously Plural World,* London & Oxford, 1986, Mowbray.

CHAPTER 2

RELIGIOUS PLURALISM AS AN ASPECT OF GLOBALIZATION

THE REVOLUTION in religious consciousness with which this book is concerned, namely the change from a singular to a plural outlook, is itself an aspect of a broader revolution. Cipher's dilemma of inundation with information about religion is just one characteristic of a much more wide-ranging situation. As the historian Theodore Zeldin puts it, "what to do with too much information is the great riddle of our time."[1] Indeed, this larger scale revolution is sometimes referred to simply as the "information revolution." However, this name, like any other, is far from satisfactory.[2] Any single term or phrase used to characterize "our time," and the complex historical processes which have led to it, is going to encounter difficulties. Trying to catch the flavor of the zeitgeist in just a few words will, inevitably, fail. To do justice to it requires extensive analysis, detailed commentary, careful qualification. Here, though, for the limited purposes of placing Cipher's situation in some sort of wider context, I want to consider how this larger scale revolution may be thought of in terms of "globalization."

By globalization I mean the inter-related complex of processes—industrial, economic, technological, cultural and cognitive—which have resulted in regional boundaries (whether of individual, family, class, religion, or nation) being rendered permeable to more distant influences.[3] Such permeability means that the destruction of rain forest in Brazil may lead to protests in London, Tel-Aviv or Brisbane; that the purchase of computers in Vancouver or Hamburg will have an effect on employment prospects in the Philippines and Korea; that an act of terrorism in rural Ireland will be seen on TV screens on every continent; that a software package written in California will be disseminated world-wide; that an Asian financial crisis will have an impact on the livelihood of whelk fishermen in Wales; that agricultural decisions which will massively shape the environment and economy of Kenya or Bolivia will be made in board rooms in London and New York; that the same films, pop music, TV programs and best-selling novels, will enjoy cultural currency in scores of different countries, among an audience of billions; that the same products will be offered for sale in shops almost everywhere.

The immediately noticeable signs of globalization in an individual's life may seem commonplace and religiously uninteresting—the fact that our supermarkets routinely stock exotic fruits and vegetables flown in from other continents, or that the same event is viewed by millions, more or less simultaneously, as constituting the news of the day, or that we encounter familiar brand names, logos, designs everywhere from Utah to Ulan Bator—but in fact such things are indicators of very radical changes in human affairs, and these changes raise profound questions about purpose, value and responsibility.

Communications systems constitute a key feature of globalization and the networks of interdependence and interconsciousness which it creates. They have had an enormous impact on the integrity of regional boundaries, boundaries that once kept different individuals, nations, races, classes and religions so self-contained that effectively (and often actually) they were unaware of each other's existence. A mushrooming of technical invention has seen photography, the telegraph, telephone, radio, TV, video, fax, computers, satellites and other media, transform the way in which communications happen. Such developments have created an increasingly interlinked network whose intricate criss-crossing of electronic capillaries have threaded their way through societies which were once separate, autonomous, isolated, making them (unevenly) interconscious and interdependent. Instantaneous communication across distances that once meant long delays and uncertainties between the sending and receipt of messages is a key feature of globalization. At the same time, developments in transport systems, and the impetus given to travel by business, politics, tourism and education, have likewise acted to make people increasingly aware of the world beyond their own indigenous place in it.

To see the networks which create our increasingly "wired" world only in terms of facilitating communication, or as conduits of data neutrally providing access to information, would, of course, be extraordinarily naïve. Terms such as "global village" and "world civilization" (like "information revolution") are dangerously cosmetic and tend to obscure important (and often distasteful) aspects of the phenomena they seek to label. A more accurate picture of their nature is suggested by Ben Bagdikian, when he talks about the "troika" of global media corporations, multinational industries and the world-wide banking establishment creating "a new power in world politics and economics."[4] This is a new power that has challenged traditional conceptions of national sovereignty and done much to shape the social, cultural and political contours of our time (by, for example, transferring capital to areas of the world where workers' rights and incomes are low). Indeed, Bagdikian considers modern mass media to be "one of the most powerful forces in history,"[5] and sees in the integration of such media and world-wide mass advertising (financed by the multinational manufacturers of consumer goods) a threat to cultural diversity, local autonomy and individual freedom.

In terms of *religion*, globalization's major impact has been a hugely increased awareness of number and diversity not previously recognized (or not recognized on the same scale). Pluralism, in other words, is the most religiously significant upshot of globalization. In real terms, the hall of mirrors in which Cipher finds himself, and with which this book is concerned, exists independently of globalization. It is there, has always been there, because different religions are there. But in cognitive terms, in terms of Cipher's *awareness* of its existence, it could be seen very largely as an outcome of the globalizing processes which have done so much (and are doing so much) to shape the contours of our time.

As well as fostering an awareness of religious pluralism (an awareness which naturally has an impact on how the different religions define themselves and plot their relationship to other faiths), globalization also affects religions in a range of other ways. For instance, the agenda of concerns voiced by any local religious group is now likely to include global dimensions. A village church in remote rural Ireland, for example, may campaign on behalf of an international relief organization such as Christian Aid, while a Buddhist group in New York may try to heighten awareness of human rights abuses in Tibet; Jews and Muslims in the Middle East may engage with a range of environmental issues whose impact extends far beyond their immediate locales, while Zen monks and nuns in Taiwan may work to foster religious tolerance world-wide through the setting up of a museum of world religions.[6] As Fiona Robinson succinctly puts it, "globalization means that we are increasingly confronted with moral dilemmas about our relationship with strangers."[7] That confrontation has had a significant effect in terms of the moral and social preoccupations of religions. But beyond this kind of obvious globalizing of their agendas of concern, there are other less easily measured, but highly significant, influences as well.

For instance, we are now surrounded by images to an extent that is quite unprecedented, courtesy of the world-spanning communications systems that are such an integral part of the whole process of globalization. Pierre Babin has gone so far as to suggest that in fact we are living at a "difficult interim period between two ages,"[8] in which an era of print is fast giving way to the triumphal ascendancy of images. Whether or not we really are on the cusp of so epochal a change as Babin suggests, is uncertain. But it is clear that images are a principal characteristic of the media that have come to cultural dominance in this century. The urge to picture things is not something new of course. It is, rather, an indelible feature of our species, evident from the caves at Lascaux to the latest web-site. What is new, and what takes us into uncharted territory, is the way in which modern mass media project images with such number, vibrancy and insistence into our lives.[9] Even in 1970, in his pioneering study *Theology Through Film*, Neil Hurley was talking about our being "literally barraged with images," to the extent that we experience a "saturation" of visual communications. He estimated that the average New York commuter (a useful statistical fiction) receives some 5,000 audio-visual impressions on any given weekday.[10] History provides us with few reference points to gauge the precise impact of this heavy rain of images upon the psyche. Does it matter what we look at, for how long, under what conditions? How does what appears before the eye inform the mind and heart? In what relationship to believing or valuing does seeing stand? No one knows for sure how great a weight of meaning is carried by the different images which, moment by moment, meet our gaze. We do not have an ethics, still less a metaphysics, of seeing to guide us. The impact of the image-deluge on religion remains to be seen, but we need to be aware of the enormous epistemological potential that it carries.

A glimpse of this potential can be seen in a remark of Kenneth Woodward, religion editor for *Newsweek* magazine. Increasingly, he says, "the quality of pictures available for illustrating articles determines (as it does on television) which stories get published and at what length."[11] Woodward's observation pinpoints a common trend which now shapes the content of many media. But the idea of an image-led epistemology taking root, in which what is unpictured (or unpictureable) is simply ignored, treated as if it does not exist or matter, clearly has some very serious religious implications, given the high valuation religions give to purported entities and states which are apparently beyond the reach of any word or picture (not to mention their concern with values which defy easy pictorial expression). One might also wonder about the way in which our ability to handle abstract issues, our understanding of complex processes that do not readily admit to being pictured, may be affected by this relentless emphasis on the image.

Some further idea of the likely dimensions of the epistemological potential carried by images may be guessed at by looking at an earlier revolution. This allows us to see the way in which, when the dominant medium of communication changes, there are massive concomitant shifts in religious thinking. Thus Walter Ong has convincingly shown how the shift from oral to literate culture involved a massive change in people's conception of the world. According to Ong, "more than any other invention writing has transformed human consciousness."[12] Embedded in such media revolutions as that which marked the onset of written language are wide-ranging cognitive consequences whose impact religion cannot hope to escape. In oral cultures, for example, a word like "God" "may hardly be conceived of as a separate entity, divorced from both the rest of the sentence and its social context. But, once given the physical reality of writing, it can take on a life of its own."[13] By objectifying words and by "making their meaning available for much more prolonged and intensive scrutiny than is possible orally," writing "encourages private thought."[14] Jack Goody sees religion as being profoundly influenced by writing. Religions associated with writing can become "world" rather than just "local" or "national" faiths (reminding us that writing is an important factor in globalization). Literacy not only facilitates the development of world rather than local religions, it also gives rise to some of the characteristics of such religions (just as the absence of literacy helps to shape less encompassing traditions). Literate religions tend to be "religions of conversion, not simply religions of birth."[15] Their ethical framework is universalistic in scope and their teachings are not limited to particular times or places.

Just as writing shapes religious thinking according to the cognitive contours afforded by it as a medium, so we can expect other media to likewise influence religion. As Neil Postman says:

> Introduce the alphabet to a culture and you change its cognitive habits, its social relations, its notions of community, history and religion. Introduce the printing press with movable type, and you do the same. Introduce speed of light transmission of images and you make a cultural revolution.[16]

If we are indeed experiencing the kind of epochal change that Babin suggests, then it is unlikely that religion will be left unaffected. Jorge Schement and Hester Stephenson, for example, have speculated on the extent to which "the religions of the Word are on the verge of being conquered by a new kind of orality, in which multimedia environments will frame the religious experience."[17] They pose the interesting question of whether the shift away from print culture which this involves, "to a new visual 'virtual reality' culture," will "undo the foundation from which Protestant Christianity grew."[18] Religion is not immune to the changes which have happened (and are still happening) as the various processes involved in globalization take ever wider effect.

Susan Sontag, whose meditation *On Photography* offers a powerful insight into modern/postmodern spirituality and the ways in which it has been moulded by pictures, has suggested that "the omnipresence of photographs has an incalculable effect on our ethical sensibility."[19] It may, as she suggests, simply be too soon to try to calculate the extent to which the ocean of images in which we swim has changed our sense of self and others, our sense of our place in the universe, our sense of time and memory, our sense (if any) of God. We need, again, to remind ourselves of the recentness and revolutionary nature of our situation. The revolution in religious consciousness is one aspect of a larger revolution, one key aspect of which is the prevalence of images in our lives. This sets our experience apart from that of previous generations. We see things daily that would have left them amazed. This is a point that Thomas Martin has very effectively emphasized, drawing attention to the massive impact on our outlook which photography has had. After briefly reviewing the enormous expansion of our awareness brought about by slow motion, microscopic, telescopic, underwater and other forms of photography, Martin concludes that "Human consciousness cannot be the same today as it was prior to the extension of its vision through film. Neither can religious consciousness ever be the same."[20] Not only are we experiencing a revolution in religious consciousness in terms of our awareness of religious pluralism, but the religions themselves, under the impact of globalization, are also likely to succumb to quite radical change.

The upshot of all this for Cipher is that he needs to remember the hall of mirrors is not somewhere static and unchanging. On the contrary, it is a place in which there is considerable movement. Religions are likely to feel the impact of globalization in a range of ways. When it comes to changes in media, for example, (and such changes are very closely associated with globalization) it is quite clear from historical precedent that we can expect them to spark a whole series of quite fundamental changes in the societies where they happen. Precisely what religious changes will attend recent media change remains to be seen; we are too close to the event to offer more than tentative assessments of its impact. However, it is clear that Cipher would be profoundly deluded were he to imagine that the religions which surround him in pluralism's hall of mirrors are timeless, unchanging, unaffected by history. On the contrary, he is dealing with images which are fluid, organic and adaptable.

Cipher also needs to be aware of the stereotypical potential of media portrayals of religion. If, for example, the image of Islam in his hall of mirrors is one that is drawn from what he sees about this religion on TV or reads about it in the press, then the mirror in question may be grotesquely distorting. The extent to which this faith has been presented as a fanatical, fundamentalist religion, given to intolerance, violence and extremism, has been highlighted in the work of scholars such as Edward Said, Akbar Ahmed, and S.A. Schleifer[21] (whose books Cipher would do well to read). According to Ahmed, "nothing in history has threatened Muslims like the Western media."[22] If Cipher draws his ideas about Muslims from the negatively stereotypical images of an Islamophobic worldview, it will scarcely be conducive to his quest for understanding and evaluation. (And Islam is by no means alone among the faiths in receiving a bad press.) In exploring the hall of mirrors Cipher will need to be alert to where the reflections come from which show him the different religious outlooks on the world.

Optimistically read, globalization has resulted in "global consciousness and citizenship,"[23] a sense of the interdependence of nations and individuals, a heightened feeling for the human family, increased opportunities for travel, a wider range of choices for the consumer, a vast increase in the wealth of information available to individuals. From a pessimistic point of view, globalization has led to "a Cocacolonization of the world"[24] where, instead of facilitating communication, media facilitate commerce, where information becomes a carefully controlled commodity rather than a freely available resource, where freedom of expression is curtailed by economics, where stereotypes obscure the truth, and where the right to communicate is as unevenly enjoyed as other human rights. George Gerbner's vision sums up what many fear this will bring:

> Fewer sources fill more outlets more of the time with ever more standardised fare designed for global markets. Global marketing streamlines production, homogenises content, and sweeps alternative perspectives from the mainstream. Media coalesce into a seamless, pervasive and inescapable cultural environment, with television its mainstream, presenting a world that is iniquitous, demeaning, and damaging to those born into and living in it.[25]

This book is not concerned to comment on whether globalization is, overall, a good thing or a bad thing. It is easy to specify both positive and negative aspects of it. What I am concerned with in the pages that follow is how the individual might cope with the major religious upshot of globalization, namely the increased and increasing awareness of living in a religiously plural world. Whether we should welcome or decry our new found multi-religious awareness, or the circumstances that have given birth to it, is a secondary consideration compared with how we are going to deal with it. This is the way things are. This is the situation in which we now have to live.

It should be stressed again that I am merely using globalization as a shorthand device to try to place in a wider context the revolution in religious consciousness which has given rise to our awareness of religious pluralism. There are all sorts of other ways in which this kind of context-setting might be attempted, and it is as well to be aware of some of the limitations which the vocabulary of globalization carries with it. The vast processes that it tries to name, or at least some aspects of them, might equally well be described in other ways. For instance, as Tim O'Sullivan points out, "the cultural experience of globalization and the mishmash of world cultures which result, can be seen as a telling aspect of the postmodern condition."[26] Likewise, one might prefer to think in terms of the dominance, spread and implications of Western capitalism. Though Peter Beyer, for one, argues strongly against seeing globalization as just another word for Western expansion. In his view it is:

more than the spread of one historically existing culture at the expense of all others. It is also the creation of a new global culture with its attendant social structures, one which increasingly becomes the broader social context of all particular cultures in the world, including those of the West. The spread of global social reality is therefore quite as much at the "expense" of the latter as it is of non-western cultures.[27]

Or one might see consumerism, or, perhaps, technological imperialism (or "technopoly"[28]), or the irresistible march of scientific rationalism, or the unfettered practice of free-market forces and mass production, as more deftly pinpointing the trends which have increasingly come to characterize the our century than "globalization" does. Herbert Schiller, for example, specifically rejects "globalization," suggesting that the situation it is seeking to describe is more accurately seen as "the spread of unchecked trans-national corporate activity and the retreat of national accountability."[29] Majid and Katharine Tehranian, on the other hand, suggest that the global communication network is "globalizing local issues at the same pace that it localises global issues such as the environment, human rights, and population control."[30] As such, it has been suggested that the hybrid term "glocalization" more aptly describes what is happening.[31] Globalization is not an exact term, nor is it the only one that might be used. Certainly it would be hard to date any absolute point of beginning for the processes it seeks to name. Its roots lie embedded variously in literacy, capitalism, industrialization, technology, mass production, and so on, and its increasing impact is closely linked to changes in the size and power of business corporations and the massive increase in the geographical scale of their operations (the key catalyst behind such changes being the development of world-spanning communications systems). As John Tomlinson points out, "no matter how generalised a description is given to it, globalization remains a difficult process to get to grips with, either theoretically or empirically."[32] Perhaps Ali Mohammadi comes closest to the mark when he dubs it a kind of "myth of our times"[33] (remembering the enormous influence which myths of one sort or another have always had on human history).

Whatever way one decides to describe these world-shaping trends—globalization, postmodernism, free market capitalism, consumerism, technological imperialism (and for simplicity's sake I have chosen the first of these terms, even though it is far from ideal), we need to appreciate that increasingly "there is a common social environment shared by all people on earth."[34] To ignore this fact and its profound implications would be to miss "a key aspect of the human condition in our contemporary world."[35] Most importantly, we need to recognize that "the present world order is not ordinary but extraordinary,"[36] such that we are witnessing "one of the turning points in human history."[37] Such a turning point has given rise to the religious situation with which this book attempts to deal.

Notes

1. Theodore Zeldin, *An Intimate History of Humanity,* London, 1995, Minerva, p. 18.
2. The idea of an information revolution is effectively critiqued in Michael Traber, (ed.), *The Myth of the Information Revolution: Social and Ethical Implications of Communication Technology,* London, 1986, Sage. Traber suggests that far from making citizens better informed, the information explosion has resulted in a rapid growth of misinformation and disinformation. As such, he questions the extent to which it is accurate to think in terms of an information "revolution" at all.
3. I have, quite deliberately, avoided any neat, dictionary-type definitions of globalization, preferring instead to characterize it in very general terms as an inter-related complex of processes which render regional boundaries looser, more flexible, more permeable—the permeability allowing a two-way flow of influences, and then to offer some illustrative instances of its impact. Neater definitions do exist. For instance, Hamid Mowlana tells us that globalization is "a process of structuration

that encompasses homogenization and heterogenization—a process in which agencies operating under different temporal sequences interact to connect and alter varying structures of social existence to create a structurally oligarchic, but interconnected, world," *Global Communication in Transition: the End of Diversity?* Thousand Oaks, 1996, Sage, p.198. And Ali Mohammadi suggests that "globalization" refers to "the way in which, under contemporary conditions especially, relations of power and communication are stretched across the globe, involving compressions of time and space and a recomposition of social relationships," in Mohammadi, (ed.), *International Communication and Globalisation,* London, 1987, Sage, p.3. It is worth bearing such technically accurate definitions in mind for future reference and orientation. However, they do not strike me as appropriate to the very general, introductory picture of globalization I am attempting to give here.

4.   Ben Bagdikian, *The Media Monopoly,* Boston, 1992, (1983), Beacon Press, p. 247.

5.   Ibid., p. 250.

6.   On the Museum of World Religions see my "The Art of Exhibiting the Sacred," forthcoming in Crispin Paine (ed.), *Religion in Museums,* Leicester, 1999, Leicester University Press.

7.   Fiona Robinson, "Rethinking Ethics in an Era of Globalisation," International Relations & Politics Subject Group, University of Brighton, *Sussex Papers in International Relations* no. 2, 1996, p.1.

8.   Pierre Babin, *The New Era in Religious Communication,* tr. David Smith, Minneapolis, 1991, Fortress Press, p. 203.

9.   The fact that so many of these images are violent is also something that concerns many people. It has been estimated, for example, that the average American TV viewer (of course there is no such person, but the statistic is usefully indicative nonetheless) has witnessed some 18,000 deaths on TV by the age of 14 (this statistic is quoted by John Hick in his *Death and Eternal Life,* London, 1976, Collins, p.86). Can we safely assume that such exposure may be considered morally and religiously neutral?

10. Neil P. Hurley, *Theology Through Film,* New York, 1970, Harper & Row, pp. 191-192.

11. Kenneth Woodward, "Religion Observed: The Impact of the Medium on the Message," in John Coleman and Miklos Tomka (eds.), *Concilium* 1993/6, p. 106.

12. Walter J. Ong, *Orality and Literacy: The Technologising of the Word,* London, 1982, Methuen, p. 78.

13. Jack Goody & Ian Watt, "The Consequences of Literacy," in Jack Goody (ed.), *Literacy in Traditional Societies,* Cambridge, 1968, Cambridge University Press, p. 53.

14. Ibid., p.62.

15. Jack Goody, *The Logic of Writing and the Organisation of Society,* Cambridge, 1986, Cambridge University Press, p.5.

16. Neil Postman, *Amusing Ourselves to Death: Public Discourse in the Age of Show Business,* London, 1986 (1985), Methuen, pp. 162-3.

17. Jorge Schement & Hester Stephenson, "Religion and the Information Society," in Daniel Stout & Judith Buddenbaum (eds.), *Religion and Mass Media: Audiences and Adaptations,* Thousand Oaks, 1996, Sage, p.277.

18. Ibid., p.278.

19. Susan Sontag, *On Photography,* Harmondsworth, 1978 (1977), Penguin, p. 24.

20. Thomas Martin, *Images and the Imageless; A Study in Religious Consciousness and Film,* Lewisburg, 1981, Bucknell University Press, pp. 54-55.

21. See Edward Said, *Covering Islam; How the Media and the Experts Determine How We See the Rest of the World,* London, 1981, RKP (the new 1997 edition includes material on the Gulf War); Akbar S. Ahmed, *Postmodernism and Islam, Predicament and Promise* (in particular Chapter 6, pp. 222-265, "The Evil Demon: the Media as Master"), London, 1992, Routledge; S.A. Schliefer, "An Islamic Perspective on the News," in Chris Arthur (ed.), *Religion and the Media; an Introductory Reader,* Cardiff, 1993, University of Wales Press, pp. 163-175.

22. Ahmed Akbar, op. cit., 223.

23. Majid and Katharine Kia Tehranian, "That Recurrent Suspicion: Democratization in Global Perspective," in Philip Lee (ed.), *The Democratisation of Communication,* Cardiff, 1995, University of Wales Press, p. 42.

24. Ibid.

25. George Gerbner, "The Cultural Frontier: Repression, Violence & the Liberating Alternative," in Philip Lee (ed.), op.cit., p. 170.

26. Tim O'Sullivan, John Hartley et. al., *Key Concepts in Communication and Cultural Studies,* London, 1994, Routledge, p. 130.

27. Peter Beyer, *Religion and Globalisation*, London, 1994, Sage, p. 9.

28. "Technopoly" is Neil Postman's term for the "totalitarian technocracy" which he sees assailing human consciousness and leading to a distortion of values. See his *Technopoly: the Surrender of Culture to Technology*, New York, 1992, Knopf.

29. Herbert I. Schiller, *Information Inequality: the Deepening Social Crisis in America*, New York, 1996, Routledge, p. 135.

30. Majid & Katharine Tehranian, in Philip Lee (ed.), op. cit., p. 61.

31. See Roland Robertson, "Globalisation or Glocalisation?," *Journal of International Communication*, Vol. 1 1994, pp. 33-52.

32. John Tomlinson, "Cultural Globalization and Cultural Imperialism," in Mohammadi (ed.), op. cit., p.171

33. Mohammadi, in Ali Mohammadi (ed.), op. cit., p. 5.

34. Peter Beyer, op. cit., p. 7.

35. Ibid.

36. Hamid Mowlana, op. cit., p. 39.

37. Ibid.

CHAPTER 3

INTRODUCING CIPHER AND THE HALL OF MIRRORS

IN THE early pages of that oddest of books, Flann O'Brien's *At Swim Two Birds*, we read how the proprietor of the Red Swan Hotel, Mr Dermot Trellis, gives birth to a fully grown man. An extract from the local press reports this bizarre matter prosaically enough:

> the new arrival, stated to be "doing very nicely", is about 5 feet 8 inches in height, well-built, dark and clean shaven.[1]

Trellis is, of course, a writer and the new arrival—one John Furriskey by name—is the intended villain in his book. However, the author's plans go seriously awry when he becomes so involved in his own fictional world that he seduces his leading lady. He is eventually put on trial for his life by a self-appointed court of rebellious characters, who are ill-pleased with the lot assigned to them by their author-creator. At that trial Trellis is cross-examined about the nature of Furriskey's birth:

> "In what manner was he born?" the court asks.
> "He awoke," replies Trellis, "as if from sleep."
> "What were his sensations?"
> "Bewilderment, perplexity. He was consumed by doubts as to his own identity."[2]

In an effort to dispel these doubts, Furriskey is seen, shortly after his impromptu entrance into the world,

> searching his room for a looking glass or for a surface that would enable him to ascertain the character of his countenance.[3]

The court is particularly enraged at Trellis' seeming indifference to the severe mental anguish he has occasioned by creating a character who is left so uncertain about who he is and what he ought to do.

"Why," they ask him, "did you not perform so obvious an errand of mercy as to explain his identity and duties to him?"[4]

To this, Trellis has no answer.

Miles away from Flann O'Brien's riotous imagination, in David Hume's *Enquiry Concerning Human Understanding*, we find a not entirely dissimilar process of birth when Hume introduces the man brought into the world "on a sudden,"[5] fully adult and with all his sensory faculties functioning correctly, yet with absolutely no prior experience of the empirical world. Hume's creation is brought on to support the argument against necessary connection. He is given no name, allowed no benefit from custom, "the great guide of human life,"[6] and once he has served his role as dumb (and, we must assume, utterly disorientated) advocate of Hume's philosophical point of view, he disappears without trace. Unlike the unfortunate Trellis, Hume—as far as we know—was never brought to book for so capricious an act of creation.

It is from a birth not unlike that of John Furriskey, or of Hume's man brought into the world on a sudden, that I wish to begin this exploration of commitment in an era of globalization, an era in which the religiously plural nature of our planet has become (and is still becoming) an increasingly inescapable fact. The character I wish to bring to life, and whose fortunes I will examine in the chapters which follow, will be similar to Furriskey in that he will feel bewilderment, perplexity and immense doubt about his identity and purpose, and, like Furriskey, he will search for a mirror which may reveal the "true character of his (and the world's) countenance." He is similar to Hume's abruptly born man in that he has been deliberately created to serve a particular purpose.

I shall call my creature Cipher. The name is chosen simply because so many of its resonances of meaning are appropriate to his situation. To begin with, Cipher, in the sense of nought or zero, suggests neutrality, something bearing neither plus nor minus value. Second, although this neutral zero may have no value in itself, it is something which, placed after any integer, any whole number, multiplies its value tenfold. Third, Cipher can be suggestive of code, of some secret mode of writing where the meaning is uncertain until we find the key which acts to decipher what is said. Fourth, Cipher suggests a person of little significance, a non-entity, someone whose existence and individuality tend to be dwarfed by the immensity, or multiplicity, of the environing phenomena. All these senses are quite deliberately implicit in the name I have chosen. I will explain their aptness in due course.[7]

Who, then, is Cipher, and in what situation does he find himself? Adopting Martin Hollis' neat formula for "in a nutshell" replies,[8] a miser summarizing an answer to these questions by telegram could do so in ten words: *Cipher is someone perplexed by a situation of religious plurality.* In this chapter I want to go beyond such a miser's reply and concentrate on making clear the nature of his perplexity. We can then go on to consider how it might be resolved.

Cipher is an individual whose life is regularly punctuated by an unnerving sense of apparent *insignificance, mystery* and *meaninglessness.* His life appears insignificant when it is viewed against the backdrop of space, time, other persons' lives, and the apparent accidentalness of fate. Cipher knows something of the smallness of our planet and the scale on which individual existence upon it may be seen. In his informed mind's eye he sees the earth as an infinitesimal spark of light in a surrounding immensity of darkness. He knows that on its surface millions upon millions of human beings have passed the briefness of their hurried finitude, leaving scattered behind a cumulative history which dwarfs any single contributory existence such as his. And in the same way, human history itself is dwarfed by the millions of years before its advent, when the globe was untroubled by any human movement and bore only the unreflective tread of giant reptiles and amphibians upon its already ancient contours. He realizes that, during his brief existence, his life may go through pendulum swings of fortune so vast and inexplicable as to disturb the comforting equilibrium that a more reliable routine might suggest. To borrow a potent example recounted by George Steiner, one moment may see him as a comfortably housed academic gently pursuing the life of knowledge, the next as a tortured inmate of some dark place like Treblinka.[9] Less dramatically, one moment he may be healthy and whole, and the next reduced by an accident, whether of natural or human origin, to a pitiful state of pain and incapacity.

At the same time as it may appear insignificant, Cipher's life also seems mysterious—indeed, the very sense of its insignificance may act to trigger a sense of wonder and mystery. Is it not profoundly strange that, amidst the ponderous immensities of time, space and circumstance, this one unique and fragile path which is his life should have emerged out of all the flux of a seemingly accidental creation? Why *this* path and not some other? That he should have been born at all, and that being born he was born *thus*, as a particular individual, seems so improbable that the mere fact of his existence is replete with mystery.

Cipher has a wealth of knowledge at his disposal concerning the physical nature of the world he lives in, and about the structure and function of the organism which he thinks of as "me." Around him science produces sophistication upon sophistication, which can subdue and control much that was hitherto beyond all but the most minimal human influence. In terms of both sciences and humanities, his understanding of many aspects of his experience is subtle and profound. Yet there remains a sense of mystery which seems impervious to all the information he can muster, to all the power—practical and intellectual—which is at his disposal, and which seems even to mock the most accomplished technological achievements as being somehow beside the point. Why does he exist at all? And, existing, why in this particular form? Why is there something rather than nothing, existence rather than unbroken emptiness? And, more pressingly, what view ought he to take of this mysterious place in which he briefly finds himself, such that his life may be lived in the most appropriate fashion?

Cipher's insignificant and mysterious life often seems meaningless. Although he has many plans and ambitions, many likes and dislikes, much that he wishes to do and much he would prefer to avoid, Cipher feels an underlying emptiness which does not allow such things to provide a fully satisfactory sense of value for his existence. Beneath his search for a better job, for increased wealth, for a happy family life, Cipher feels a deep absence of purpose. This sense of meaninglessness, like that of insignificance and mystery, is sharply accentuated by his encounter with the fact of suffering. He is aware that, although his own situation may presently be benign, peaceful and enjoyable, this is a precarious state. Moreover, there are always others in the grip of some variety of pain and horror. And, of course, no matter how pleasant existence may be, it will eventually be aborted. Death casts a shadow of futility even into Cipher's summer.

I will refer to Cipher's feelings of insignificance, mystery and meaninglessness collectively—since there is considerable overlap between them, both in terms of cause and expression—simply as his sense of *lostness*. This is a feeling that he does not belong in the world, that he possesses no comfortable sense of a place in it which assures him of his identity, value and purpose. Virginia Woolf once remarked that:

> the strange thing about life is that though the nature of it must have been apparent to everyone for hundreds of years, no one has left an adequate account of it.[10]

Cipher shares this sense of perplexity. No matter how at home he may often feel in the world, no matter how well acquainted with the familiar calm and turbulence of the human condition, he is periodically aware of his lack of any adequate account of life, of some statement about it, some outlook on it, some means of living it, which would quieten his feelings of insignificance, mystery and meaninglessness, and comfort his lostness with an unshakable sense of homecoming.

Alongside his sense of lostness, Cipher is well aware that there exist many versions of the "adequate account" of life which he seeks. He recognizes that, since the dawn of history, people have found a sense of belonging in some form of religious outlook on life. From the burial ceremonies of early man to the complexities of Vedic ritual, from the sacrifices (sometimes human) which the Iron Age peoples of Europe made to Nerthus, their earth goddess, to the Buddhists' Eightfold Path, from the teachings of Jesus to Islamic submission to the will of Allah, Cipher sees glimpses of various, "adequate accounts" which seem to make sense of human existence and seem to provide those who hold (or held) them with an effective defense against that intrusive sense of lostness which troubles him.

Cipher sees many threads of purported sense which have variously led men and women through the labyrinth of existence, plotting guide-lines across even such desolate places as those occupied by pain and loneliness, separation and death. The problem is, which, if any, should he follow? Do any of the religions offer an adequate account of life which he can accept as such and, if so, which one? Moreover, if such an account is to be found in the religious realm, which one—or which combination—offers the most adequate account? Cipher's situation is problematic, not simply because of a sense of lostness, but because this is coupled with an awareness of numerous versions of curative meaning which might counteract it. At this point anyway, his problem is not so much that of a man suffering from some ailment who is looking for a cure, as that of someone faced with trying to decide among many pos-sible treatments. He does not know which one is best, or if a combina-tion would, perhaps, be better. Nor is he sure if they offer the same diagnosis, or if any of them are, in fact, efficacious.

To a large extent, Cipher's world is that of an educated twentieth century Westerner. Now this is *not* to say either that *every* contempo-rary educated Westerner may be characterized thus, or that in other times and places there was no such thing as religious pluralism, or that one must be educated before being stung with a sense of life's insignifi-cance, its meaninglessness or mystery. However, our present century and culture do have certain features which render Cipher's situation problematic in a more insistent way than had I decided to bring him to birth in some other setting. The first century Mediterranean world would doubtless have provided him with an interesting pluralism of beliefs as the Christian religion budded towards its eventual global dimension in modest local settings of considerable spiritual diversity. A genesis some centuries earlier in the midst of the plague in Athens, described so elo-quently by Thucydides,[11] or in the turbulence of revolutionary France or Russia, might well be supposed potent enough environments to stir even the most complacent and untroubled outlook to thoughts of the insignificance and apparent senselessness of human life. Such settings would provide many interesting problems, but they are not ones I wish to investigate here. *Cipher is very much a late twentieth century creation, located firmly in the present.*

Cipher's present-day status means that, rather than seeing no further than the next village or city or continent, his perspective is global. He is aware of the earth as a single planet and of its tinyness in space. And through the various cognitive telescopes and microscopes afforded by modern learning he can see, almost at a glance, the diversity of the present, and, stretching out before it, he can eavesdrop far beyond those ancestors whose lives and beliefs are still held warm in living memories, to generations long forgotten by any self-conscious familial survivor. Ninian Smart has drawn attention to the change in religious awareness from local to global dimensions which has been witnessed in the last century. Whereas in times past a religious consciousness could develop in relative isolation, in ignorance of what Smart calls "other worlds," existing beyond the horizon of its awareness, the present outlook can take virtually the whole gamut of human religiousness into its purview. Previously it was possible to be aware of religious diversity on a local scale, presently such awareness is of potentially global extent. As Smart writes in *Beyond Ideology*, his study of religion and the future of western civilization:

> when Jesus walked with his comrades beside the hot blue shore of the lake, the Buddha's message was [unbeknownst to them] already centuries old in the minds of the shaven-headed monks of Sri Lanka. And men who went for a change of soul to the shining mysteries of Isis knew nothing of Confucius or the Tao. But now there is no world beyond our world. Our *oikumene* is spherical, closed, and there is no new frontier.[12]

Until the arrival of those extra-terrestrial beings whose existence some are so sure of, our outlook on religion may be considered complete, in a sense that was not possible for previous ages. In this global village, Cipher is aware of more religions than would have been possible at any other time, not because there *are* more, but because of the overview which is now available to him.

In the general context of "modernity," Peter Berger has drawn attention to the "multiplication of options"[13] facing people today. Indeed, he suggests that "modern consciousness" entails a movement from fate to choice"[14] (and the same point holds with even more force for "postmodern" consciousness). Cipher is situated very much in the context of choice amidst multiple options. Fate has not dictated what account of the world he will accept as adequate; rather, it has informed him of a range of possibilities and the decision is left to him. George Rupp has pointed out the way in which such a state of perceived pluralism poses a challenge, as it impinges ever more forcefully on the mind. In his *Beyond Existentialism and Zen* he argues that:

> Greater self-consciousness about pluralism has the effect of radicalizing its impact. Unreflective awareness that other people adhere to different traditions becomes instead a recognition of multiple perspectives as alternatives competing for the individual's allegiance.[15]

Moreover, for Cipher the impact of pluralism is further radicalized by the fact that he approaches it from a perspective which is "unanchored." He is not a Christian or a Jew or a Hindu or a Muslim surveying the teachings of faiths other than his own—or, indeed, the variety of outlooks *within* his own faith—and coming to *theological* terms with the diversity. Rather, he is aware of the different religions' "adequate accounts" of the world from an essentially uncommitted perspective. He holds no specific *religious* guidelines to which appeal might be made.

Let it be emphasized that, although he is definitely contemporary, I am not casting Cipher in any widely representative, let alone prescriptive, role. He does not stand for the plight of twentieth century religiousness, if indeed there is one; he is not meant to show how we *ought* to react to a situation of religious pluralism, even supposing such a single right way exists; his dilemma is not that of "modern man in search of a soul," if that is indeed what modern man is looking for; he has not been designed to symbolize any problems which faith may encounter in a secular setting. I would hope that the situation in which I place him is not implausible, to the point of finding no resonance of interest or sympathy from his readers; but, at the same time, it must be stressed that his situation is to some extent artificial and contrived. Thus, if I had cared to make him modern in the sense of representing one widespread modern attitude towards religion, I ought, if Hendrik Kraemer's analysis is accurate, to have ensured that Cipher manifested that "mysterious phenomenon" of complete indifference to religion—indifference in the face of extensive information—rather than the interest and concern which he will, in fact, show.[16] I would expect many people to see Cipher's whole character as improbable, and his search for some curative response to his sense of lostness to be fundamentally misguided. Indeed, I shall consider some powerful objections to it in a moment. It is, however, my intention to focus closely on this particular situation— for it seems preferable to discuss a single clearly demarcated example and let others draw their own conclusions about the extent of its relevance, rather than to make pronouncements on such elusive entities as "modern religiousness," "twentieth century spirituality" or whatever. Although it might seem unduly restrictive to focus so closely on a particular figure, and an imaginary one at that, I would argue that, in so doing, quite apart from side-stepping the considerable perils of addressing highly contentious generalities, we may make appeal to various persuasive literary precedents as justifying such a strategy. Surely a great deal may be learned by looking closely at carefully constructed fictional settings, even if they are not, indeed perhaps especially if they are not, wholly typical of a particular age or group. Although Cipher can lay no claim to the status of a Hamlet, a Raskolnikov, an Anna Karenina or a Kristin Lavransdatter—beside them he is a mere shadow of ideas—he can claim credibility by appeal to the educative aspect of such fictions, which is unimpaired even when their situation is non-representative and their behaviour eccentric or indeed mad. It would, in short, be rather rash to question the usefulness of taking Cipher as a point of focus simply on the grounds of his individual fictional status.

From birth, albeit of the artificial ready-made kind which Flann O'Brien dubs "aestho-autogonomy,"[17] let us go momentarily to death. In one of P. D. James' rather superior "whodunnits," *Death of an Expert Witness*, we find Commander Adam Dalgleish and Detective Inspector Massingham searching through the room of a murder victim. Among his books are volumes by Teilhard de Chardin, Jean Paul Sartre and Plato, as well as numerous titles in the field of comparative religion. Massingham remarks to his chief:

> "It looks as if he was one of those men who torment themselves trying to discover the meaning of existence."
> "You find that reprehensible?" Dalgleish asks.
> "I find it futile. Metaphysical speculation is about as pointless as a discussion on the meaning of one's lungs, they're for breathing."
> "And life is for living. You find that an adequate personal credo?"
> "To maximise one's pleasures and minimise one's pain, yes Sir, I do. And, I suppose, to bear with stoicism those miseries I can't avoid."[18]

If Cipher were to meet an untimely end under suspicious circumstances and attract the attentions of such philosophical policemen, they would doubtless find in his room a similar preponderance of books on comparative religion, and it is clear that he would fall squarely into the category of "one of those men who torment themselves trying to discover the meaning of existence." Equally clear is the fact that there are many who would simply dismiss such an effort as futile and misconceived. How would Cipher reply to such criticism (supposing he encountered it while still alive)?

He might well end up *agreeing* with it. Perhaps, in the end, his zero of neutrality will take its stand behind whatever integer indicates that there is no meaning to existence beyond day-to-day criteria of sense, and that to look beyond these for some sort of *ultimate* purpose is simply misguided. It must be stressed that, as we join him, Cipher is uncommitted. His problem is not just to decide which religious outlook is true, for among the multiplicity of options apparently available to him is that which queries the reliability of *any* religious outlook. He does not begin by assuming *a priori* that some religious outlook on the world is true and that he only has to decide which one (which, obviously, would not be an easy task). Rather, his question is: which, *if any*, of these outlooks can offer an adequate account of life? Cipher's main assumption is that for many of their millions of believers, religious outlooks on the world provide precisely that antidote to a sense of lostness that he is looking for. Whether or not he will reach a similar conclusion about any of them, however, remains uncertain.

For convenience I will refer to that state of mind in which no decision has been taken about the overall meaning and nature of existence, or about whether such a meaning exists, as "*world uncertainty*," to the resolution of this sense—in whatever form—as the discovery of "*world certainty*," and to the movement between former and latter states as making a "*world decision*." Not all world certainties are religious, but I will be restricting my attention here to those of them that are. Thus, it is important to remember that making a world decision may as easily involve a rejection of any form of religious outlook as the acceptance of one.

Further, when we identify Cipher with the man who torments himself looking for the meaning of existence, we must avoid thinking in simplistic terms of his expecting a neat, clearly formulated answer, such as the proverbial "42" in *The Hitch Hiker's Guide to the Galaxy*.[19] As Karl Britton puts it in his study of *Philosophy and the Meaning of Life*, "To say that there is a meaning in life is to say that there is something that may serve as a guide in our lives."[20] Cipher is not looking for some sort of easy verbal formula, but rather for some guidelines by which he might navigate a sense-giving course through the various elements of that feeling of lostness which prompts his sense of world uncertainty in the first place and which, together with his multi-religious informedness, lies at the root of his dilemma.

Rather than presenting Cipher as someone looking for "the meaning of life"—which in the current zeitgeist, given such phenomena as Zaphod Beeblebrox and Monty Python, has become a topic as much in the preserve of the clown as the contemplative, we might simply say that Cipher is looking for *peace of mind*. According to the present Dalai Lama, this, in the last analysis, is "the hope of all men."[21] If such peace of mind does indeed exist, however, it should be stressed that most of the varieties of it offered in religious contexts do not exactly conform to an over-literal understanding of this phrase. Like that exemplar of educatively misleading titles, *Zen and the Art of Motorcycle Maintenance*,[22] a book which has little to do with either Zen or motorcycle maintenance, the "peace of mind" offered by the world's religions is often neither particularly peaceful nor primarily intellectual.

In terms of his religious environment, Cipher finds himself located in a *hall of mirrors*. Rather than standing before any single mirror—whether of Buddhism, Christianity, Hinduism, Islam, Jainism, Judaism, Sikhism, or some less easily labeled faith—Cipher finds himself surrounded by mirrors, on which appear many differing reflections, all purporting to show how he should see himself and the world he lives in and, in consequence, how he ought to conduct his life. The hall of mirrors is the first of many metaphors which I shall employ in exploring Cipher's situation. Indeed, as a general epigraph applicable to this book as a whole, had I not opted for Sallie McFague TeSelle's observation, I might have chosen Max Black's remark on the unique usefulness of metaphor:

> Metaphorical thought is a distinctive mode of achieving insight, not to be construed as an ornamental substitute for plain thought.[23]

Since the hall of mirrors is the central metaphor to which I will refer, it is important to see how it can be used to symbolize many of the important aspects of the milieu in which Cipher is located. There are six points about it which I want to consider now.

First, as we have already noted briefly, the hall of mirrors has always been there, though its extent and content will vary somewhat from age to age. It is not a twentieth century construction. Being in a position to see its existence is, however, a relatively recent phenomenon. Like the sky, religious pluralism has always been a characteristic of the human environment. But just as the jet aircraft is a comparatively recent innovation, so too is the ability to travel through the hall of mirrors to the extent and with the ease that it is now possible for us to do. That is not to say that previous generations never got airborne—but their passage through the religious hall of mirrors was of limited duration and questionable value, so imperfectly did they perceive the images which were there. Even so skilled a pioneer aviator in the interreligious stratosphere as William Beveridge, can be seen crashing through a low altitude survey of Judaism, Hinduism and Islam, before landing back where he had started from, almost as if he had never taken off. This is in no way to denigrate his efforts. That a passage from his *Private Thoughts Upon Religion*, published posthumously in 1709, was chosen to preface that epoch-making entry into the hall of mirrors, *The Sacred Books of the East* series, is testimony to the enduring applicability of his *intentions*, even if the right equipment to carry them out properly simply did not exist. Beveridge writes:

> The general inclinations which are naturally implanted in my soul to some religion, it is impossible for me to shift off; but there being such a multiplicity of religions in the world, I desire now seriously to consider with myself, which of them all to restrain these my general inclinations to.[24]

Similar sentiments might be voiced by Cipher. There are three main differences between him and Beveridge. First, whilst Beveridge moves out from—indeed never really leaves—a solid Christian base, Cipher has no such secure spiritual anchorage. Second, whilst Beveridge considers it impossible that he should ever shake off the "general inclinations" to some religion that are "implanted in his soul," Cipher's inclinations to some religious outlook on the world are strongly connected with his desire for peace of mind. If he finds that no such peace of mind is available, *his* inclinations will be to dismiss religion and look elsewhere. The third (and perhaps the greatest) difference between them is that the meagerness of information available to Beveridge simplifies his quest considerably, whilst the range and depth of Cipher's information makes his search a much more complex affair. Beveridge writes,

> the reason of this my inquiry is not that I am, in the least, dissatisfied with that religion I have already embraced; but because it is

natural for all men to have an over-bearing opinion and esteem of that particular religion they are born and bred up in ... to profess myself a Christian, and to believe that Christians are only in the right because my forefathers were so, is no more than the heathens and Mahometans have to say for themselves. Indeed, there was never any religion so barbarous and diabolical, but it was preferred before all other religions whatsoever, by them that did profess it. ... The Indians that worship the devil, would think it as strange doctrine to say that Christ is to be feared more than the devil as such as believe in Christ think it to say the devil is to be preferred before Christ.[25]

For Cipher, the reason for his inquiry is similar to Beveridge's in that birth alone does not serve to decide the matter of his religion. He has not been born Jewish, Hindu, Christian, Buddhist or whatever, and thought no more about it. Unlike Beveridge, though, whose realization of the inadequacy of mere indigenousness as a justification for his faith does not, at the same time, mean that he abandons his world-certain position for one of neutral investigator (in anything more than an artificial methodological sense), for Cipher there is no such point of reference from which to set off or to which to return. Moreover, while Beveridge can dismiss the "heathens" and "Mahometans" fairly easily as worshipping devils, or being otherwise grossly and obviously misled, Cipher has abandoned such an instantly dismissive vocabulary, with all its easy theological implications, as he discovers more and more about the religions in question and recognizes their status as serious attempts to offer an "adequate account of the world." The hall of mirrors is not new, but never before have so many of its polished surfaces been accessible to the inquiring eye.

The second feature of the hall of mirrors which I want to stress is that it may have either a theoretical or concrete locus, or a mixture of both. In other words, Cipher might be informed about Buddhism, Christianity, Hinduism, Islam, Jainism, Judaism and other religions in a theoretical fashion only, without having actually encountered any living representatives of these faiths, or he might have no knowledge about the different religions beyond that which can be directly observed in the people around him. I will assume that for Cipher the hall of mirrors is perceived in both ways. Not only does he read and think widely in the general area of religious studies and comparative religion, but he encounters living representatives of the different faiths as he goes about his business in a multi-cultural, and therefore multi-religious, globalized society. Moreover, he sees the different religions reported on television and in the press, and has visited some of the world's great holy places on his travels. Indeed, one of the things that makes his quest more difficult and complex is the tension which sometimes exists between Buddhism, Christianity, Hinduism, Islam, Judaism, *etc.* on the street, as it were (and even more so on the screen), and the theoretical, text-based versions of these faiths. How is Cipher to decide what counts as Buddhism if the Buddhists he encounters, although calling themselves Buddhists, sometimes flout some of the Five Precepts, or if some Christians behave in ways which are out of line with the moral code they claim to adhere to?

Third, the religious hall of mirrors must not be seen in the simplistic terms suggested by the fairground version of this phenomenon, from which the metaphor is, admittedly, derived. It is not as if we enter some dim-lit tent and walk between a row of mirrors showing four deviations from the norm: fat, thin, squat and tall, knowing all along what we really look like, and feeling amusement rather than puzzlement. Cipher has not chosen to enter the hall of mirrors, and he can see no easy exit from it which marks a return to "normality." He does not know all along what the correct image is, nor are there a mere handful of reflections before him. It is not as if he is flanked on one side by Hinduism, Buddhism and Taoism and on the other by Judaism, Christianity and Islam, such that there are six distinct images, six adequate accounts of the world, offering the possibility of peace of mind in the face of his feelings of insignificance, mystery and meaninglessness.

Apart from the fact that inter-religious diversity extends beyond those faiths just mentioned to Jainism, Shinto, Sikhism, Zoroastrianism, and into the uncertain area of new religious movements and what Tillich termed the quasi-religions (such things as humanism, national-ism and Marxism), there is considerable *intra-religious* diversity as well. Each mirror which we might at first sight take to be single is, in fact, fragmented into many facets. The various religions do not simply present a series of single unitary reflections which would enable us to say without qualification, *that* (referring to some precisely specifiable set of phenomena) is Hinduism, Buddhism, Christianity, Islam, or whatever. Rather, within each of these broad (and by no means clear or necessarily exclusive) categories, there are successively smaller divisions (Vedantic and Tantric; Hinayana and Mahayana; Shi'ite and Sunni; Catholic and Protestant), until eventually we come down to the individual and find an almost person-to-person variation in belief. Cantwell Smith has pointed to this "further fact" (i.e. further to inter-religious diversity) of diversity within each tradition.[26] Every faith, he says, "appears in a variety of forms,"[27] to the extent that "it is no longer possible to have a religious faith without *selecting* its form."[28] Focusing on Christianity in particular, he suggests that the modern Christian faces a situation, within his or her own faith, of "open variety,"[29] or "optional alternatives,"[30] in which they must come to a decision regarding what form their commitment is to take, rather than assuming that this is something which is automatically settled simply by being a Christian in the first place. Under the general heading of "Christian," (and the same goes for "Hindu," "Buddhist," "Muslim" etc.), there are many possible outlooks that can be taken. In a sense, each of the mirrors in the hall of mirrors leads off into a hall of mirrors of its own. Indeed, we might suppose that Cipher has many fictional first cousins, each engaged in a quest similar to his own—Christians, Hindus, Muslims and Buddhists who, within the confines of their own particular faith, are trying to decide where, precisely, to locate their individual commitment and what to make of those surrounding alternatives to the choice they finally arrive at. We might think of Cipher as being one stage behind these first cousins, for he has not yet narrowed down the area of choice into the slightly more manageable bounds of a single particular religion. Although Cipher may, from time to time, cast an eye towards the progress of these first cousins, it must be stressed that his problems, although similar, are not the same as those posed by religious plurality for commitment within a Christian or Hindu or other particularized setting.[31] Alternatively, depending on the course they followed to get to their position of choice set amidst mono-religious diversity, it might be argued that, far from being behind them, Cipher is in fact one step *ahead* of them. If they have failed to appreciate the logic of religious plurality and are confining their attention to single traditions for unreflective reasons of sectarian loyalty, then clearly this is so. They are in that case merely reflecting Beveridge's maxim that it is natural for people to have "an over-bearing opinion and esteem of that particular religion they are born and bred up in."

The fourth point I wish to mention about the hall of mirrors is, simply, that not all of its reflective surfaces will bear images of the same size and intensity. It seems likely that the "adequate accounts" of the world which may have been offered by the various "dead" religions will not constitute such significant reflections for Cipher as those offered by the great world religions which are still very much alive today. Similarly, the various localized religions which still flourish around the globe, different forms of tribal animism for example, may be supposed to exert a less potent force than that emanating from the more international faiths. Moreover, according to Cipher's personality, his likes and dislikes, some mirrors will exert a stronger fascination than others.

Fifth, the religious mirrors must not be seen as straightforward two-dimensional looking-glasses. In one sense, of course, they can be taken as such. After all, generally speaking, at the level of introductory textbooks on the major world faiths, there is a large clearish surface image which announces "Buddhism," "Christianity," "Hinduism," "Islam" (or some other religion) to the observer. But simply to stop before such images and to proceed no further would be to take a superficial and ultra-literal view. The mirrors consist of groups of individual believers, and really to see what the images of "Buddhism," or "Christianity," or "Hinduism" offer, in terms of the peace of mind that he is looking for, Cipher must try to see how such committed individuals, who term themselves "Buddhists," or "Christians," or "Hindus" see the world. He must try to move from the point of view of external observer, standing outside and looking at superficial pictures of religions, to the perspective of internal observer who is in a position to share more closely the outlook of those who have made a world decision and align themselves to (and so help to constitute), a particular faith. In short, his focus of interest in the religious hall of mirrors will be more on *persons*, rather than the abstract religious systems within which they might happen to stand. At the end of the day it is the lives and thought of individuals who claim to have found some curative response to the sense of lostness which they and Cipher feel that constitute the particular area he wishes to investigate. That the lives and thoughts of the individual may sometimes be at odds with the traditions in which they claim to stand is, as mentioned earlier, a further complicating factor.

The sixth and last point about the hall of mirrors simply has to do with the implications both of "hall" and "mirror." These ought, I think, to be made explicit, since part of my reason for choosing this metaphor was because of what they suggest. "Hall" can mean either the main room of a great house or a passage through which one passes to one's destination. It is important to remember that, although Cipher may feel he is at the beginning of his search, he may, in a sense, have reached his destination already. Perhaps his investigative journey will merely involve a change of perspective, so that the passage is seen as the room he wants to get to. This is a point I will return to in a later chapter. "Mirror," on the other hand, is derived from the Latin, "to wonder at," and serves as a useful reminder of the importance of wonder as a basic religious sense. If Cipher is to see in any depth through the eyes of those whose world decisions interest him, he will often need to share their sense of wonder at the fact of being.

As well as the objection that, in looking for some sort of peace of mind in the various "adequate accounts of the world" apparently offered by the religions, Cipher is in fact seeking something which simply does not exist, there is also the complaint or caution that, unless he is very careful, he may end up focusing his attention on abstractions which have little to do with the varieties of faith by which men and women

have actually responded to the human situation. Wilfred Cantwell Smith
has argued that:

> Neither religion in general nor any one of the religions ... is in
> itself an intelligible entity, a valid object of inquiry or of concern
> either for the scholar or for the man of faith.[32]

According to Smith's analysis, the concept "religion", and the various
religions subsumed beneath it—Buddhism, Christianity, Hinduism and
so on—are all relatively recent Western reifications of personal faith
into impersonal ideological structures, which act to misdirect our attention away from the actual lived religiousness of individuals and towards apparently mutually exclusive systems which stand quite apart
from each other. The word "religion" should, argues Smith, be dropped
from our vocabulary because it is "confusing, unnecessary and distorting."[33] Likewise, since modernity has "conferred names where they did
not exist,"[34] terms such as "Buddhism", "Hinduism", "Islam" and so on
ought to be done away with. Smith is not suggesting that the entities
that have been called religions do not exist but, rather, that they exist in
a form which is distorted by any attempt to consider them in terms of
unitary, exclusive entities subsumable under single headings. In place
of religion and religions, Smith argues that we should talk in terms of
two interrelated factors, an historical *cumulative tradition*, and the *personal faith* of men and women. The use of terms like "Muslim" and
"Christian," at least as nouns, should be abandoned since they impose
boundaries where none need, in fact, exist. As Smith puts it, arguing for
their purely adjectival usage:

> A man cannot be both a Christian and a Muslim at the same time.
> The nouns keep us apart. On the other hand, it is not, I suggest, as
> ridiculous or fanciful as might be supposed, to ask whether in the
> realm of adjectives it may not be possible for a man to be both
> Christian and Muslim at the same time. I for one can understand
> and countenance meanings for the terms in which not only is this
> possible, but even in which one could say that to be truly Chris-
> tian is ipso facto to be truly Muslim.[35]

Clearly, if the hall of mirrors is perceived as a series of distinct surfaces whose reflective areas do not overlap, then it falls foul of Smith's analysis and stands accused of seriously misrepresenting the whole religious realm. If we see Cipher's situation as one in which he faces many unitary images reflected from discrete mirrors which can be termed "Buddhism," "Christianity," "Hinduism," "Islam" *etc.*, then there may indeed be the danger that his quest for peace of mind will degenerate into a survey of precisely those aspects of religion which might be least valued by those who profess themselves faithful to some religious world certainty.

I hope that by enlarging and clarifying the nature of the hall of mirrors metaphor I have already allayed any fears that Cipher is going to misdirect his search into an assessment of illicit and simplistic reifications. The mirrors are complex, three dimensional and constituted by the faith of *individuals*, on whom Cipher's focus of attention will be firmly set. This is not the place to embark either on an appreciation or a critique of Smith's thought. My concern is simply to consider those aspects of it which might be relevant to Cipher's situation and which might, perhaps, be considered to constitute a serious objection to the intelligibility of his intended quest for peace of mind. Perhaps we can best sum up the direction in which his criticisms point and show how Cipher does not stand with those accused, by developing a rather unsatisfactory metaphor which Smith himself suggests in his influential study, *The Meaning and End of Religion*. Complaining of irreverent and insensitive studies of religion, Smith argues that the scholars concerned:

> might uncharitably be compared to flies crawling on the outside of a goldfish bowl, making accurate and complete observations on the fish inside, measuring their scales meticulously, and indeed contributing much to a knowledge of the subject, but never asking themselves, and never finding out how it feels to be a goldfish.[36]

Such scholars imagine that there are a series of separate goldfish bowls on which they stick the labels, "Buddhism," "Christianity," "Hinduism," and so on, and proceed to focus their attention as much on the bowls themselves as on what happens inside them. And when they do look inside, their vision is refracted through the distorting glass of the reifications which they have imposed. Cipher, on the other hand, might be seen as being adrift on the sea of possible world certainties, aware of the various currents and seeing those who call themselves Jewish, Sikh or Parsee as voyaging in particular directions. He is less interested in plotting divisions in the ocean than in discovering where the various navigational possibilities lead, so that, eventually, he may decide which, if any, to follow.

While accepting Wilfred Cantwell Smith's point that it is misguided to suppose that we can draw neatly exclusive lines around individual expressions of religiousness and proceed to juggle intellectually with "Buddhism," "Hinduism," "Islam" as if they were so many discrete, easily graspable entities, I have, however, absolutely no intention of changing my vocabulary accordingly. To excise "religion" and the names of the various faiths from what follows would leave many embarrassing gaps which I doubt even Roget could fill convincingly, and which would certainly leave me quite lost for words. Indeed Smith's apparently serious suggestions about removing such words from the language shows a strange insensitivity to the mechanics of linguistic change, which tends to come about through reformed usage rather than instant extermination and replacement.

I hope that the appropriateness of Cipher's name may now be fully apparent. He is Cipher in the sense of nought or zero because at this point he feels that his life is without real direction. He has made no world decision, he is uncommitted, in a state of world uncertainty. He wishes to search in the hall of mirrors for the possibility of a religious integer to place before his existence, so that his life might take on some value which is not eroded by his sense of lostness. The problem is, just as there are many numbers so there are many religions. He is not sure whether they offer the same or different values, or if any of them offer the value that he is looking for (or whether he should adopt one integer, several, none, or a series of fractions drawn from different sources). He is Cipher in the sense of code, in that he feels his life is mysterious, that, were he only able to discover the key, he would find a deciphering meaning. Again, the problem is, *which* key? He is Cipher in the sense of being someone insignificant, because he feels lost and dwarfed by the environing immensities of time and space in which the fragile planet of his birth seems scarcely larger than a dust-speck, on which his sense of lostness sometimes seems more appropriate than any scheme of sense.

Cipher may seem to be something of a religious outsider and yet there is, perhaps, a loose sense in which, despite the uncommitted, searching stance, he might still be described as being religious. Certainly some comments of Wittgenstein's would seem to categorize him thus. "The meaning of life," wrote Wittgenstein, "i.e. the meaning of the world, we can call God.... To pray is to think about the meaning of life...to believe in God means to see that life has a meaning."[37] According to these criteria, Cipher certainly prays (i.e. he thinks about the meaning of life), though he does not believe in God, even to the not necessarily theistic extent of seeing that life has a meaning. Whether or not such a meaning exists is precisely what he wants to find out. As we shall see in the next chapter, however, his search in the hall of mirrors for meaning which can offer peace of mind will share at least some of the more troublesome aspects of an overtly religious quest.

Notes

1. Flann O'Brien, *At Swim Two Birds*, London, 1966 (1939), Hart-Davis, MacGibbon Ltd., p. 54.
2. Ibid., p. 57.
3. Ibid., p. 59.
4. Ibid.
5. David Hume, *An Enquiry Concerning Human Understanding*, Oxford, 1894, (1748), Oxford University Press, Selby-Bigge edition, Section 4 Part 1, p. 28.

6. Ibid., Section 5 Part 1, p. 44.

7. In choosing to call my imaginary character "Cipher" I do not want to bring to mind, beyond noting its occurrence and possible future relevance, the concept of the same name which plays an important part in Karl Jaspers' philosophy. For Jaspers, the centrally important cipher of "foundering" "signifies the fruitlessness of all endeavours to reach, from a finite basis…a satisfactory access to Being, i.e., to arrive at the absolute." So, the character Cipher might, eventually, in some future philosophical stage of his search, consider whether or not what he is attempting falls under such a condemnation. However, for the purposes of that part of his search which will be dealt with in this book, Cipher and his readers can simply lay to one side as accidental any implications which may be read off Jaspers' remarks on "ciphers" or "cipher-script." My choice of "Cipher" as a name for the heuristic fiction herein created occurred long before I learnt of Jaspers' use of the term. Since the identical nomenclature is coincidental, no significance should be read into its occurrence in two such different contexts. On Jaspers' concept of foundering, see Johannes Thyssen, "The Concept of 'Foundering' in Jaspers' Philosophy," pp. 297-235 in Paul Arthur Schilpp (ed.), *The Philosophy of Karl Jaspers*, New York, 1957, Tudor Publishing Co. The quotation above is taken from p. 312 of Thyssen's article.

8. See Martin Hollis, *Models of Man, Philosophical Thoughts on Social Action*, Cambridge, 1977, Cambridge University Press, pp. 20-21.

9. George Steiner, *Language and Silence, Essays 1958-1966*, London, 1985, (1967), Faber, pp. 180-181.

10. Virginia Woolf, *Jacob's Room*, Harmondsworth, 1971, (1922), Penguin, p. 90.

11. Thucydides, *The Peloponnesian War*, see in particular Book 2 Chapter 5.

12. Ninian Smart, *Beyond Ideology: Religion and the Future of Western Civilization*, London, 1981, (the Gifford Lectures at the University of Edinburgh, 1979-1980), Collins, p. 21.

13. Peter L. Berger, *The Heretical Imperative, Contemporary Possibilities of Religious Affirmation*, London, 1980, (1979), Collins, p. 11.

14. Ibid.

15. George Rupp, *Beyond Existentialism and Zen: Religion in a Pluralistic World*, New York, 1979, Oxford University Press, P. 10.

16. Hendrick Kraemer, *Religion and the Christian Faith*, London, 1956, Lutterworth Press, p. 22.

17. Flann O'Brien, op. cit., p. 55.
18. P. D. James, *Death of an Expert Witness*, London, 1983 (1977), Sphere Books, p. 186.
19. Douglas Adams, *The Hitch Hiker's Guide to the Galaxy*, London 1979, Pan Books, p. 135f.
20. Karl Britton, *Philosophy and the Meaning of Life*, Cambridge, 1969, Cambridge University Press, p. 12.
21. The Dalai Lama, *My Land and My People, the Autobiography of His Holiness the Dalai Lama*, edited by David Howarth, London, 1962, Weidenfeld & Nicholson, p. 211.
22. Robert Pirsig, *Zen and the Art of Motorcycle Maintenance*, London, 1974, The Bodley Head.
23. Max Black, *Models and Metaphors, Studies in Language and Philosophy*, New York, 1962, Cornell University Press, p. 237. Lest Black's remark be dismissed as a nugatory philosophical apothegm with little relevance to religion, consider Heinrich Zimmer's claim that "the gist of Buddhism can be grasped more readily and adequately by fathoming the main metaphors through which it appeals to our intuition than by a systematic study of the complicated superstructure and the fine detail of the developed teaching." (*Philosophies of India*, New Jersey, 1969, Princeton University Press, pp. 474-475). I would argue that although metaphor is weighted quite differently in different religions, it provides a key locus for understanding. It is uniquely well suited to cast light on areas which are traditionally thought to be "beyond words."
24. William Beveridge, *Private Thoughts Upon Religion*, Glasgow, 1753, (1709), William Duncan Junior, p. 9.
25. Ibid.
26. Wilfred Cantwell Smith, *The Meaning and End of Religion*, London, 1978, (1962), SPCK, p. 2.
27. Ibid.
28. Ibid.
29. Wilfred Cantwell Smith, *Questions of Religious Truth*, London, 1967, Gollancz, p. 35.
30. Ibid.
31. The problems posed by religious plurality for Christian commitment have received extensive treatment. Among the volumes which Cipher's Christian first cousins might look to for advice are: Stephen Neill, *The Christian Faith and Other Faiths: The Christian Dialogue with Other Religions*, London, 1970, 2nd edition (1961), Oxford University Press; A. K. Cragg, *The Christian and Other Religions*, London, 1977, Mowbray; Alan Race, *Christians and Religious Pluralism: Patterns in Christian Theology of Religions*, London, 1983, SCM; Paul Knitter, *No*

Other Name? A Critical Study of Christian Attitudes Towards the World Religions, London 1985, SCM; Gavin D'Costa, *Theology and Religious Pluralism: The Challenge of Other Religions*, Oxford 1986, Basil Blackwell.

32. Wilfred Cantwell Smith, *The Meaning and End of Religion*, p. 12. Smith's point is helpful in making us more critically aware of the limitations of viewing religions as independent monolithic realities with easily speci- fied and mutually exclusive identities. It also draws attention to the impact that studying religions can have on the object of study, creating structures that may not exist independently of such study. Jonathan Z. Smith stresses this point, arguing that "religion is solely the creation of the scholar's study." It is, he suggests, "created for the scholar's analytic purposes by imaginative acts of comparison and generalization," to the extent that religion "has no independent existence apart from the acad- emy." (see his *Imagining Religion: From Babylon to Jonestown*, Chicago, 1982, Chicago University Press, p. xi). Such perspectives are valid up to a point. However, I think the balancing rebuttal is well made by Ninian Smart (in his *The World's Religions: Old Traditions and Modern Transformations*, Cambridge, Cambridge University Press, 1989, p. 556): "Many modern historians of religion wish to deny that there is some one thing called Hinduism or Buddhism; they think that these are at best labels for a whole slew of differing religious movements, cults, beliefs and so on. But modern conditions have made religions more self-consciously global in character. They have increased a degree of homogenization through mutual contact, and have also bred ecu- menical movements which are quite influential in exchange of ideas and mutual feelings of support. So though Buddhism may not quite have existed before, it does now; and the same for all the other reli- gions. Self-definition is becoming the order of the day." Smart reiter- ates this point in his *Reflections in the Mirror of Religion* (London, Macmillan, 1997, edited by John P. Burns, p ix), where he suggests that those who deny there is any such thing as Hinduism should try this idea out on a group of Hindus.

33. Ibid., p. 50.

34. Ibid., p. 60.

35. Wilfred Cantwell Smith, *Questions of Religious Truth*, p. 107.

36. Wilfred Cantwell Smith, *The Meaning and End of Religion*, p. 7.

37. Ludwig Wittgenstein, *Notebooks 1914-1916*, Oxford, 1961, Basil Blackwell, edited by G. H. Von Wright and G. E. M. Anscombe, trans- lated by G. E. M. Anscombe, pp. 72-73e.

CHAPTER 4

INFORMATION AS AN INIMICAL FORCE

IN HER interesting study of "the Way" in the religions of the world, Edith B. Schnapper sets out to show the centrality of this concept in religious thinking. She argues that every religious tradition offers a path designed to lead towards the kind of destination envisaged by the writer of that famous prayer from the Upanishads, who implored:

> Lead me from the unreal to the real,
> Lead me from the darkness into light,
> Lead me from death to immortality.[1]

To suggest, as she does, that religion and the Way are synonymous, and that all the apparent variations in direction in fact lead to the same place, would seem to involve a rather serious underestimation of the diversity of phenomena subsumed beneath the heading "religion." And it simply ignores the view of scholars like Pietro Rossano, who argue that it is, as he puts it, "scientifically certain"[2] that the ways found within the different faiths are *not* the same. However, though I would question some of her conclusions, Schnapper does make many astute observations in the course of her investigation. Most importantly, she identifies several important shared landmarks which do seem to be encountered on the routes proposed by the different religions. Thus, in a chapter dealing with the notion of *wilderness*, passage through some form of which seems to be a common phase of "the Way" (however it may be envisaged), she remarks:

> It is a well known phenomenon that almost immediately we set out on the religious quest inimical forces, from without and within, suddenly appear.[3]

Two very famous examples come to mind immediately: the attempts of

Mara to lure Siddhartha Gautama, the Buddha, off his meditative path towards enlightenment; and Jesus' temptation by Satan. Leaving aside questions of their internal or external status, and the extent of their comparability, both Mara and Satan constitute inimical forces. Their appearance in the wilderness (whether of actual desert or of meditation) constitutes a threat of potential diversion from the Way which is being sought.

The apparently unconditional triumph by Gautama and Jesus over their tempters cannot be expected by the ordinary pilgrim. Their paths will follow a rather more circuitous route, full of unwanted delays and detours, mostly occasioned by their own frailties, which, in the end, will probably leave them some distance from their desired destination. St. Paul's lament, "the good that I would do, I do not; but the evil which I would not, that I do,"[4] finds widespread echo across a wide range of religious settings and is a more common outcome of temptation than the triumph of a Buddha or a Christ. Indeed, in his study *Religious Truth and the Relation Between Religions*, David Moses argues that Paul's "experience of moral failure, his feeling of estrangement, of alienation from the heart of reality,"[5] is a fundamental human experience. In similar vein, Aldous Huxley (harking back to a saying of Ovid's) has suggested that every human biography, regardless of whether or not its course is considered to be religious, can be summed up in the words, "I see and approve of the better things, but I follow the worse."[6] In other words, I have given in to inimical forces that I am unable or unwilling to resist, I have followed a way at odds with a deeper sense of direction.

Cipher is a pilgrim in the hall of mirrors. His quest is to determine if, among the multiplicity of images, there is some mapping of a Way which might provide the peace of mind he seeks, a peace of mind which will act curatively upon those feelings of insignificance, mystery and meaning-lessness that punctuate his life and threaten to swamp him with a sense of futility. But immediately he sets out, indeed even as he *contemplates* setting out, Cipher is going to encounter the equivalent of what Schnapper aptly terms "inimical forces"—forces which threaten to halt and obstruct the path that he seeks to take, paralyzing his proposed investigation of the diverse religious outlooks with which he is surrounded.

Cipher's proposed investigative journey may not contain such epochal confrontations as those between Buddha and Jesus and their tempters. It may lack something of the action and excitement of the sort of archetypal religious quest found in, say, Gilgamesh's search for immortality, for the hazards he will encounter are unlikely to be as obviously dramatic or colorful as those met with by this ancient Mesopotamian hero. Not for Cipher the terrible scorpion man of Mount Mashu, "whose terror is awesome and whose glance is death."[7] Nonetheless, Cipher's quest for peace of mind in the disturbing context of a religiously plural world is an urgent one. The difficulties which seem to bar his path, and to stand in the way of a successful world decision (i.e. a resolution of his neutrality into some form of commitment), although neither grotesque or picturesque, appear both numerous and formidable. Moreover, the possibility of one's life appearing futile and absurd, or of remaining perpetually in a state of indecision, are not exactly negligible risks. Indeed, they might well carry a sting as lethal, if less immediately apparent, as that of the scorpion man.

This book is concerned with religious commitment in an age of pluralism. It seeks to anticipate, identify, and explore some of the issues and difficulties with which Cipher will have to contend in his wilderness of neutrality set in a context of potentially multiple choice. In this chapter, however, I will confine my attention to an inimical force that seems to come into operation even before he proceeds any further than *contemplating* the religious reflections that surround him. This inimical force centers around the scale of information involved. It threatens to stop Cipher's quest even before it gets started. It poses the temptation of supposing that his quest for a world decision is hopeless. The scale of the task necessary in order to make such a decision is presented as being so great that it would make Cipher's whole endeavor unrealistic. Giving in to this temptation would mean abandoning the attempt to find out which, if any, of the outlooks in the hall of mirrors might offer peace of mind. Let me try to spell out in a little more detail what this inimical force involves.

In *Mankind and Mother Earth*, a work which he presents as a bird's-eye view of human history, Arnold Toynbee writes:

> Religion is, in fact, an intrinsic and distinctive trait of human nature. It is a human being's necessary response to the challenge of the mysteriousness of the phenomena that he encounters in virtue of his uniquely human faculty of consciousness.[8]

Mircea Eliade, writing in the first volume of his *History of Religious Ideas*, offers a similar diagnosis concerning the inevitability of human religiousness. The sacred, says Eliade, "is an element in the structure of consciousness and not a stage in the history of consciousness."[9] Whether we are, by nature, fundamentally religious animals is not a question I wish to discuss here. Trying to prove that all human beings conform to any particular characteristics, beyond the most obvious physical ones, is an exercise fraught with difficulty. In a species of such diversity as to crowd the pages of its history with figures as different as Genghis Khan and Georgia O'Keefe, Madonna and Mozart, Cleopatra and the Dalai Lama, Pol Pot and Mother Teresa, Hildegarde of Bingen and Charles Darwin (the list of contrasting pairs is endless), it can be hard to find convincing common denominators beyond the shared elements of blood, breath and other biological fundamentals. However, regardless of our verdict on their accuracy, remarks such as those of Toynbee and Eliade point unwaveringly towards the massive extent of human religiousness. And this is the root of the inimical force of information which Cipher faces.

From the anonymous cave paintings which throng the caverns at Altamira and Lascaux and still delight us (aesthetically, if no longer religiously) with their graceful sinuousness and color, to Mark Rothko's looming empty panels in the non-denominational chapel named after him in Houston; from the millions of Muslims who have made the pilgrimage to Mecca, to the mass suicide (or massacre) of hundreds of the People's Temple sect in Guyana; from the bloodthirsty frenzied dancing of the Indian goddess Kali, to Confucian mores of firm gentleness and poise; from the elaborate opulence of the Hindu temples of Khajaraho, to the emptiness of a Zen garden; from Kurrichalpongo, the aborigines' creator deity, to Milton's Satan; from Gregorian chant to recitation of the sacred syllable Om; from Aum Shenrikyo to the Salvation Army, humankind has marked out clearly in a multiplicity of different ways, and in different mediums, its deep concern with the sacred. Our religiousness seems to be coterminous with our species, regardless of how individuals, movements, sometimes whole nations, may wish to distance themselves from allegiance to any faith.

But why should the cargo of information carried by the colorful descriptivism of a natural history of religions, the polychromatic richness of which is evident even from such a random and truncated excerpt, constitute an inimical force for Cipher? In examining this inimical force, I want to do two things: first, emphasize the way in which this fundamental fact of religion's extensiveness and diversity creates a situation of profound dilemma for my fictional hero; second, to glance beyond Cipher for a moment and see how the study of religion has generated, and how it responds to, the mass of information about religion which affords the hall of mirrors its depth. This will usefully reiterate the point that although Cipher and the religious studies scholar do share some common territory (for example, the desire to see the way in which religions are perceived by their adherents), their motivations and methods are by no means identical.

In the previous chapter, listing some of the things which might be found in Cipher's room were he to meet with a suspicious end and so attract the attentions of careful professional searchers, mention was made of a preponderance of books on comparative religion. But among them the searchers might also find works by Amiel, Barbellion, Bashkirtseff, de Guerin and other famous exponents of the art of journal writing. Cipher will have an interest in the thoughts of others who have pondered deeply on the nature of being, and who have left behind meticulous records of their struggle to find meaning in the world. Indeed, beside such classics of the genre, it is by no means improbable that the searchers would find Cipher's own writings, a meditative record of his struggle to make sense of things in a religiously plural world, an attempt to come to some point of decision which would release him from his unwanted state of neutrality. As Mircea Eliade says in the first volume of his own autobiographical journal, this type of writing may be "anything from a calendar to a diatribe, to a table of contents for the next *Summa Theologica.*"[10] Cipher's writings certainly will not aspire even to the most embryonic Thomistic synthesis. They may, however, provide us with a closer realization of what it is like to be in the hall of mirrors, of how having access to information about a whole range of human religiousness, from the prehistoric to the present, severely complicates the issue of personal commitment. Let me use an extract from this imaginary journal to try to show, in more personal, individual-centered detail, just how perplexing awareness of the information which constitutes the hall of mirrors can be.

Cipher writes:

> I am dazzled by a glittering mosaic of religious lights, though—paradoxically—I feel as if my eyes are covered with a heavy blindfold. All across the blindfold's surface are numerous rips, gashes, pinpricks, of various shape and size. From them issues light of different color, duration and intensity. Seen cumulatively, with my eyes wide open, the effect is confusing, almost blinding. By closing my eyes to a slit, and squinting resolutely in one direction, I can imagine what it must be like to see the light through a single aperture only. Searching back in time, history reveals occasions when individuals were conscious only of that source of light which was sanctioned by whatever society they belonged to; their path through life was lighted by a single faith. There were often huge variations within it, but beyond its circle of radiance no alternative illumination was perceived, only the darkness of denial. No other sources of light were seen, or, if they were, it was so dimly that they could be rejected automatically as inadequate and inferior. Sometimes I wish that I too existed in so straightforward a context of commitment. But beneath this tattered blindfold my eyes are wide open and I can turn my gaze in all directions. My view is not seriously restricted by obstructions of distance or ignorance or *a priori* condemnation. Faced thus with a myriad of possible pathways, illumined from a seeming galaxy of lights, I stand

undecided, uncertain how, or in what direction, to proceed. Light pours from the life of Jesus and millions try to walk in the course which it illumines. Light pours from the teachings of Gautama Buddha and millions guide their way according to this beacon. The Qur'an burns with a singular intensity which draws submission from millions of Muslims. The wisdom of the Hindu Vedas points a beam which seeks to cut a swathe through the illusions of existence; millions direct their steps accordingly.

Looking across the religious spectrum there is a blaze of luminosity—Christianity, Buddhism, Islam, Hinduism, the light of Jainism and Sikhism, the incandescent history of the Jews, the alluring iridescence of Taoism, the glow of Shinto and the spark of the Parsees. Further off, and dimmed into a subdued glow, the smoldering embers of the dead religions are still just visible, vanished searchlights whose beams once probed the darkness of uncertainty for Aztecs, Egyptians, Sumerians, Dravidians, and those nameless tribes before them who trace our history back to the caves (where we still find flickering traces of a religious consciousness). Coming up the stream of time again, the new religions of the present provide a cacophony of colored light, psychedelic, bewitching, fantastic, troubling, set amidst the background illumination of those traditional outlooks we have grown used to (and which have sometimes lost something of their original sheen).

Is there, from any of this host of sources, a light which can cast its brightness on my life? Can I see anything in the light of the world's religions which makes sense of my individual existence, which allows it to be anything other than transient, unimportant, troubled and confused? Or am I simply looking towards a mesmerizing fantasy kaleidoscope which offers nothing but distraction from the uncomfortable truths of the human situation? Am I looking at things the wrong way round? Are the religious lights, far from being Ways of insight through a blindfold, simply blind spots of ignorance and credulity on the fabric of everyday existence? Are the different points of light truly derived from some sense-giving "wholly other" entity or state, or are they simply painted on the fabric of the world, like smiling masks on a frightening face put there by children who are intimidated by the ogres of darkness, pain and death? Ought I to ignore them all, paint over them with realistic colors, accept that I have come of age and that the religious lights have all gone out, that they illumine only our history, tell us something about the past, but offer no insight into how we ought to live today? Or is there, somewhere in the glittering array, a thread of truth and meaning which can lead the deepest sense of lostness to the homecoming it yearns for? Does God or Brahman, Nirvana or the Tao, shine through the fabric of the everyday mundane existence that I lead? If so, are their several radiances ultimately unitary or irreducibly diverse? Or are such points of blinding light, attested to by the millions who have followed life-ways apparently lit up by them, merely the cumulative phosphorescence of minds consumed by dazzling illusion?

As he stands on the threshold of the hall of mirrors, the view as far as Cipher's eye can see is one of dazzling extent and complexity. Such is the range of relevant material open to him that the first inimical force he faces is simply that constituted by the *scale* of his informedness. What creates his dilemma, and seems to frustrate any attempt to resolve it, is an awareness, already extensive and capable of massive potential development, of the varieties of human religiousness. Faced with such a daunting scale of material, Cipher may conclude that he is, quite simply, hopelessly ill-equipped to undertake the work which his predicament seems to demand. If he is to make an effective investigative journey through the hall of mirrors, then surely he must be multi-lingual, gifted in theology and philosophy, possessed of a clear historical overview and willing to embark on an extensive program of world travel, otherwise he may see only the most superficial aspects of the various images which hold him in neutralistic thrall. While he is no dullard, Cipher is no polymath either, and it would go far beyond the bounds even of his fictional status to suppose that he has the necessary powers of perception and retention adequately to survey the whole. It would, of course, be ideal if Cipher could understand all that met his gaze, and if his gaze was of sufficient depth and breadth as to be able to encompass the whole range of religious phenomena sparkling before him, but this is simply not the case. Were it imagined to be so, we would have moved from very low key fiction to the most exaggerated fantasy. Cipher's powers are limited and his life is short. He cannot hope to understand or to cover everything, even with the help of his whole library of books on comparative religion.

Recognizing his limited abilities in the face of the vastness of his task may be disheartening. However, we must remember that Cipher is not being asked to produce an encyclopedia but, rather, to make a world decision. The two exercises are not identical (though they will overlap here and there). He is interested in peace of mind, not the painstaking detail of scholarship (though again, obviously, there will be essential shared areas of common concern). If certain things lie beyond his competence and understanding—as they are bound to do—that is no reason for Cipher to abandon his proposed quest. Such things will simply have to be bypassed as irrelevant. If he genuinely cannot understand something, if it is expressed in a language he cannot master and of which there is no translation, or if it involves ideas which he simply cannot grasp, then such a thing would seem unlikely to be able to provide the peace of mind he is looking for. Cipher must adopt a Cartesian pragmatism here and, like Descartes, recognize the limitations of his abilities and the briefness of his life. These are the conditions he is operating under. He needs, in other words, to accept the inevitable limitations which attend his situation and just get on with the job, to the extent that, as Descartes might put it, "the mediocrity of his talents" and the "brief duration of his life"[11] allows, rather than concluding that such mediocrity and finitude provide a valid excuse for not trying. They are important defining features of his problem, not crippling limitations which mean he can never hope to solve it. Obviously no individual can produce some sort of all-encompassing natural history of religion. But, even were it possible to do so, this would not resolve Cipher's situation. Writing such a natural history is not the same as arriving at a world decision.

The first aim of this chapter has now, I hope, been met. Information may seem to constitute an initial inimical force of paralyzing dimensions, tempting Cipher to abandon his quest for peace of mind. As we have seen, although his situation in the hall of mirrors does involve a daunting scale of information about religions, this should not in itself be taken as providing grounds for abandoning the search for peace of mind. The second aim of the chapter involves looking beyond Cipher for a moment. I think at this point it may be useful to try to place him in some sort of perspective *vis-a-vis* the disciplinary area whose work has been largely responsible for facilitating the kind of view he has of the hall of mirrors. It seems reasonable to suppose that some clues about how to approach the immense mass of religious information stretching out before him might be found within the work of those disciplines which have collected that information in the first place and have thus directly fostered the conditions for his troubling awareness.

Cipher's view of the hall of mirrors may be immediately framed and facilitated by the media, by daily encounters with members of a range of different faiths, and/or by traveling to areas of the world in which the religious environment is very different from that of his indigenous setting. But it acquires its depth and detail through the work which has been carried out under such subject headings as "comparative religion," "history of religion," "science of religion," "phenomenology of religion" and so on. I will, for convenience, refer to these variously named endeavors by the single title "religious studies." In doing so I am guilty of considerable simplification. Each label carries sufficiently different nuances of meaning for them to have become flags of methodological allegiance, under which different tribes of scholars conduct their business (and occasionally wage war on each other). I do not wish to get involved here in debates about disciplinary identity or procedure. Such matters are irrelevant to someone who is looking for peace of mind in the hall of mirrors. The several variations occurring beneath the broad general heading of religious studies, despite their undoubted differences, may be considered similar in terms of their outcome for an individual such as Cipher. They all act to increase such an individual's awareness of the extent and diversity of religions.

The awareness of, and possession of information about, religions in a plural sense could be seen as going through three fundamental stages. These might be called *the three ages of religious studies*. Looking at them will, I hope, help to identify areas of possible interest for Cipher within this broad area of academic concern.[12] First, there is a phase of discovery, largely undertaken—or rather occurring—in a non-deliberate and somewhat haphazard way. In it occurs the acquisition of information about hitherto unknown areas. Such information is often not particularly accurate and gathering it may be quite accidental. This first age lays the initial seeds of an awareness that the religion with which we happen to be most familiar is not the only one in the world. Second, there is a phase of deliberate and systematic investigation of a more definitely circumscribed area. The first age acts to alert us to—and disseminate initial information about—the *existence* of new religious phenomena while the second age begins the process of gaining reliable and detailed knowledge about them. Third, there is a phase of reflection that marks a loss of confidence in the unselfconscious fact-gathering of religious studies' second age. Questions relating to method now tend to be given more prominence than those referring solely to aspects of the material under study.

In these three ages, religious studies tends, respectively, to display what might be termed its *primitive, classical* and *modern* forms. Such a rough threefold model can be applied both to the study of religion as a broad disciplinary area and to an individual's approach to religions. Indeed, to some extent, ontogeny repeats phylogeny here (to put it in evolutionary jargon). That is to say, the stages of awareness found in individual consciousness mirror those occurring in the subject as a whole. I will consider phylogeny first, looking at religious studies in its primitive, classical and modern manifestations, before turning to ontogeny and considering how such different forms of individual outlook might influence Cipher's situation.

In its most primitive form, religious studies (though it is, of course, extremely doubtful if the name is accurately applicable to much of this early phase) begins with travelers' accounts of what appear to the writers concerned as utterly alien and often damnable phenomena. If, for example, we turn to those early works recording Europeans' first experiences of India, we can find some good examples of the sort of outlook primitivism allows. In William Finch's account of his travels in India in

1608, we find descriptions of sacred sculpture which, in the absence of any understanding of the symbolism involved, perceived them as demonic and disgusting. Finch saw gods:

> with long hornes, staring eyes, shagge hair, great fangs, ugly pawes, long tailes, with horrible deformity upon deformity.[13]

As Partha Mitter has pointed out, even if we thoroughly searched the Hindu pantheon, "we would be hard put to find such a monster."[14] The frequent non-correspondence of description to the actual existence of anything so described is a common feature of the primitive form of religious studies. New things are first conceived of very largely in terms of existing categories, quite regardless of how good a fit they might be, or according to wildly inaccurate preconceptions. The first Western accounts of Eastern religiousness viewed temples as churches, consecrated maidens as nuns and so on, across a wide range of translations which are often understood quite literally by those who encounter them at second hand, such that the illustrators of early travel volumes have come up with some marvelously incongruous pictures. At the same time, stereotypical descriptions of monsters and devils, all the dark side of the early Christian psyche, crop up again and again, foisting on the novelties of Hindu iconography an interpretation which had its origin more in the Western subconscious than in any observable features of the phenomena concerned. Commentators have spoken of the virtual "inability of the Europeans to describe a religious system except in Christian terms"[15] and of the way in which early Western observers "created Hinduism in their own image."[16]

The extent to which expectations can color actuality is remarkable. Another striking example is recorded by Jonathan Spence in his brilliant study of Matteo Ricci, the Jesuit missionary who visited India en route to China, where he lived from 1583 until his death in 1610. Spence notes how the first Portuguese navigators to reach South India actually worshipped before images of the goddess Kali, because they believed her to be the Virgin Mary.[17] This identification of Kali with the Virgin presumably took place largely because of their vague knowledge of the so called "Malabar Christians" and their expectation that Christianity would be the religion of this area. Given that Kali is almost invariably portrayed in what, to Western eyes, are the most lurid terms—as a savage, demonic, bloodthirsty figure, wearing a necklace of skulls or freshly severed heads, wielding a sword, and often dancing on a prostrate body, this particular instance of mistaken identity suggests a quite remarkable failure of observation.

It is easy to be patronizingly amused by the mistaken assumptions of primitivism. However, the extent to which presuppositions determine what we actually see is a human attribute which is observable throughout history. Mention was made in Chapter 1 of Thomas Kuhn's theories about the way in which we tend to see the world according to socially sanctioned models or "paradigms." Anything which does not fall into line with whatever paradigm happens to be dominant is difficult to see as such. It tends to be assimilated into the familiar picture, whether it really fits there or not. Thus Kali becomes Mary, a temple becomes a church, and so on.

A neat illustration of this tendency—and one which Cipher will need to bear in mind as he explores the hall of mirrors—is the so called experiment of the anomalous cards. In this experiment, "anomalous" cards, that is, cards that do not fit into the standard color-coding of the suits, such as a black four of hearts, are introduced into a normal pack. When the pack is dealt through to an observer, he or she invariably fails to identify these "rogue" elements. Instead, the anomalous cards are perceived as entirely normal. They are, as Kuhn puts it, "immediately fitted to one of the conceptual categories prepared by prior experience without any awareness of trouble."[18] "Seeing is believing" is a saying which seems to have an important reverse sense as well. As he looks into the images which surround him in the hall of mirrors, Cipher needs to be critically reflective as to the nature of his own seeing, otherwise the religious equivalent of color blindness may picture everything he sees according to one dominant accustomed model, rather than allowing the different images to take shape in their own undistorted uniqueness before his eyes.

The often amusing misconceptions of the primitivism displayed in the first age of religious studies are gradually weeded out and corrected as the classical form of the discipline comes to assert itself, gradually gathering momentum so that its increasingly accurate collection and cataloguing of religious facts covers an ever wider area. Scholars now talk confidently about a *science* of religion, which will lead unerringly to a clear understanding of the entire religious realm. Gone is the wholesale rejection of "other" religions as comical, false or iniquitous—an attitude common in primitivism. Instead, we find the kind of belief expressed by Max Müller, editor of the *Sacred Books of the East* series (perhaps the literary pinnacle of religious studies in its classical form), that:

> Every religion, even the most imperfect and degraded, has something that ought to be sacred to us, for there is in all religions a secret yearning after the true, though unknown God.[19]

It is realized that the accumulation of sufficient data to perceive this unknown deity is yet in its infancy, the science of religion is still only in embryonic form, but no doubts are expressed about its successful development. Though it may not be possible *yet* to specify the exact nature of such a discipline in all its details, classicism is characterized by a confidence in its own powers to bring about a golden future in which we will have all the facts about religion and will understand them perfectly. Thus James C. Moffat talks of "marking out the ground-plan on which the final structure (of the science of religion) is to stand."[20] His two volume *Comparative History of Religions* (1875) is, presumably, intended to make a substantial contribution to laying the foundations.

That the ground-plan Moffat marks out may itself contain such difficulties of procedure as to prevent any stone from being firmly laid (or to question the stability of any eventual edifice which he and like-minded workers envisaged building on it) is a worry which only seriously troubles those in the third age of religious studies, when the subject assumes its modern form. Moffat still belongs to an intellectual milieu where two great world religions may be compared in a matter of pages and one of them be found wanting. Whilst in retrospect one may admire the bold strokes of such intellectual audacity and envy their apparent conclusiveness, at the same time one realizes that the methodological naiveté with which they were carried out renders the final result untrustworthy. The massive structures of classical religious studies still provide much of the stage upon which the concerns of its modern form are acted out, but it is a stage upon which there are many separate structures and much controversy. It does not bear upon it anything resembling the single, monolithic and triumphant science envisaged by many of those who built it.

The contrast between the mood of classical and modern religious studies may be quickly illustrated by juxtaposing two quotations. The first is Emile Burnouf's famous methodological prophecy which envisages a future for the subject in similar terms to Moffat's, the second is Ralph Wendell Burhoe's assessment of the methodological status of the subject a century later. First Burnouf, writing in 1870:

> This present century will not come to an end without having seen the establishment of a unified science whose elements are still dispersed, a science which the preceding centuries did not have, which is not yet defined, and which, perhaps for the first time, will be named science of religion.[21]

Second Burhoe, writing in 1974:

> It could be said that the scientific study of religion is today in a more primitive state than was biology two centuries ago. We have not yet had our Darwin; we have hardly had our Linnaeus to sharpen our basic descriptive terms and their classifications.[22]

Symptomatic of the growing doubt that such things as Moffat's confidently staked out ground-plan can, in fact, be built on, or that Burnouf's prophecy can ever be fulfilled, we find in the modern form of religious studies much discussion as to whether any sort of clear-cut methodology is possible in this area. The conclusions reached are often pessimistic in terms of allowing the sort of wide-ranging and conclusively answer-giving discipline which classical scholars seem to have envisaged. Georg Schmid sums up something of the mood of modernism when he observes:

> As paradoxical as it may sound, the more we know, the less we
> know. The more extensive and detailed our knowledge is, the greater
> is the problem and the more reserved are all our statements about
> religion.[23]

Religious studies in its modern form might, in fact, be characterized by
an uncertainty about how to proceed, given the extent of its information about religions. As early as 1905, Louis Henry Jordan noted with
some alarm that a particular difficulty in the study of religions is "the
overwhelming mass of detail, still rapidly increasing, which confronts
every investigator."[24] By 1958, G. F. Woods had realized that "we are
standing near an explosion of knowledge"[25] which has left us somewhat
shell-shocked; and, some twenty years later, Eric Sharpe characterized
religious studies as involving "rapidly increasing accumulations of material"[26] in search of some method to make sense of it. In a similar vein,
Schmid saw the contemporary situation in the subject as one of "bound-
lessly broadening acquaintance with religious data."[27] Many take the
view that such accumulation of data is not a satisfactory end in itself. As
Bleeker put it, though we have increased our knowledge about religions
dramatically, there still remain "many blind spots on the map of our
insight."[28] (In other words, information in itself does not guarantee
understanding.) There is also a growing awareness of the effect such
information may have on individual religiousness. Frederick Streng, for
example, draws attention to the threat such material poses for the stability of any *particular* faith stance.[29] The picture of modernism which
emerges is almost that of a rather dazed band of miners who have accu-
mulated a huge amount of precious ore, yet are unsure just how to
process or refine it, and are beginning to realize that it may not be a
safely inert substance, but rather that it might exert an almost radioac-
tive potency.

In the introduction to the English translation of that classic of Eastern spirituality, *The Tibetan Book of the Dead* (a book whose growing
popularity in the West offers a small index of the extent to which our
religious horizons have become permeable to non-indigenous influences),

W. Y. Evans-Wentz declared that the hope of all sincere researchers in the field of comparative religion:

> ought always to be to accumulate such scientific data as will some-day enable future generations of mankind to discover Truth itself—that Universal Truth in which all religions and all sects of all religions may ultimately recognise the Essence of religion.[30]

The accumulation of data has progressed apace since Evans-Wentz made this comment in 1927. However, far from having assisted in the perception of some common truth, such information seems to have acted to increase our uncertainty about the nature of religions and the truths which they proclaim, the relationship between the world's faiths, and the way in which the study of religion should itself be conducted. Few of those working in the field today would endorse Evans-Wentz's mission statement.

This suggestion of three ages in religious studies, with their corresponding dominant moods of primitivism, classicism and modernism, is intended as a very rough thematic model rather than an accurate historical analysis. In terms of the discipline as a whole, it would not be easy to establish clear chronological watersheds which effectively separate the three ages. We might, perhaps, see the first as extending up to about 1700 or so, the second to the late 1800s or early 1900s, and the third from then until the present. But this crude trisection of the past should not be relied on as offering more than an indication of some of the general features which we might expect a work falling within any of its divisions to display (in terms of its perception of a religiously plural world). Inevitably, some works will come "out of sequence," so to speak, belonging more properly to the intellectual climate of a past or future age. A work belonging chronologically to the third age may, in fact, be more primitive in outlook than a work actually dating from the first age, in which such an outlook might be expected.

The historical validity of this very crude model is not something that I would wish to present as being much more than a useful device for initial orientation. It serves to put Cipher's situation into a broad context which affords some points of reference in giving an idea of the likely evolution of his particular perspective on the religious hall of mirrors. Its historical limitations notwithstanding, the notions of primitivism, classicism and modernism are useful, I think, on the ontogenetic level, *i.e.* on the level of individual attitudes to religious pluralism. But, again, we ought not to see them as three consecutive stages in a developmental model which everyone passes through, but rather as attitudes of mind which may be held singly, or serially, or in unpredictable combination.

Had Cipher been born into the first age of religious studies, and had he displayed all the marks of the primitivism normally associated with it, it would have been impossible for him to have perceived the hall of mirrors in the way in which he does. The information necessary would simply not have been available. The chances are that his situation would have been similar to the one looked back on rather wistfully in the extract quoted from his journal, where only a single source of religious light was visible. Any illumination straying into the visual field of primitivism from other religions would likely be seen as faint, and probably fantastic. Something which could not, at any rate, be taken seriously as constituting an alternative.

In so information-soaked a culture as ours, it would be difficult to pinpoint precisely Cipher's ontogenetic recapitulation of primitivism, his slowly dawning perception of the fact that there are different religions in the world. In one version of an imaginary biography that we might suppose Cipher to have lived through, his first awareness of the fact that there are "other" religions in the world could be seen as being mediated via television or newspapers, or through his encountering the visibly different customs of the various religious groups which occur in a multicultural society, or through holidays, business trips and educational exchanges abroad.

Had Cipher been born into the second age of religious studies, and displayed all its typical classical features in his own outlook on religions, then it is more likely that he would have been concerned with pressing ahead and discovering more and more about the religious images in the hall of mirrors, rather than with feeling perplexed by them.

He might also have shared Evans-Wentz's assumption about some essential universal truth underlying all religions (an assumption that is much harder to maintain as the real differences between the faiths become apparent). On an ontogenetic level, Cipher would pass from a primitive to a classical perspective only supposing that what he perceived, albeit dimly, in the earlier phase was of sufficient interest to encourage him to find out more about it. If he had little interest in what religions say about the world, then it would be most unlikely that he would ever engage in the systematic study which is the hallmark of classicism.

Cipher is, however, a typical child of the third age of religious studies and displays all the characteristics of the modernism associated with it. As such, he is deeply perplexed by the information which he has at his disposal about the religions of the world. No longer are the "other" religions something so faintly perceived, so distant, and so alien, as to constitute a matter for curiosity and condemnation rather than perplexity. No longer can the information which he gathers about them appear to be an end in itself. He displays what might be taken as the three key features of modernism: extensive informedness about religions; no firm base in terms of commitment to any particular outlook; and an uncertainty about how to proceed. (Those who prefer to think of the contemporary situation in terms of postmodernism can easily adapt this model, since, crudely stated, postmodernism involves an exaggeration and amplification of these three key features.)

Let me repeat that it would have been quite possible for Cipher, contemporary though he is, to have had a primitive outlook on the hall of mirrors, with its various images being darkly perceived through the distortions of a religiously xenophobic outlook. For example, although chronologically she is located near the boundary between classicism and modernism, Gervee Baronté writes of Hinduism as a conglomeration of superstitions and myths, full of what she calls "beastly rites." In her analysis, these are simply based on what she terms a widespread "sex hysteria."[31] I suspect that any hysteria in her fascinating book, *The Land of the Lingam*, in fact derives, not from the phenomena under study, but from an outlook and style of writing worthy of the most retarded primitivism. Although in terms of history we would expect her to show signs of classical or modern approaches, in terms of psychology she is very much a primitive. There would be many interesting problems to consider were Cipher born into the first or second age of religious studies, or if he displayed a primitive or classical outlook rather than a modern one. However, these are not the settings that I want to focus on here.

Ernest Becker has spoken of the overproduction of information which assails us. In his interesting psychoanalytic study of our time, *The Denial of Death*, he suggests (echoing Otto Rank) that the man of knowledge is currently "bowed down under a burden he never imagined he would have: the overproduction of truth which cannot be consumed."[32] Becker's general comment very much applies to the situation faced by Cipher in the hall of mirrors. Clearly the overproduction of information about religion is, to a large extent, a glut that should be welcomed. After all, one can see its accumulation as having the benign effect of blasting away the ignorance and parochialism in this area which has had such a destructive impact on history. But such information, as Cipher knows to his cost, seems to have a distinctly negative side too, in relation to what I suppose we might loosely term human spirituality. Anselm Strauss has warned of the way in which an individual can become "spiritually dispossessed."[33] How he can, in effect, "lose his world,"[34] if he cannot find a way through the multiplicity of options, the immensity of information, that constitutes the experience of being in a locus like the hall of mirrors. Such a loss is:

> tantamount to saying that his commitments—to significant others and to himself—have been tremendously weakened. [For] when a man questions his central purposes, he is asking himself: to what, for what, to whom am I committed?[35]

The "overproduction of truth" about religion—the result of the accumulation of scientific data which Evans-Wentz and others urged on modern scholars—has led to a situation where the individual's "central purposes," which might once simply have been assumed as a given (because they were unchallenged by any alternative), come under serious threat. The hall of mirrors is an uncomfortable place. As far as Cipher is concerned, the accumulation of data about religion that early research-ers imagined would lead to the "Truth," and so decisively clarify our ultimate commitments, has instead created an uncomfortable relation-ship between religious information and individual religiousness. Ci-pher feels impelled by his sense of lostness to try to make some world decision, to align his central purposes behind a sense of certainty. Of-ten, the specialization that has sparked the explosion of information about religions seems at odds with that desideratum.

In an attempt to see how he might cope with the first inimical force which stands in his way, that is, the sheer extent of available infor-mation about religions, the vast expanse of the hall of mirrors, we have considered how Cipher stands in relation to religious studies—the dis-ciplinary area which has been largely responsible for allowing him ac-cess to a perspective of extensive plurality in the first place. Going back to the passage quoted from his journal, the work of religious studies has acted to remove various obscurities of ignorance so that the different religious lights may shine brightly across almost the whole of their re-flective surface. It seems clear that, in a sense, Cipher is repeating at an individual level some of the problems which the subject itself now seems to be encountering. We have seen how scholars belonging to the third age of religious studies are often puzzled about how to cope with the massive amount of information they have at their disposal. The key task of present-day religious studies, according to Schmid, quite simply consists of "finding the thread which leads through the enormity of the evidence."[36] In the course of his exploration of the hall of mirrors, Ci-pher will refer to religious studies again for guidance on more particu-lar questions. Clearly, though, as a source of possible advice about how to cope with the sheer mass of material around him, there seems to be no clear advice given. To some extent the subject itself is grappling with the selfsame problem, and it is often "solved" (though, arguably, "avoided" might be a better choice of word) by making a complete division between professional and personal concerns. The task of religious studies is to understand religion in all its forms. Whether any religion is true, whether any offers valid guidance about how one might live, whether in the mass of information unearthed by the discipline there may be personally relevant material, all this is left to the individual.

The difference between Cipher and the student of religious studies may be underlined by reference to one of the stories collected by Paul Reps in *Zen Flesh, Zen Bones*, a source book of material drawn from the Zen Buddhist tradition. The story in question concerns a mother's advice to her scholar-monk son. To her dismay, he has begun to establish a reputation for himself as a lecturer:

> Son, I do not think you became a devotee of the Buddha because you desire to turn into a walking dictionary for others. There is no end to information and commentation. I wish you would stop this lecture business. Shut yourself up in a little temple in a remote part of the mountain. Devote your time to meditation and in this way attain true realization.[37]

Her remarks serve as a reminder of the tension which is often seen to exist between learning about a religion and being religious, between intellectual endeavor and spiritual attainment. She is concerned that her son, mesmerized by the specialized data which scholarship endlessly handles, will be diverted from his spiritual goal. Or, in other words, her fear is that information will get in the way of the saving transformation which the Buddha's teaching purports to offer. Cipher is not seeking to become a devotee of the Buddha (though this is, of course, one possible upshot of his search), but this unnamed Japanese mother's advice can, with slight adjustment, be applied to his situation. He does not want to become a scholar (caricatured as becoming a walking dictionary for others), or a devotee of a particular faith (caricatured as self-incarceration in a remote mountain temple). His path, with regard to information, is more of a middle way lying between these two extremes.

The first inimical force encountered by Cipher suggests that if his goal of reaching a world decision is not rendered unrealistic by the inadequacy of his skills, then it is surely rendered impossible by the sheer extent of the phenomena which need to be considered. Will Cipher succumb to the temptation to abandon his search, concluding that it is something that is beyond the power of any individual to deal with, that there will always remain images which he simply will not have time to consider, that if he is fated to deal with only a small part of the hall of mirrors, then why bother unduly about a decision which, given the scale of the situation, is going to have an element of incompleteness, arbitrariness and provisionality anyway? No doubt, realistically, in certain moods and moments Cipher will feel like giving up. Like everyone else, there will be some days in which he will just immerse himself in the business of day to day routine and try not to "remember death/life" in the sense explained in Chapter 1. However, this book is concerned with those days when he does so remember and when the search for some sort of peace of mind in the hall of mirrors seems imperative. The inimical force of information need not be considered an insuperable obstacle. It can, I think, be dealt with in a commonsensical sort of way, similar to that voiced by Descartes at the outset of a similarly daunting journey. Cipher must simply deal with the brightest mirrors first, deal first with those images which he finds the most dazzling and appealing, and proceed from there as time and energy, ability and opportunity allow. This is by no means a completely satisfactory answer. It must, however, suffice in terms of getting the job *started*, if not completed.

We might, perhaps, sum up and conclude this chapter—and anticipate something of the next one—by likening Cipher to that most celebrated solver of apparently intractable dilemmas, Mr. Sherlock Holmes. Holmes' approach to information further emphasizes the sort of practical outlook which Cipher will need to adopt if he is not to be halted in his tracks before even setting out. Consider this assessment of his friend by the worthy Dr Watson:

> His ignorance was as remarkable as his knowledge. Of contemporary literature, philosophy and politics he appeared to know next to nothing. My surprise reached a climax when I found incidentally that he was ignorant of the Copernican theory and of the composition of the solar system.

"You appear to be astonished," he said, smiling at my expression of surprise. "Now that I do know it I shall do my best to forget it."

"To forget it!"

"What the deuce is it to me?" he interrupted impatiently: "You say that we go round the sun. If we went round the moon it would make not a pennyworth of difference to me or to my work."[38]

While I would not wish to subscribe to a theory of education based on Holmes' assertion, much of what Cipher sees in the hall of mirrors would *not* make a pennyworth of difference to his attempts to reach a world decision. Like Holmes he may, therefore, display a startling ignorance. We need to remember that he is simply not interested in accumulating data as an end in itself, but rather in solving a particular problem (and, as we shall see in the next chapter, this does not require as a pre-requisite an acquaintance with all the facts). It should be stressed once again that Cipher's objective is to make a world decision, not to compile an encyclopedia of religions. The two exercises are not coterminous.

At the beginning of this chapter I contrasted the responses made to temptation by Gautama and Jesus with those of the ordinary individual embarking on some "Way." The temptation which the inimical force of information places before Cipher is that of abandoning his whole endeavor to make a decision about commitment in the context of a religiously plural world, on the grounds that he is insufficiently talented, or that the field is simply too extensive to cover properly. Cipher does not respond to such temptation like a Buddha or a Christ, such that the problem of information is heroically and conclusively overcome. The way in which he does respond to it may be unsatisfactory when measured against some scale of absolute victory, but in terms of the ordinary pilgrim's common (rather than sublime) sense, it has, I hope, at least the merit of being realistic.

Notes

1. Brihadaranyaka Upanishad, 1.3.28. Shree Purohit Swami and W. B. Yeats (trs.), *The Ten Principal Upanishads*, London, 1971, (1937), Faber, p. 119.
2. Pietro Rossano, "Christ's Lordship and Religious Pluralism in Roman Catholic Perspective," in Gerald H. Anderson and Thomas F. Stransky (eds.) *Christ's Lordship and Religious Pluralism*, New York, 1981, Orbis Books, p. 98.
3. Edith B. Schnapper, *The Inward Odyssey: the Concept of The Way in the Great Religions of the World*, London, 1980, (1965), George Allen & Unwin, p. 86.
4. *Romans* 7.19.
5. David Gnanaprakasam Moses, *Religious Truth and the Relation Between Religions*, Madras, 1950, The Christian Literature Society for India, Indian Research Series 5, pp. 91-92.
6. Aldous Huxley, *Eyeless in Gaza*, Harmondsworth, 1974 (1936), Penguin, p. 12.
7. Quoted in Mircea Eliade, *From Primitives to Zen, A Thematic Sourcebook of the History of Religions*, London, 1979, (1967), Collins, p. 326.
8. Arnold Toynbee, *Mankind and Mother Earth*, London, 1976, Oxford University Press, p. 4.
9. Mircea Eliade, *A History of Religious Ideas, Vol. 1: From the Stone Age to the Eleusinian Mysteries*, London, 1979, (1976), Collins, p. xiii.
10. Mircea Eliade, *No Souvenirs, Journal 1957-1969*, London, 1978, (1973), Routledge & Kegan Paul, p. viii.
11. See René Descartes, *Philosophical Works, Vol. 1*, Cambridge, 1973, (this edition 1911), Cambridge University Press, tr. Haldane and Ross, p. 82.
12. Readers who want to plot a history of religious studies in more detail than that afforded by this very crude model, will find useful material in Jan de Vries, *The Study of Religion: a Historical Approach* (translated and introduced by Kees Bolle), New York, 1967, Harcourt, Brace & World Inc (original Dutch edition, 1961); Eric Sharpe, *Comparative Religion: a History*, London 1975, Duckworth; and Walter H. Capps, *Religious Studies: the Making of a Discipline*, Minneapolis, 1995, Fortress Press.
13. Quoted in Partha Mitter, *Much Maligned Monsters, A History of European Reactions to Indian Art*, Oxford, 1977, Clarendon Press, p. 20.

14. ibid.
15. P. J. Marshall (ed.), *The British Discovery of Hinduism in the Eighteenth Century*, Cambridge, 1970, Cambridge University Press, p. 20.
16. ibid., p. 43.
17. Jonathan D. Spence, *The Memory Palace of Matteo Ricci*, London, 1985, Faber, pp. 111-112.
18. Thomas S. Kuhn, *The Structure of Scientific Revolutions,* second (enlarged) edition, Chicago, 1970 (1962), University of Chicago Press, p.63.
19. Max Müller, *Chips From a German Workshop, Vol. 1: Essays on the Science of Religion*, London, 1867, p. xxx.
20. James C. Moffat, *A Comparative History of Religions*, New York, 1875, Dodd & Mead, Vol. 1, p. vi.
21. Emile Burnouf, *The Science of Religions*, London, 1888, (1870), Swan, Sonnenschein, Lowrey & Co., p. 1.
22. Ralph Wendell Burhoe, "The Phenomenon of Religion seen Scientifically," in Allan W. Eister (ed.), *Changing Perspectives in the Scientific Study of Religion*, New York, 1974, Wiley Inter-science, p. 15. Burhoe's opinion echoes that of Edwin Starbuck, voiced some seventy five years earlier in his *Psychology of Religion* (London, 1899). Starbuck contrasts the study of religion with the history of science and concludes that "the study of religion is today where astronomy and chemistry were four centuries ago" (p. 3). Alister Hardy would, apparently, disagree with this assessment of the situation, suggesting that in William James and in Starbuck himself we already have parallels, in what he calls "the biology of God," to Darwin and Wallace in (non-theistic) biology. See *The Biology of God, a Scientist's Study of Man the Religious Animal*, London, 1975, Cape, p. 20. This variation in opinion as to the state of the subject underlines the point made in the text—that the "three ages" model is very much a generalization. It is not difficult to find voices which disagree with the schema it proposes.
23. Georg Schmid, *Principals of Integral Science of Religion*, The Hague, 1979, Mouton, p. 5.
24. Louis Henry Jordan, *Comparative Religion, its Genesis and Growth*, Edinburgh, 1905, T & T Clark, p. 163.
25. G. F. Woods, *Theological Explanations, A Study of the Meaning and Means of Explaining in Science, History and Theology*, Welwyn, 1958, James Nisbet & Co. Ltd., p. 2.
26. Eric J. Sharpe, *Comparative Religion, A History*, London, 1975, Duckworth, p. 2.

27. Georg Schmid, op. cit, p. 19.

28. C. J. Bleeker, *The Sacred Bridge, Researches into the Nature and Structure of Religion*, Leiden 1963, E. J. Brill, p. 11.

29. See Frederick J. Streng, "Religious Studies: Process of Transformation," in *The Proceedings of the American Academy of Religion*, Academic Study of Religion Section, 1974, p. 118.

30. W. Y. Evans-Wentz (ed.), *The Tibetan Book of the Dead*, London & New York, 1977, Oxford University Press (this edition first published 1927), p.2, note 1.

31. Arthur Miles (pseudonym of Gervee Baronté), *The Land of the Lingam*, London, 1933, Paternoster Press, pp. 7 and 9.

32. Ernest Becker, *The Denial of Death*, New York, 1973 The Free Press, p. x.

33. Anselm Strauss, *Mirrors and Masks: the Search for Identity*, London, 1977, Martin Robinson, p.38.

34. Ibid., p.39

35. Ibid.

36. Georg Schmid, op. cit., p. 18.

37. Paul Reps (compiler), *Zen Flesh, Zen Bones*, London, 1971, Penguin, p. 34. From Story no.20 in *101 Zen Stories*, "A Mother's Advice." Reps' source book, which gathers material from as early as the thirteenth century, was first published in 1957 and has seen numerous reprintings. It is a deservedly popular, and extremely effective, introduction to the spirit of Zen.

38. Arthur Conan Doyle, *A Study in Scarlet*, Harmondsworth, 1981, (1887), Penguin, reprinted in *The Penguin Complete Sherlock Holmes*, p. 21.

CHAPTER 5

THE SLAP AND THE SALAMANDER

THE NATURE of Cipher's situation in the religious hall of mirrors has now been stated in general terms and, in considering information as a potentially inimical force, something of the extent and complexity of his environment has been further illustrated. Cipher's own nature and desiderata have been roughly sketched as well. His situation *vis-a-vis* the disciplinary area of religious studies has been noted, and we have seen his common-sense response to the daunting scale of the task he is faced with. Cipher is thus poised to proceed on an investigative journey among the many perplexing religious images with which he is surrounded. He will look first at those that make the strongest impression on him and investigate as he may, accepting his limited time and abilities as part of the situation with which he must cope (rather than as a disqualification which prevents him from setting out). Cipher's sense of zero, in other words, one of the strands of meaning in his name which I wish to stress, is ready to explore some religious integers to see if they might offer a source of peace of mind, according to which his life might be given a new sense of value and direction.

In another journey, whose course I cannot map out in this brief volume, Cipher might have chosen to survey the various available *explanations* of religion rather than the religious images themselves. For it might well be supposed that the religious hall of mirrors is but a glassy mirage which modern thought has effectively shattered. After all, are there not philosophical, psychological and sociological accounts of precisely those images before which Cipher stands uncertain and mesmerised, which reveal them to be things of no significant substance, about which he ought not to concern himself beyond a purely academic interest? Cannot the existence of God be seriously queried by logic, or the nature of such a supposed entity be shown to be no more than a projected father figure, or a social emanation, or a source of narcotic escapism in a heartlessly unjust world? Have Hume, Freud, Durkheim, Marx, and others not effectively shattered all the religious mirrors which surround Cipher? And, rather than bringing untold years of bad luck for the generations who followed in their steps, could it not be argued that in so doing they have provided freedom from enslavement to misleading ideas, directing eyes squarely to the realities of the human condition and away from the distracting dazzle of the illusion of transcendence?

If they are accepted as being accurate, such explanations of religion lead unerringly to the conclusion that whatever peace of mind this realm of human experience might *seem* to offer, it is founded on the sand of muddled thinking, illusion, or quite contingent societal circumstances, and is therefore, to that extent, unreliable and untrustworthy. Any peace of mind which religion may seem to offer is undermined by an investigation of the *nature* of religion. It pays out counterfeit comfort which may, sure enough, provide a sense of well-being—but only so long as we do not inquire too closely into its origins. Given the possibility that he may not, in fact, be facing an apparent multiplicity of genuine formulae for achieving peace of mind, but rather a set of figures which have been rigged, albeit unconsciously, to provide the sort of answers he is looking for, ought Cipher not to begin with a consideration of those auditing accounts of religions which seek to expose their arithmetic as highly dubious, rather than wasting his time trying to work out which sum, if any, adds up to the right answer?

I do not wish to suggest that the various critiques of religion which explain it in terms that believers would consider destructive are irrelevant to Cipher's intended quest, or that such criticisms as they level are mistaken. On the contrary, such critiques are both highly relevant and often persuasive. However, this is simply not the area on which I wish to focus here. At some point in a quest such as Cipher's, attention must, obviously, be given to the various avenues of criticism—philosophical, historical, scientific, etc.—which might be made of any religion being considered as a source of peace of mind. If such a task were ignored, Cipher might well accept as a Way something that was, in fact, directly at variance with the directions desired by that Upanishadic prayer which I quoted at the start of Chapter 4 (that is, which would lead him from the real to the unreal, from light into darkness). At the stage of his deliberations to which *these* chapters give access, though, Cipher's emphasis will be on asking why those who hold to a particular religious outlook accept it as a source of peace of mind. His primary interest will be on the explanations *which they themselves consider valid* for their so doing, not on causative accounts of why they happen to think and act in the way they do. To contrive a very simple example: suppose someone told Cipher that Hinduism provided them with peace of mind, such that their feelings of insignificance, mystery and meaninglessness received an adequate, sense-giving antidote through, say, devotion to the goddess Kali. In reply to the question *why* they believe such devotion offers peace of mind, *why* it is curative of a sense of lostness, the Hindu might simply reply that it feels as if it does, that to them, self-evidently, it is peace-of-mind-giving and requires no further substantiation beyond this. Or they might say that their belief is based on that most ultimate of experiences, the identity of Brahman (the world soul) and Atman (the individual soul), and the realisation that all else is illusion, a perspective on things which they find effectively afforded via the mythology and symbolism of the cult of Kali. In reply to this same question, a sociologist might suggest that they are Hindus because they were born into a community where what Peter Berger calls "the cognitive majority"[1] held similar views, where adherence to such views receives strong peer group approval and divergence from them strong disapproval. Alternatively, it might be argued that the peace of mind offered by such devotion as they display offers only some small nectar of comfort in bitter surroundings, whether of grinding rural poverty or urban hardship and squalor, and that it would disappear in a sweeter environment where the compensations it offers would be rendered unnecessary. Or, were he to ask a philosopher rather than a sociologist, Cipher might find belief in Kali dismissed as erroneous, something logically insupportable, the outcome of flawed thinking, such that attitudes of devotion are unfounded. At this stage, Cipher's attention is firmly set on investigating the answers given by the Hindu him or herself. His interest is on the self-understanding of those who variously accept religions as offering peace of mind, not on critical explanations of such acceptance which might be formulated from outside the faiths in question.

So, rather than considering the various explanatory accounts of the origin and nature of religion, accounts which might act to dismantle the whole structure of the hall of mirrors as a locus which legitimately offers "answers" of the sort which interest him, Cipher's *first* steps will be concerned with seeing the various images as they appear to those who do accept them (whether at face value or not) as somehow providing peace of mind. This may well be the wrong way to tackle things and it might be objected that Cipher is making very heavy weather of a matter which could be solved comparatively simply—in a sense just by looking behind the mirrors and seeing that there is something non-religious there creating the perplexing picture. Presumably this sort of objection will be made if one happens to take, say, a Freudian or Marxist view, or if one believes that logic has already demolished such ideas as God even before we reach for our empirical guns. To some extent, Cipher's choice of initially focusing on the hall of mirrors' various images, as these are experienced by the people who accept them as genuine, is simply a choice. It is one way of doing things, a possible response to his situation. It is not necessarily the best one and certainly not the only one. It is, however, the one which I, as his creator, have chosen to dictate and which I wish to explore—and in a sense that is justification enough; it simply has to do with setting reasonable bounds for a particular inquiry. However, were such a choice to need further justification beyond authorial fiat, it might be pointed out that for all the destruction which the various critiques of religion may sometimes seem to have wrought, if we bother to pick up the apparently shattered religious images in the aftermath of some particular attack, it is often difficult to piece together anything which anyone would seriously accept as a picture of religion as it is held to and practised by believers. As Leszek Kolakowski has remarked,

> More often than not the philosopher discusses problems which, though perfectly valid in themselves, are very remote from the real worries of...religious people.[2]

The philosopher is not alone in preparing intrinsically interesting but rather off-target critiques. Psychological and sociological efforts too often seem wide of any mark which a believer would recognise as characterising his or her faith. It seems clear (to put it in Cantwell Smith's terms) that at least some of this inaccuracy comes as a result of aiming at cumulative tradition and claiming to have "hit" personal faith. The explanations of religion offered by Freud and Marx and the criticisms put forward by philosophy are, moreover, almost invariably directed to a monotheistic type of religion. But many of the images in Cipher's hall of mirrors are not even *theistic,* let alone subscribing to the idea of a *single* deity. It is by no means clear if a Freudian critique of religion would apply to Buddhism, or if Hume's superbly crafted critique of the design argument would be applicable to a conception of the world as *mayic* or *samsaric.* Before such questions can be answered we need a clear view of what the religious images in question actually involve. This is not to cancel critical accounts of religion from the syllabus of Cipher's quest, but rather to postpone an examination of them to some place outwith the scope of this particular book.

Cipher's quest, so far as we shall focus on it here, is to clarify the nature of the images which perplex him, *as they are actually perceived and held to be of value and authority by those who subscribe to—indeed who make up—the various religious mirrors.* For until he has seen clearly how they are accepted as offering peace of mind by those who accept that they do act in this way, he will, in a sense, not really know what he may be accepting or rejecting when he comes to make a decision, either about them or about some critique of them which he might consider in the future.

Attempting to see clearly the way in which people accept the religious outlooks they do as offering peace of mind, could, of course, be a lifetime's endeavour. Cipher could use this point of focus to transmute his search for an answer into a situation where the search itself became, if not the answer, at least the excuse for never arriving at one. Phenomenology could displace and deaden perplexity as he strove to discover in minute and exhaustive detail what makes someone a Hindu or a Buddhist or a Christian; how, precisely, their outlook pictures the world; what value they accord to human life; their moral teachings, and so on, gradually forgetting, in the course of this research, that in fact he set out to get more than just a super-accurate description of the different religious images which are accepted as peace-of-mind-offering entities. He might well come to a quite brilliant understanding of the history and mythology of, for example, Hinduism. But, in so doing, he may move little closer to a decision as to whether or not he could commit himself to a Hindu view of things. In a sense, information once more exerts an inimical force, this time threatening to draw Cipher into that situation where, in effect, he would be left constructing a full-scale replica model of the religious landscape which he really only wished to map and pass through. And, for the purposes of his particular journey, as we shall see in a moment, a fairly simple map will suffice. Information here offers the temptation of deferring decision indefinitely, in favour of complete description. And Cipher, a child of the third age of religious studies, has at his disposal an accumulation of data such that this kind of painstaking reconstruction would never run short of material.

As the French diarist Amiel put it, summarizing an obvious but sometimes overlooked truth:

> The man who insists upon seeing with perfect clearness before he decides, *never* decides. Accept life and you must accept regret.[3]

Cipher has already come to terms with two regrets. First, that his abilities are far from perfect, that he has by no means the ideal intellectual equipment to carry out his quest. Secondly, that the extent of the information and the briefness of his life mean that there will always be a sense in which his search will be incomplete and any conclusion reached therefore incurably provisional. Now he must come to terms with a third regret. Namely that for any particular area of investigation he cannot wait for complete description (which is, after all, never really complete) before making a decision. Given the briefness of his life, the immensity of his task, the limitations of his abilities and the urgency of addressing his sense of lostness in the world by reaching some decision about commitment, he cannot attempt some sort of exhaustively comprehensive study of every aspect of those parts of the hall of mirrors that he *does* have time to focus on.

Fascinating though it might be, and important for understanding the way in which the religious images are seen by those who accept and help to constitute them, Cipher cannot embark on elaborate explorations around the vast circulatory systems which channel the life-blood coursing through each religious body. If he did so, he would reach many vital organs, see how the various religions hold together as living organic structures, feel himself carried along by their vital energies, but such a wide-ranging exploration would be ill-suited to solving his particular dilemma. He must seek some means of getting straight to the heart of the matter, ruthlessly pushing aside scores of phenomena as being various degrees of periphery, which will only become of interest to him if the central core about which they orbit is sound.

Cipher's main concern in exploring the religious images in the hall of mirrors is to establish if he can accept any of these images, in whole or in part, singly or in some kind of combination, as offering peace of mind, as providing some adequate response to those feelings of insignificance, mystery and meaninglessness which trouble him. In this phase of his exploration, which is focused on religion as it is perceived by religious believers, the key question which he will use to steer his inquiries towards the heart of the matter will simply be to ask of the Buddhist, the Christian, the Hindu or the Muslim: "What makes you profess this faith? On what grounds does your acceptance of it as a legitimate source of peace of mind rest?" Alongside his desire to find out the nature of the religious outlook they think offers peace of mind is the more urgent desire to find out *why,* in their own terms, they think it does so. In this way Cipher hopes to drive towards the linchpin of the whole religious structure, that point which the believer would regard as of crucial importance, such that, were it discredited, his or her faith— if continued—would be in some sense radically changed or devalued. Of such linchpins, which hold together the whole weight of the various images which dance before him in the hall of mirrors, Cipher will ask: "Is it true? Can I accept it?" If he can, *then* the whole structure which depends upon it will become worthy of extensive—if not exhaustive— study. If he cannot, if a linchpin is found to be in some sense faulty or illusory, or if it remains imperceptible, then the image which depends upon it may be dismissed, *not* as something of absolutely no value (that would be a ridiculous and simplistic over-reaction) but as something which will no longer be of such first-order interest to Cipher as a potential source of peace of mind.

It may be objected that, if he brushes many phenomena aside as peripheral and tries to get to some kind of linchpin, Cipher's intended focusing on religious images will end up doing worse violence to the pictures of Buddhism, Christianity, Islam, and so on than any external critique. This sounds suspiciously like the crudest separation into essence and manifestation. But Cipher is not denying that all religious phenomena contribute to an overall, cumulative sense of meaning which is deeply embedded in cultural and symbolic forms. He accepts that each phenomenon is important in as much as it provides access to, constitutes a doorway opening onto, is expressive of, that which gives the whole structure life. This is *not* to say that every religious phenomenon is *similarly* grounded in some originative life-giving experience. Clearly the twentieth century lay-Buddhist who only meditates occasionally, whose knowledge of the Buddha's life and teaching is somewhat sketchy, and whose undertaking of the Five Precepts is uneven, and a close and devoted disciple of Gautama, stand at somewhat different distances from the arterial system of Buddhism. In the same way, the nominal present-day Christian, whose religion finds little expression beyond Sunday church going and formal rites of passage at birth, marriage and death, would seem to be located nearer the periphery of this faith than, say, St. John of the Cross. Both they and he will give access to the same originative source of authority that provides final sanction for the outlook they variously adhere to, but, in terms of the analogy with the circulatory system, in one case we are at the very extremities of the body, in the finest of the capillaries, in the other we are nearer to a strong source of pulse. Cipher is assuming that if contact with this pulse is finally broken, or if the heart of the matter turns out to be other than it is perceived by the believer, then the status of their outlook as offering legitimate peace of mind must be questioned. Within any particular expression of religiousness, Cipher will look for the channels which link it to the heart and attempt to work his way back towards it.

Obviously Cipher is likely to receive many different types of answer to the question: "Why do you accept this particular image as a legitimate source of peace of mind?" (or, conversely, "What would make you reject it?"). The linchpin of a religious outlook, as it is perceived by someone who accepts its vision of the world, may be explained as being pragmatic—"I accept it because it works" (and would reject it if it stopped working); traditional—"I accept it because countless others have done so in the course of a long and venerable history;" contextual— "I accept it because I know of no other way" (things might be different if the context was different); or absolute—"I accept it because it's true" (and would reject it if it were found to be otherwise). I take it as axiomatic that Cipher could not accept something as a curative formula for his troubled mind, for his sense of lostness, if he knew it to be false, or indeed if it was founded on a linchpin which could continue to function independently of the truth—that would be like accepting as a cure for malaria something which in fact left all the symptoms unaltered. He will focus his attention on answers which make reference to an absolute linchpin, not on those of a pragmatic, traditional or contextual nature. These would not take him to the heart of the matter nor provide a conclusion, for he might quite reasonably continue his questioning in the face of the answers which they offer (*Why* does such and such an outlook work? *Why* did previous generations believe it?). Unless he is to be led into some sort of ultimately self-destructive circularity, reference must be made to something else. Cipher's focus will be on that something else, the originative, absolute justifying point which explains why a believer accepts a particular outlook to be valid, and *in the face of which it would be inappropriate to ask further, "Why do you so believe?"*

Cipher's attention will, then, be keenly focused on the linchpin of those actual experiences which will be referred to as the final authoritative element in most attempts to justify faith in a particular religious structure. Once he has located such linchpins, he will have to try to decide for himself whether or not they are as they are presented and relied upon, whether they are trustworthy as possible foundations for peace of mind. Cipher will not be asking of Hinduism or Buddhism or Christianity, "Is it true?," but rather, "On what is the faith acceptance of individual Hindus, Buddhists and Christians ultimately founded?" and "Can that linchpin of their faith be accepted in the terms in which they present and understand it?" To ask of Hinduism, Buddhism or Christianity "Is it true?" or "Can I accept it as a peace of mind offering entity?" is somewhat simplistic and naive, given that beneath these undoubtedly misleading general headings there is gathered such a multiplicity of things. Cipher will be concerned, rather, with the basis on which individual believers found their faith, and sooner or later this will, inevitably, take him towards a focus on some form of religious experience. For, as R. C. Zaehner put it:

> If religion is to have any meaning at all [and Cipher accepts that it does, though he is not sure of what type or whether it will suffice to give meaning to *his* existence] there must be an element of experience in it: there must be some apperception of what, for want of a more precise word, we must still call the divine, the holy or the numinous.[4]

I agree with Zaehner on our lack of a precise word for the object of religious experience. However, I think "transcendent" has fewer theistic overtones than "divine," "holy" or "numinous," so I shall use that term instead of the selection which he offers.

Left unqualified, "religious experience" could mean anything from lighting a joss stick to going on pilgrimage, singing hymns, fasting, reciting the nembutsu, or countless other activities in the huge spectrum of possible behaviours which a glance through the hall of mirrors reveals. I am using this term specifically to mean that which constitutes the internal explanatory root of the phenomena which go to make up a particular religious outlook on the world. In other words, religious experience in this sense refers to the ultimate sense-giving validation of their beliefs which would be offered by a believer. It is that which, so to speak, gives life to their faith, such that the diverse phenomena which go to make up a Hindu or a Buddhist or a Christian or an Islamic or a Taoist outlook on things cohere together as organic wholes, their existence ultimately claiming whatever life-force they manifest from an experiential core (variously named as Brahman, Nirvana, God, Allah, the Tao). This life-giving experience of the transcendent extends throughout the religious realm, though it underlies different phenomena at vastly varying depths. It provides the ultimate internal validation for religion as a source of peace of mind. Religious experience understood in this sense provides the linchpin which holds together the various images in the hall of mirrors. It is the heart of the matter which Cipher hopes to reach.

Buddha, Zoroaster, Jesus, Muhammad, the writers of the *Vedas*, Lao Tzu—all provide examples of individuals who have had religious experience of such power and vitality as to leave each generation since them struggling to find adequate ways of putting it into words and action. Such interpretations have been many and varied and constitute the major part of the history of religion. But though they may have held sway for years, and influenced the lives of millions, no single interpretation of such experiences has seemed entirely satisfactory, to the extent that succeeding ages are left theologically replete and silent. On the contrary, the religious experiences of the great holy figures of history, at once both ineffable and generative of seemingly continual interpretations, seem to provide an inexhaustible quarry of *possible* understandings. Such experiences stand at the root of centuries of religious practice and give it the sense it claims. No matter how explicit the doctrine, no matter how tangible the edifice, no matter how time-honoured the ritual, every religious phenomenon seems to recede (in terms of meaning) to a central and apparently irreducible opaqueness which is variously named "God," "Brahman," "Nirvana," etc. Within that opaqueness the heart of religion seems to beat in an endlessly recurring rhythm of systolic ineffability and diastolic attempts at expression and understanding, its pulse apparently generating that situation of diversity, at least in much of its intra-religious sense, with which Cipher is concerned (as we shall see further in Chapter 7). It is towards this heart that Cipher will have to try to proceed, since it is only according to the nature of its pulse that a decision can be reached about the quality of life which spreads through its arterial system, offering a structure which purports to give peace of mind. If the religious heartbeat does indeed stem from a genuine encounter with some transcendent state or entity, then its reverberations may, perhaps, lull all of Cipher's disquiet to sleep, providing a sense of belonging and homecoming that will cure his feeling of lostness in the world. If, on the other hand, that pulse is merely an echo which we have imagined from straining our ears too long in a wilderness whose emptiness, silence and meaninglessness appals us, or if it is the drumming of mere wishful thinking, then Cipher may quit the hall of mirrors and let his search take other directions.

Given this experiential linchpin, Cipher will be relatively unconcerned with the extremities of the religious body. His immediate task must be to get as close as possible to the heart, or at least to some strong source of pulse, and to *listen* with all the attention he can muster.

It may seem, however, that—crucial though it is—this source is just not reachable. If, for instance, in the course of exploring a particular image in the hall of mirrors, Cipher finds he is referred back to the experience of some single long-dead historical figure, it may be located in the distant past, and between it and Cipher may stretch centuries of partial deafness and dubious interpretation. But although we may look to them for its classic and defining instances and for the provision of some sort of specialised vocabulary or set of reference points, it is important to remember that religious experience is by no means confined to these key figures of the major traditions. Accordingly, there is no reason for Cipher's investigation to be confined only to them. The religious experience of the ordinary person in the street may leave little imprint on recorded history (whether because of its lesser power or that person's reticence or inarticulateness in dealing with it), but its occurrence may well blaze its way indelibly, if privately, across the path of the individual's biography. Such ongoing individual experiences serve to reinvest traditional accounts of religious experience with an aliveness they could not hope to have were such experiences located solely in an unrenewable, culturally-remembered past. It is towards such incandescent present moments that Cipher will direct his inquiries. His interest will be in the point of ignition rather than the subsequent flames, and he will assume that those flames would long ago have been extinguished, or at least have faded, were there but a single point of ignition at some historical moment of beginning, which, thereafter, never sparked out again.

Such an assumption receives strong backing in David Hay's *Exploring Inner Space,* a book which attempts to assess the extent of religious experience in modern British society. Hay writes:

> What is unique to religions is that they always assert the possibility
> of getting in touch, directly, with whatever is ultimately "real."[5]

Such a getting in touch with what is variously taken to be ultimately real is, I think, what gives religions the peace-of-mind-offering status which they display and which scientific and humanistic alternatives often seem to lack. As J. C. A. Gaskin puts it:

> most religious experience can be described in terms of an awareness
> of something other-worldly *in relation to which man finds his greatest
> joy and peace.*[6]

Readily acknowledging the "decay of [many] publicly available symbols of religion,"[7] Hay focuses attention on what he calls "the sacred dimension to human experience which is prior to all symbols"[8] and without which it might be argued that "all other dimensions of religion are emptied of meaning."[9] His conclusions are startling for those who might imagine that in the late twentieth century we have become secularised to the point of denying the existence of the transcendent altogether, or of allowing only the very faintest "rumour of angels" any credence. Thirty-six per cent of the sample of people approached by National Opinion Polls answered affirmatively to the question: "Have you ever been aware of, or influenced by, a presence or power, whether you call it God or not, which is different from your everyday self?" "On that basis," remarks Hay, "we can predict that about 15 million adults in this country would say the same; that is to say, over a third of the population aged 16 or over."[10] Similarly, thirty-one per cent of the sample responded positively to the question, "Have you ever felt as though you were very close to a powerful spiritual force that seemed to lift you out of yourself?" Hay concludes his careful and interesting study by suggesting that:

> Probably a majority of the more intelligent, saner and socially responsible people in our secular nation would claim, perhaps rather shyly, to have had these experiences. They may fear they are in a minority, and will be thought by most people to be stupid or mentally unbalanced; but they are merely claiming the kind of contact with ultimate reality which lies at the heart of Western culture and of every great historical culture.[11]

Unless Hay's results are *altogether* wrong, it would seem clear that Cipher's focus on religious experience need not be restricted to a handful of historical cases which may lie so far beyond the reach of effective investigation as to guarantee an "open" verdict. Moreover, in justifying his location of the linchpin of a religious image in this sort of experience, it would seem quite plausible for him to argue that, were this "contact with the heart" actually severed, were this experiential spark to be extinguished, the status of religion as offering peace of mind would then be vastly diminished. If Hay's exploration of inner space had perceived no confirming echoes in modern consciousness of the ecstatic shouts of the ancients, if no religious outlook today could claim some sort of direct unmediated contact with some absolute point of ignition and confirmation, then it might surely be supposed that the hall of mirrors would simply have become misted over. As such, it would very rapidly cease to be the perplexing place that Cipher finds it to be. It causes him such puzzlement precisely because it appears to be a living repository of profound experiences which seem to be suggestive of radically different outlooks. Were the hall of mirrors not rooted in such continuing experiences, it would soon become like a vast museum offering a catalogue of outmoded outlooks, not a workshop of world-views offering live and present ways of living and thinking.

Cipher's focus will not, therefore, be on those religious persons whose reference to an experiential basis for their outlook is a second- or third-hand referring back, but on those for whom it is immediate. This is not to say that the faith of the individual which is founded on purportedly direct personal experience of the transcendent is superior to that founded on trust that someone else has experienced the transcendent, or trust in some recorded, historically distant, moment of revelation—they simply offer Cipher a quicker way of getting to the heart of the matter and therefore making a decision about commitment.

A focus on religious experience may also provide Cipher with a basis on which to begin to answer the question of the extent to which the different religious images are the same and the extent to which they are different. Is there one uniform experience being interpreted variously, or are there various similar but different experiences eliciting a range of descriptions? Or are the experiences entirely different and non-overlapping? It is self-evident that at a surface level the different religions are different. But does the difference run uniformly from the outermost periphery to the innermost heart? Can we locate any underlying similarity which might act to qualify any subsequent difference as secondary and relatively unimportant, or are the different images in the religious hall of mirrors underlain for all their depth with the same radical dissimilarities which so blatantly and problematically characterise the faces they show the world?

Of course, even if Cipher could establish that all the different religions had, ultimately, the same experiential source, this would not end his dilemma (though it would make it a little less complicated). He would still need to know if such a source provided a reliable foundation for achieving peace of mind and he would have to decide which of the still different routes to follow towards it. As the Abbott of a Zen Buddhist Priory in the North of England puts it:

> I get rather tired of people telling me that all the ways are the same. They are spectacularly not the same. If you want to travel to the priory from the South coast, it does not make much difference whether you go via the M5 and M6 or around London and up the M1. But you must make up your mind and stick to it. If you make a mistake and end up in Cornwall then you reassess the situation and start again from there. Too many people like nothing better than going round and round 'spaghetti junction' in the Midlands, admiring all the roads that lead off from there, but never going any further themselves.[12]

In a sense, of course, Cipher is circumambulating a kind of spaghetti junction in the hall of mirrors. The problem is, he is not sure if the roads go where the signposts say they go, or if their destinations are, in the end, the same. His immediate concern must be to investigate the claims of travellers who say they have been there, to try to decide if the routes they recommend really follow the contours they claim and offer the perspectives they say they have seen. Cipher does not want to end up wasting time and energy disappearing down some blind alley which in fact leads nowhere, or which may simply go round in a wider and less honest and obvious orbit than that of his spaghetti junction of informed and inquiring neutrality. In a sense, he will seek to go a little way with those travellers who seem to follow the fastest and most direct route, questioning them carefully and subjecting their reports to the closest scrutiny, before deciding if he wishes to make any of the journey at all. And to reiterate the point that he is not interested in *everything* in the religious realm, we might note that he will accept without question all kinds of claims about the quality of the vehicle and the fellow travellers;

he accepts that there is much of worth in any religious community in terms of, for example, various social and aesthetic parameters, but *his* question remains: does the road lead to legitimate peace of mind?

"Man's religiousness," as Willard Oxtoby rather clinically put it, is "a response to a stimulus commonly called 'the sacred.'"[13] Joachim Wach, using the same terms as Oxtoby (and echoing John MacMurray), has complained that "a great deal of our modern study of religion attempts to give an account of a response without any reference to the stimulus."[14] It is the *stimulus,* as the validating source of the various religious responses which perplex him, on which Cipher will try to focus his attention. Needless to say, though, he will not approach it with any *a priori* assumptions about its nature. Focusing on religious experience does not mean that he gives credence to the way in which it is read by those who report it.

Cipher's emphasis on the validating stimulus or stimuli behind the religious responses, on the linchpins of those massive religious structures which purport to contain peace of mind and which together constitute the hall of mirrors in which he is situated, can be memorably expressed by referring to a passage from the autobiography of Benvenuto Cellini. This will also (and you may think at long last) explain the otherwise rather odd sounding title of this chapter. In Book One, Section 4 of his colourful and fascinating life story, Cellini relates the following incident:

> When I was about five years old my father happened to be in a basement chamber of our house, where they had been washing, and where a good fire of oak logs was still burning; he had a viol in his hand and was playing and singing alone beside the fire. Happening to look into the fire, he spied in the middle of those most burning flames a little creature like a lizard, which was sporting in the core of the intensest coals. Becoming instantly aware of what the thing was, he had my sister and me called, and pointing it out to us children, gave me a great box on the ears, which caused me to howl and weep with all my might. Then he pacified me good humouredly, and spoke as follows: "My dear little boy, I am not striking you for any wrong that you have done, but only to make you remember that the lizard which you see in the fire is a

salamander, a creature which has never been seen before by anyone of whom we have credible information." So saying, he kissed me and gave me some pieces of money.[15]

Transferring the imagery of Cellini's story to the hall of mirrors: religious experience is cast in the role of the salamander, and the various interpretative and expressive words and actions which have sprung up around its claimed sightings are cast in the role of the slap—as reminders, often systematised into a formal corpus of ritual and doctrine, of what Eliade terms "hierophany" (that is, what is taken to be an irruption into our present experience of the transcendent[16]). The salamander is the internal validating source without which the slap ceases to have the meaning which it was intended to have (which is not to say that it would have no meaning at all if the salamander turned out to be in some way unreal or illusory). Cipher's emphasis will be on the salamander rather than the slap, though obviously his approach to it will be mediated through careful study of the various mnemonic forms which are immediately visible and accessible to him. Thus, for example, Cipher will only be marginally interested in the forms of ceremony, the artefacts used, the sacred places involved in worship. His attention will be focused, albeit *through* these secondary phenomena, on the experience which lies behind an act of worship, whether immediately or at some distance, and on which the sense of the worship undertaken ultimately depends. Whereas a student of comparative religion might devote all his or her energy and attention to an examination of the slap (the *response* to the stimulus of the transcendent), describing its various forms and unravelling its history in terms of various typological categories, Cipher will be interested in the claimed reality to which prayer, sacrifice, devotion, worship, etc. purport to point. As such, he may be breaking the cardinal rule of some scholars' notions of what religious studies is all about (namely, a neutral, descriptive approach which does not get involved and offers no opinion as to the truth or falsity, the authenticity or the illusoriness of the focus of religious phenomena). He will, however, be following a course of action more consonant with his dilemma than "pure description," however accurate, could ever be.

Just as, had Cellini's father not seen a salamander in the fire, the blow he struck his son would have been pointless in the way in which it was intended, so the various religious phenomena in the hall of mirrors might be dismissed as similarly meaningless, at least in the way that they are intended to be meaningful, were there no experience corresponding to the salamander behind them. Moreover, had Cellini's father been mistaken about what he saw, it is clear that the status of his subsequent action would have to be called into question. There is no point in providing someone with a reminder of what neither you nor they have seen. Likewise, if religious experience is not of what it was originally taken to be, subsequent accounts of it and actions based on it may have to be reviewed. From Cipher's point of view, were there no salamander somewhere in the image at which he looks, then most of what he sees could be dismissed as not constituting the conditions necessary to provide a formula for peace of mind.

This is not to say that religious experience lies immediately and obviously below *every* religious phenomenon. Sometimes the outgrowth of the response, the slap, has moved so far from the stimulus, the salamander, that there is only the most tenuous connection between the two. Indeed, one gets the feeling that at some points the response would be distinctly embarrassed to be reminded of its originating stimulus. Many of the various religious structures with which Cipher is concerned would probably survive even a clear-cut proof of the non-existence of their particular "salamandric" source, though clearly this would change their tone of meaning, shifting it from absolute to relative, from metaphysical to social. As such, they might still offer peace of mind, but it would be a somewhat watered down variety, diluted to the point where it was more an acknowledgement of the insignificance, mystery and meaninglessness which craves peace of mind in the first place, rather than the relationship with ultimate reality which might cure it. Cipher would consider such dilutions only after any remaining full-strength formulae had been looked at.

Nor ought it to be supposed that Cipher's emphasis on the salamander commits him to considering only the most literal interpretations of religious experience. He will follow *any* religious response back to its stimulus in an effort to check its linchpin, in an effort to get to the heart of the matter. Some responses will be more straightforward than others, offering reasonably quick access to a perspective from which the believer's view of the salamander may be seen and shared. Others may seem so far removed from it that they act almost to obscure it from view.

As Lesslie Newbigin once put it: "A study of the eye is useful in its proper place, but it cannot replace the use of the eye for seeing what is to be seen."[17] Thus, in Newbigin's opinion, the study of religion might risk being somewhat pointless if "it is only concerned with the study of the 'religious dimension of human experience' and not with the realities which religious experience tries to grasp and respond to."[18] There are many differing views as to where the focus of comparative religion or religious studies *ought* to put its emphasis—on personal faith or cumulative tradition, on the parahistorical or the historical aspects of religion, or on what Schmid, very confusingly, terms the reality of religion or the religious reality.[19] Newbigin offers another way of putting this stimulus:response/salamander:slap dichotomy. In terms of *his* metaphor, Cipher must try to determine if the religious eyes gaze out on a vista in which some being such as God, or some state such as Nirvana, can be perceived, so that the apparent senselessness of human existence is thereby revealed as purposeful by reference to them, or if their field of vision is blank, or focused on some non-transcendent mirage which they mistakenly perceive to be the ultimately real.

Some interpretations of religious experience, however, or, to continue in terms of Newbigin's metaphor, some accounts of the religious vision of things, will not be of much interest to Cipher. What J. C. A. Gaskin, looking at the work of figures like D. Z. Phillips and Don Cupitt, has dubbed the personalist theologies[20] (which, incidentally, he sees as being indistinguishable from atheism), will not be of primary importance in his quest. Such theologies offer an interpretation of religion which is so far removed from what most believers take the referent language of their faith to be talking about, that they deposit the stimulus, the salamander, the transcendent—call it what you will—in an abstract theoretical stratosphere, where the religious atmosphere becomes so thin as to be virtually indistinguishable from that of a non-religious understanding of the world and of religion's place in the world. Such interpretations provide no linchpin for the religious structure. They offer no absolute grounding for accepting their particular variety of faith as offering peace of mind. It is one thing to say that the salamander is, in fact, a non-figurative, awesome experience which, in symbolic language, sometimes appears as a mythical reptile, and still to justify the slap (for something memorable has still been encountered). It would be quite something else to found such a reaction on a sighting of what was accepted as no more than the death-throes of an unfortunate lizard.

To sum up: in the grand tradition of methodological prolegomena, it may appear as if we have moved very little further forwards. Still, I am not concerned at this stage with following Cipher's quest, but with considering what procedural difficulties attend the kind of journey he is planning to make, and how best that journey might be directed. We are at the stage of route-planning rather than actually going on the journey (an account of the journey itself must wait for another book). Cipher's priority has now been firmly focused. He is primarily interested in discovering how religious believers perceive their religion as offering peace of mind, and proceeding from such a vantage point to consider if he could accept it as such himself. Such a focus could end up as an exercise in endless phenomenology were it not for the insistent stress on the experiential linchpins which Cipher will make. There is much in the hall of mirrors that is of only academic interest to him and which he will thus pass by. His experiential focus may also provide him with a means of determining how different the various religions really are.

Thus we leave Cipher still standing free of the inimical force of information, and with his proposed investigation of the hall of mirrors now clearly targeted on the stimulus, the salamander, which he will seek to approach through the more immediately visible phenomena which constitute the various responses (or "slaps"). In the next chapter we will begin to consider more closely how this approach might be effected. Perhaps we should end on a note of warning and reassurance, since Cipher's quest may carry with it considerable potential to make him sad (in much the same way as Michael Novak has argued that religious studies poses this risk for its practitioners).[21] For, if he can, at the end of the day, perceive no salamander, no incandescent stimulus, for the religious responses with which he must wrestle, then perhaps his quest for peace of mind will consist of encountering a number of slaps or body blows which will result in little more than a severe case of spiritual bruising. In view of such a possibility, it is perhaps worth remembering that there are various non-religious sources of peace of mind (art and science, for example) that he might then turn to for possible solace.

Notes

1. Peter Berger, *A Rumour of Angels, Modern Society and the Rediscovery of the Supernatural*, Harmondsworth, 1971, (1969), Penguin, p. 18f.
2. Leszek Kolakowski, *Religion, If There is no God.... On God, the Devil, Sin and other worries of the so called Philosophy of Religion*, Glasgow, 1982, Fontana Books, p. 12.
3. Henri-Frédéric Amiel, journal entry dated 17th December 1856. See *Amiel's Journal, the Journal Intime of Henri-Frédéric Amiel*, tr. with an introduction and notes by Mrs Humphrey Ward, London, 1913, (1885), Macmillan.
4. R. C. Zaehner, *The City Within the Heart*, London, 1980, Unwin, p. 6.
5. David Hay, *Exploring Inner Space: Scientists and Religious Experience*, Harmondsworth, 1982, Penguin, p. 28.
6. J. C. A. Gaskin, *The Quest for Eternity: An Outline of the Philosophy of Religion*, Harmondsworth, 1984, Penguin, p. 174. My emphasis.
7. David Hay, op. cit., p. 55.
8. Ibid., p. 69.
9. Ibid.
10. Ibid., p. 118.

11. Ibid., p. 212. The work of the Religious Experience Research Unit continues today, though this research group now operates under the name of The Alister Hardy Research Centre, in memory of its founder. Readers interested in an up-to-date account of their work should contact the Director at: AHRC, Westminster College, Oxford, OX2 9AT, UK.

12. Daishin Morgan, "Choosing Your Way," *The Journal of Throssel Hole Priory,* Vol. X no. 1, Spring 1983, p. 7.

13. W. G. Oxtoby, "Religionswissenschaft Revisited," in Jacob Neusner (ed.), *Religions in Antiquity*, Leiden, 1968, E. J. Brill, p. 596.

14. Joachim Wach, *Sociology of Religion*, London, 1947, Kegan Paul, Trench, Trubner & Co. Ltd (in the International Library of Sociology and Social Reconstruction series, edited by Karl Mannheim), p. 14. Although Wach voices agreement with MacMurray in terms of the way in which the modern study of religion focuses on response rather than stimulus (citing the latter's *The Structure of Religious Experience*, London, 1936, Faber, pp. 20 and 43), he would not characterize the stimulus in the same way.

15. Benvenuto Cellini, *Autobiography*, New York, undated, Random House Modern Library, tr. by John Addington Symonds, p. 9 (1728).

16. "To designate the *act of manifestation* of the sacred, we have proposed the term *hierophany*. It is a fitting term, because it does not imply anything further; it expresses no more than is implicated in its etymological content, i.e. *that something sacred shows itself to us.*" Mircea Eliade, *The Sacred and Profane, the Nature of Religion*, New York, 1959, (1957), Harcourt Brace & World, p. 11. Many varieties of hierophany are mapped out in detail in Eliade's classic study, *Patterns in Comparative Religion,* London, 1976, (1958), Sheed & Ward, where we find hierophany described as "a manifestation of the sacred in the mental world of those who believed in it."(p. 10). Whether or not any particular hierophany does in fact stem from some transcendent state or entity separate from and independent of the mental world of the individual, remains one of Cipher's key questions.

17. Lesslie Newbigin, "Teaching Religion in a Secular Plural Society," in John Hull (ed.), *New Directions in Religious Education*, Lewes, 1982, Falmer Press, p. 105.

18. Ibid.

19. These various ways of characterizing an approach emphasizing "stimulus" or "response" are taken from the vocabularies of Wilfred Cantwell Smith (the terms "personal faith" and "cumulative tradition" are introduced in his *The Meaning and End of Religion*, see especially

Chapters 6 and 7); Ninian Smart (the terms "parahistorical" and "historical" are introduced in his *Secular Education and the Logic of Religions,* London, 1968, Faber, see especially Chapter 1); and Georg Schmid (the terms "the reality of religion" and "religious reality" are introduced in his *Principles of Integral Science of Religion,* see especially p.10f.). It would obviously be difficult, if not impossible (and it would certainly be distorting) to emphasize one element in any of these pairs to the total exclusion of the other. A stimulus would be invisible without some response and a response considered without reference to its stimulus would be meaningless.

20. J. C. A. Gaskin, op. cit., p. 16f.
21. Michael Novak, *Ascent of the Mountain, Flight of the Dove, An Invitation to Religious Studies,* New York, 1978, (1971), Harper & Row, p. xvii.

CHAPTER 6

SAME HOUSE, DIFFERENT WORLDS

IN 1885, Friedrich Max Müller, editor of the epoch-making *Sacred Books of the East* series (and sometimes called "the father of comparative religion"), remarked to one of his house guests who did not happen to share the same views on creation:

> If you say that all is not made by design, by love, then you may be in the same house, but you are not in the same world with me.[1]

Müller's remark is a reminder that although, of course, we all live in the same world, we can move in very different orbits of meaning, from which the same things are not always viewed and valued in the same way. There is a sense, given the varied perspectives found within Hinduism, Buddhism, Judaism, Christianity, Islam, Sikhism and so on, in which, despite our common habitat, it is yet quite intelligible to pose the question: "Which world do we live in?" and "Which mode of life and thought is most appropriate to human experience?" In a situation of plurality as regards world-views, any answer to such questions which results in particular, exclusive commitment has, presumably, to justify its own outlook as somehow preferable to any other if it does not wish to appear unreflective. The response of the various religions to their growing awareness of each other, whether in terms of inclusivist, exclusivist, or other strategies, will make a fascinating study as we move further into an era when only the most insular or blinkered of faiths can imagine that it exists in isolation. As Wilfred Cantwell Smith has put it:

> The religious life of mankind from now on, if it is to be lived at all, will be lived in a context of religious pluralism.[2]

Putting it in terms of the metaphor suggested by Müller's comment, the time has passed when we could simply assume that everyone who lived in the same house would also be in the same world.

The extent to which the new pluralistic context will be perceived as *theologically* problematic will vary from religion to religion and it will be interesting to see how the different faiths respond to it. Certainly within the Christian tradition the existence of religions in the plural is, increasingly, being recognized as a crucially important area of concern. Thus Cantwell Smith, for example, suggests that the question of how to account for the fact of religious diversity constitutes almost as big an issue for Christians as how they are to account theologically for evil.[3] Likewise, Langdon Gilkey considers the encounter with other religions to be "the most important new issue confronting Christian theology at the present time."[4] And Jacques Dupuis notes how the encounter of different cultures "has turned the theological debate on other religions into a primary concern."[5]

As John Hick noted in 1973, there has been a Copernican revolution in Christian theology. Where once Christianity occupied the center of a stage and allowed no other actors any part, except, perhaps, that assigned to them by Satan, the paradigm shift in thought away from this old Ptolemaic outlook, with its religiously mono-centric universe, has introduced a host of actors onto a multi-centric religious stage, though whether they are taking part in the same play, or addressing the same audience, whether they are written by the same author or are factual or fictional, remains uncertain. Hick's account of the massive change in theological thinking which he accurately identifies, assumes too much. For Hick, the change from Ptolemaic to Copernican theology:

> involves a shift from the dogma that Christianity is at the centre to the realization that it is God who is at the centre, and all the religions of mankind, including our own, serve and revolve around him.[6]

Apart from assuming that there *is* a God to revolve around in the first place, this seems to subsume the various ultimate foci of the different faiths beneath a single cognomen, "God." But *are* Brahman, Allah, Nirvana and the Tao accurately reducible to a single principle? Surely this is one of the great unanswered questions provoked by religious studies—to what extent are the vocabularies of the different faiths intertranslatable and to what extent are they unique, only admitting of accurate expression in their own terms? (Hick has, of course, refined and updated his thinking since this chapter first appeared. He would no longer advance a straightforwardly theocentric theology, but one in which the center is variously conceived as God, the Ultimate or the Real. See, for example, his *The Rainbow of Faiths* [1995]. This still leaves unanswered the question of whether it is accurate to assume that the center of each faith is filled by the same thing, whatever designation it is given.)

It would be interesting to trace within each faith the dawning consciousness of the religiously plural context in which they are all now so firmly set, examining the origin and development of their attitude to each other. Such a task would have to plot the ways in which their various orbits of meaning can be influenced by other religious bodies whose trajectories, once perceived, exert considerable force (whether of attraction or repulsion). It would also need to explore the extent to which the researches of religious studies influence theologies (and vice versa). This would undoubtedly be fascinating, but is not the area of concern which I have mapped out for exploration in this book. Since it closely adjoins it, however, it may be useful to glance in this direction from time to time, if not for inspiration then at least to remind us of our bearings. For I am not concerned here with how a Buddhist or a Jew, a Muslim or a Christian resolves whatever theological dilemmas may be posed by a situation of religious pluralism (if one can talk about "theological" in a Buddhist context to begin with). Nor am I concerned with how Buddhist, Jewish, Islamic or Christian theologies react to the information revealed to them by religious studies. Rather, I am exploring the way in which Cipher, someone who does not belong to any particular faith, may, in a religiously plural context, reach a decision about whether or not to move from a neutral state of mind to one of particular commitment. Such a religiously neutral individual, to continue with Müller's terminology, is in the same house as his variously committed neighbours, but in a sense he is in no world at all. He has not yet decided on how best to view existence, or how to live according to some chosen vision.

There is no question that, as he becomes more informed about the various alternative views of the world, there is an increasingly complex problem of evaluation facing the individual who is undecided, who has not yet committed himself to any particular outlook on things, nor yet reconciled himself to a permanent state of wide-ranging and deliberately chosen agnosticism. Hindus, Jews, Taoists and so on may all live on the same mother earth, but the expression which they see on her face seems, at least at first sight, to be very different indeed. For the individual such as Cipher, aware of all the different expressions, there is a pressing need for some sort of reliable global physiognomy. What sort of world is he in? What is the right way to live in it?

The likelihood is, of course, that someone raised in a predominantly Christian culture will see a more or less Christian expression on the face of the world, while a Hindu or Jewish milieu will tend to produce individuals for whom Hinduism or Judaism contain the most satisfying readings of their experience. Likewise, those who grow up in an environment where religion plays little rôle, beyond that of a colorful vestigial survival from what is seen as a more credulous and less technologically sophisticated age, will not, in general, see the world in overtly theistic terms. Obviously this is to simplify and therefore to some extent to distort. Within any cognitive majority there will be dissenters, and depending on the energy of their dissension (itself dependent on many different factors) so the line between majority and minority outlook will waver and change. Moreover, far from being set at each other's throats, acceptance of some religious outlook and criticism—even rejection—of it, often have an at least partially symbiotic relationship. Thus the outlook in question is kept vital by the critical consciousness born within it, and the critical consciousness is nourished by a system against which it can develop and exercise its acuity. As Gilbert Murray once put it:

> Every man who possesses real vitality can be seen as the resultant
> of two forces. He is first the child of the particular age, society,
> convention; of what we may call in one word a tradition. He is

secondly, in one degree or another, a rebel against that tradition. And the best traditions make the best rebels.[7]

Increasingly, though, we seem to be approaching a time where—at least in terms of religion—there is a self-conscious co-existence of so many different traditions that the bloodline of vitality feeds heirs and rebels alike a more puzzling, if also richer, mixture than they could expect from a single tradition existing in undisturbed isolation from serious alternatives to it. It is no longer so clear what to adhere to or what to rebel against when trying to come to some sort of decision about religious commitment.

Regardless of what stage society or the various religions may or may not have reached regarding the singularity or plurality of their religious self-consciousness, it is clear that, for Cipher, Müller's remark about different worlds sums up and re-states something of the dilemma of the uncommitted individual existing in an uneasy state of informed neutrality. It is a neutrality which knows of many possible roads but is not sure which, if any, offers the best route in the right direction. In this chapter I want to consider how such an individual might go about exploring the different worlds of religious meaning, with a view to deciding which, if any, to accept as his own. Having decided that he needs to see those worlds of religious meaning as they are viewed by those who accept them as offering peace of mind, how is Cipher to put that policy into effective operation?

I am going to use Müller's comment about how anyone with a different teleology, even if they are in the same house, even if they are standing shoulder to shoulder, are, in an important sense, in different worlds, both as a starting point and as a touchstone which will be referred to throughout the chapter. Since the terms "same house" and "different worlds" will be heavily used, and in a sense quite beyond what Müller intended in his chance remark, let me begin by explaining the expanded metaphorical meanings I am giving to them here.

The meaning and accuracy of claiming that we are all in the same house becomes clear if we reflect on three aspects of life. First, if we consider the purely physical nature of the world we can see that its basic fabric, according to any human perspective, remains constant across all the flux of personality, time and culture. Light and dark, hot and cold, wet and dry, large and small, animal, vegetable and mineral—such various general categories or states of thing have faced all *Homo sapiens* throughout history (although how these categories are perceived, understood, valued, and named does, of course, vary according to time and place). Second, the basic possible settings for a human life, strung out between its temporal defining points of birth and death, are likewise constant: male or female; childhood, youth, old age; solitude and companionship, poverty and wealth, health and sickness, and so on. Third, for life lived within these physical, biological and social constraints, the same basic structures of feeling obtain: joy, despair, contentment, fear, love, ambition, anger, and so on (though, again, the extent to which these different states are named and valued may differ enormously from age to age).

In short, what we might call "the human situation" does not vary appreciably across the centuries. Its basic constituents remain the same for the ancient inhabitants of Europe whose standing stones are the most tangible reminder of their religious presence, and for the twentieth century agnostic who may be a knower of many gods and a worshipper of none, and for every other individual spark of consciousness which flickers briefly in the awesomely diverse human multitude before it too (to use a phrase of Thomas Mann's) "disappears through history's trap door."[8]

That it is, in a similar fashion, metaphorically accurate to suggest— in spite of this basic shared condition—that we are nonetheless in *different worlds*, becomes clear when we consider what might be called the contextual details of specific lives, when we note the varieties of view on life's nature and meaning (and, in consequence, the variety of suggestions concerning the most fitting way to live). By contextual details I mean no more than the particular combination of circumstances in any individual's life—biological, social, cultural, historical, and so on— which serve to render it unique. It is unnecessary to labor the point that within the common area of the human situation, fate, for want of a better word, provides vastly different places in which we must live out our lives. Even individuals born in the same time and culture, indeed even within the same family, may be worlds apart in terms of the course along which their lives and thoughts will run. And when we consider humanity as a whole, the variety of fates is staggering in its unevenness, presenting us with such giddy and unsettling contrasts as that between, say, a Roman galley slave and a concert pianist, a millionaire business-woman and a wandering ascetic, between a shaman and a road sweeper, or an aborted fetus and someone who lives to be a hundred. In this sense we are in different worlds.

However, it is not on this sense of being in different worlds that I wish to concentrate here. Why, from the common stock of possibilities, we are dealt such unequal hands, is a question which any religious out-look must face up to in its attempt to provide a sense-giving view of things. Here we can simply include this unevenness of experience among those other common elements which make up the basic human situa-tion, subsuming the dissimilarity it results in individually beneath the fact that it is an unevenness encountered by everyone. The fact of in-equality, of difference, is as basic to the human situation as that of love, fear or finitude. As we saw in Chapter 3, it is precisely this fact of in-equality or difference, whose apparently random pendulum swings of fortune disrupt so many lives, which plays an important part in foster-ing Cipher's sense of lostness.

The sense of being in different worlds which is relevant to Cipher's situation, and which I do wish to examine here, is that which sets us apart in terms of how we look out upon this world, how we view our situation, and how, in consequence, we feel we ought to act in, and understand, whatever particular web of circumstances characterizes our biography.

Again, it is obvious that individuals view the world differently and that consequently they try to live their lives according to different ideal models. This is, after all, what constitutes Cipher's dilemma in the first place. Someone who considers their situation to be explained largely by the operation of karma and samsara will have a different view of things and a different code of conduct than someone who does not believe in the occurrence of rebirth, but sees each individual as the single creation of a personal god of love (rather than the serial outcome of a mechanistic process of moral cause and effect). Or, if the codes of conduct appear to be similar, the reasons behind them will certainly be very different.

Perhaps at this stage, though, a specific example might bring home the point more forcefully than these somewhat crude caricatures of difference. To give this I will go back to Müller and compare a brief statement representative of his world certainty, that is his outlook on the ultimate nature of existence, with that of Eugene Marais, the South African poet and naturalist who was one of the pioneers of the science of animal behaviour.

First Müller:

> How thankful we ought to be every minute of our existence to Him who gives us all richly to enjoy. How little one has deserved this happy life. What better, more beautiful, more orderly world could we wish to belong to than that by which we are surrounded and supported on all sides? It is a perfect sin not to be happy in this world.[9]

And now Marais, writing in *The Soul of the White Ant*:

> We seek in vain in nature for love, sympathy, pity, justice, altruism, protection of the innocent and weak. From the very beginnings of life we hear a chorus of anguish. Pain is a condition of existence, escape from pain is the purpose of all striving. If nature possesses a universal psyche, it is one far above the common and most impelling feelings of the human psyche. She certainly has never wept in sympathy, nor stretched a hand protectively over even the most beautiful and innocent of her creatures.[10]

Logically, but none the less tragically for that, Marais took his own life in 1936. As Huston Smith has pointed out, the acceptance or rejection of some such concept as God is sometimes, at root, very much a matter of facing life in an attitude of hope rather than despair.[11] For Müller, the face of mother earth bore a warm and welcoming smile, for Marais a snarl of remorseless savagery. For Cipher, informed about a wide range of such opinions, the question is: which one is he to accept?

I have suggested that we are similar in terms of the basic elements of which our lives are composed, and have collectively termed these elements "the human situation." The accuracy of claiming that we are in the same house is based on the fact that, whatever shape the individual biography we happen to live through may be, it is lived within the defining constraints of these basic shared conditions. We could, for convenience, symbolize these common elements as the letters of the alphabet. Our difference lies, first, in the particular combination and alignment of these "letters," which spell out our person, place and history, and, second, in the world-view which we accept as providing an accurate overall view of things, *i.e.* which says something about the alphabet as a whole (or which provides an "adequate account of the world," to hark back to the passage from Virginia Woolf mentioned in Chapter 3). It is important to emphasize this rather obvious point about our being in the same house lest Cipher's critics think he might disappear down a relativistic bolt-hole, or rather a series of such bolt-holes, such that he "becomes" Hindu, Buddhist, Christian, Muslim, atheist, *etc.* according to environment rather than assessment, and allows, without further reflection, that there is no problem posed by the existence of such religious variety. "When in Rome, do as the Romans," is good advice on the level of common sense, but taken too far it could leave Cipher as a religious chameleon, whose chromatic flexibility would be well nigh indistinguishable from a situation where no decision had been made about the final color of things.

This is not to deny the local color found in every variety of human religiousness. Going back to the alphabet analogy, there are elements of religion addressed to, or expressive of, the specific situations A, AB, ABC, C, CG, GHF, and so on over the immense spectrum of possible letter combinations in which individuals may find themselves, but there are also elements addressed to, or expressive of, the alphabet itself, which purport to hold good for *any* particular combination of letters, which reach beyond any specific social or cultural environment and address the common elemental aspects of the human situation. As Huston Smith put it, every religion is "a blend of universal principles and local setting. The former, when lifted out and made clear, speak to man as man, whatever his time or place."[12] (While I would agree with Smith that the local setting aspect is primarily mythological and ritual in nature, his strictures about its inaccessibility to anyone not indigenous to that religion seem somewhat overstated in the light of some recent work in religious studies.) Our focus here will be on *universal principles*. It is when these are involved that the same house/different worlds situation becomes intellectually interesting, if perplexing, and an easy relativistic solution is ruled out. It is when we are dealing with those elements of religion which seem to address *everyone*, regardless of their specific geographical or temporal setting, that the hall of mirrors has the potential to weave a dilemma such as that confronting Cipher. Of course there may be some difficulty in providing reliable criteria to distinguish between those elements of religion addressed to a universal context and those addressed to, or expressive of, a more local one, but the distinction itself seems valid nonetheless—at least as regards the great world religions. Whether it would hold for some primal religions is less sure. Certainly in the passages quoted from Marais and Müller, I think it is clear that they were intended as comments *on the world*, rather than being merely regional ontologies or purely autobiographical statements.

An important part of religion is concerned to provide universal principles by which we may understand and guide our lives in the world, that is, *any* human life in *any* contextual situation. Given that there is a variety of such principles and that, at least at first sight, they appear to be incompatible (either we are reborn or we are not; time is either cyclical or linear; the operation of karma and samsara is incompatible with the will of a beneficent and all-powerful deity; the self is either eternal or transient), then apart from the questions of why so many different religious pictures of the world appear, and how the different pictures will affect one another as they become more and more inter-conscious, the uncommitted individual such as Cipher is faced with a situation which seems to demand that he make some decision. He is faced with seemingly alternative visions of those elements of the human situation which remain constant amidst all the variations of time and place.

The religiously ambiguous nature of the world which is suggested by a comparison of the healthy-minded and sick-souled outlooks of Müller and Marais (to use William James' famous psychological categories[13]), has perhaps been presented most concisely for philosophical discussion by John Wisdom in his parable of the gardener. Let me quote part of the original version of this now well-known story, which was first told by Wisdom to the Aristotelian Society in a paper read to its members in March 1945:

> Two people return to their long neglected garden and find among the weeds a few of the old plants surprisingly vigorous. One says to the other, "It must be that a gardener has been coming and doing something about these plants." Upon inquiry they find that no neighbour has ever seen anyone at work in their garden. The first man says to the other, "He must have worked while people slept." The other says, "No, someone would have heard him and besides, anybody who cared about the plants would have kept down these weeds." The first man says, "Look at the way these are arranged. There is purpose and a feeling for beauty here. I believe that someone comes, someone invisible to mortal eyes. I believe that the more carefully we look the more we shall find confirmation of this." They examine the garden ever so carefully and sometimes they come on new things suggesting that a gardener comes and sometimes they come on new things suggesting the contrary and even that a malicious person has been at work.[14]

Wisdom's parable has had a profound effect on modern philosophy of religion. For our purposes, though, it is too simple and also misses out the main character. For neither the man who believes in the gardener, nor the man who does not believe in him, has a problem of the same order as that of the neutral observer standing between them who does not know which version of events to believe. For believer and unbeliever, respective versions of "the gardener hypothesis," as Wisdom terms it, may indeed cease to be experimental, turning out instead to be unshakable and emotionally satisfying decisions about how to see the world.

But for Cipher, the transition from hypothesis to a peace-of-mind-offering conclusion does not come about so easily.

In *The Adventures of Tristram Shandy*, Laurence Sterne warns us of precisely those characteristics of hypothesis which seem to operate in Wisdom's garden. "It is the nature of a hypothesis, when once a man has conceived it," Sterne remarks, "that it assimilates everything to itself as proper nourishment; and, from the first moment of your begetting it, it generally grows the stronger by everything you see, hear, read or understand."[15] The moment a man conceives a hypothesis seems, in the case of Wisdom's garden, to seal his outlook for good. The story seems to be set in a situation where the context of decision is determined by *fate*, not choice, in direct variance, incidentally, to Berger's analysis of the direction in which modernity has taken us.[16] But what of an individual like Cipher who seems to be faced, not with an *a priori* set of personality according to which the world appears theistic or atheistic, so that all its elements are read off accordingly, but rather with a situation of genuine uncertainty where a confusing *variety* of hypotheses jostle for the status of conclusion? And remember that Cipher is not just faced with a simple choice between two obviously opposing positions. Rather he is faced with an apparent multiplicity of hypotheses without any decisive instinctual or fate-dominated impulse towards latching on to any particular one as an unshakable certainty. He is, moreover, without a clear idea of the interrelationship between the different hypotheses, or indeed of just how many hypotheses there are.

In the same way as some people believe in God and others do not, Cipher is not sure—and these three positions (to make a theistic simplification of the multiple options in the hall of mirrors) could be seen to function as statements of personality, rather than as being constitutive of a situation of perplexity in which evaluation and decision are required. As statements of personality such outlooks would simply serve to announce the different ways in which identical evidence would be drawn into particular interpretative catchment areas. To take a simple example, the theistic believer would then interpret a numinous experience as stemming from some deity, the unbeliever would see it either as illusory or as an aesthetic response to the beauties of nature, and to someone such as Cipher, who stands midway between them, it would appear as an ambiguous experience to which either interpretation *might* apply. So every item of experience would be drawn automatically into one of these broad interpretative streams. Their currents would mold the world in their own *a priori* image as either a theistic, an atheistic or a religiously ambiguous place. This is the sort of situation which we can arrive at when an hypothesis is allowed premature conclusion-status and when the whole religious debate becomes a matter of who you are, not what the world is like. In such a situation, everyone could settle back to a life of contented fishing by the side of whatever interpretative stream happens to feed their particular psyche, pulling from its waters with reassuring predictability exactly the sort of theological catches they expect. There would be no possibility of drawing something unexpected from the depths, nor of the different streams co-mingling and causing confusion. In such a world, any religious questions would be settled from the outset, Cipher would feel no *perplexity*. Instead, among a multiplicity of autobiographical comments which related only to specific lives, the need to make a decision would be replaced by the simple act of adding his own signature, and simply signing out of the problem of commitment by saying, in effect, that there is no problem: commitment is decided just by the fact of being; "I am" already contains "I believe."

Again, this is an area of conclusion at which Cipher might, conceivably, arrive, deciding in the end that he must simply *accept* a situation of multiple religious possibilities as the hypothesis through which he will see, and according to which he will order, all that he experiences in the garden of the world. To begin with, though, he will not be content to let matters rest thus. For, while the other denizens of Wisdom's garden might be supposed to have arrived at, or to possess, satisfactory outlooks on the world, according at least to their own assessments, Cipher is not satisfied with his state of uncertainty and would be loathe to allow it to develop into a conclusion. Unlike Wisdom's characters, for whom religious outlooks are not hypotheses at all, for Cipher they are theories to be tested, mirrors which seem to reflect more than just narcissistic images. As such, they warrant further exploration.

In his potent reworking of Wisdom's parable, Antony Flew cast down the gauntlet of falsifiability to the believer. To those who accept as certainty the hypothesis that there is a gardener (or, in non-metaphorical terms, that God exists), Flew posed the question: "What would be needed in order for you to abandon that belief?" In particular, with reference to the problem of evil—which occurs if the gardener is thought to display the traditional attributes of the Christian God—"How much suffering and horror would be necessary before a belief in such a God was abandoned?"[17]

From the point of view of some varieties of theistic belief, Flew's question seems unanswerable. But Cipher has already answered it. In seeking to focus on the heart of the matter, in seeking to move to the linchpin of a religious outlook on things, he has accepted that there is some sort of religious experience, some kind of reported encounter with something transcendent, which provides the genesis and final validation of any "positive" variety of the gardener hypothesis. If it was wholly abandoned it would mean that such a hypothesis could be seen merely as one possible evaluative vocabulary for a world which is *equally* accurately described by a negative, non-gardener hypothesis (rather than being an account of how things really are, such that alternative outlooks to it would be rejected as mistaken).

Cipher's task is to consider religiously positive outlooks on the world, those which assert that "something is there" which offers peace of mind for a sense of lostness, and to consider them in such a way as to try to reach as near as possible to those moments of experience in which, ultimately, they seem to be rooted, to which the various phenomena expressive of such outlooks refer for their authority, and without which (or so it seems to Cipher) they would wither and die. This, it must be remembered, is an answer to the challenge of falsifiability made from a position of neutrality. Whether such a reply would be appropriate were it to be made from a stance of particular commitment is another matter, and not one I will discuss here.

Of course the question which asks: "What do these moments of vital, originative experience consist of and signify?" will itself be replied to with answers which may flow according to the various hypothetical streams already determined by the predilections of the experiencer, rather than according to any more objective criteria. But unless he self-consciously and deliberately returns to the source, it would be impossible for Cipher to come to a reliable conclusion about which interpretation is most accurate, or to decide if the experience is such that it may indeed bear several interpretations which compete only in terms of congeniality to personality type, not in terms of what is the case. At this stage in his inquiries, Cipher's focus of interest would seem to be clearly set on trying to share as closely as possible in the experience of the Buddhist, the Christian, the Jew, the Muslim, the Sikh, and so on, so that he may arrive at a perspective in which he may try to judge for himself the nature of their vision of the world. In terms of Wisdom's parable, he needs to see the garden through their eyes before deciding what can, in fact, be seen there.

Given the situation of religious plurality which Cipher needs to explore in moving towards some decision about commitment, with different accounts suggesting worlds as radically different as that of Müller and Marais, how is he to proceed with his investigation?

Religious studies, which has been at least partially responsible for bringing to our notice the immense variety of religious worlds inhabited by humankind and the extent to which they appear to differ has, increasingly, become concerned to provide an appropriate methodological vehicle for investigative inter-global travel between the different worlds of religious meaning. So, at this point, Cipher may again turn his attention to the disciplinary area which has done so much to create the conditions for his dilemma. This time he will focus his attention on that one particular strand, from the complex and confusing web which surrounds this whole area, which views the so-called "phenomenology of religion" as a methodological vehicle by which the different religious worlds may be explored in depth.

To use John S. Dunne's phrase, phenomenology of religion so conceived provides a means of effectively "passing over"[18] into the religious situation which one wants to investigate and "coming back" with a clearer understanding of it. It is a means of passing over to someone else's religious world of meaning so that we may try to see how things appear when viewed through that perspective. It is an attempt to place us, so far as this is possible, in the other person's shoes, so that we might stand there and walk with them, observing and feeling what occurs, with a closeness which would be impossible for an "external" study, where we stood rooted to the spot and made no attempt at passing over beyond the mere turning of an already judgmental gaze in the direction of the phenomena concerned (such as seems to be the perspective adopted by the denizens of Wisdom's garden).

Phenomenology of religion viewed as such seeks to offer to its sufficiently competent practitioner as non-secondhand an insight as it is possible to achieve into what animates the different vitalities and movements of meaning within any particular religious outlook. Its basic motivating idea is quite straightforward: to try to apprehend someone else's religion as it appears to them, rather than focusing attention on how it appears to us from a non-phenomenological standpoint. To achieve this perspective it is necessary to maintain a deliberate open-mindedness, which postpones making any value judgments, and to let oneself be moved, if only temporarily, by the same currents of meaning as stir the believer under study. Such a method thus relies to a great extent on the disciplined use of the imagination, and is focused more on individual religiousness than on religions considered as monolithic normative structures with clear-cut doctrines, rituals, mythologies and so on.

Winston L. King offers a clear statement of the goal of phenomenology of religion viewed in these terms. It is, he says, "to observe all types of religiousness from the veritable inside, and yet escape to tell all to outsiders—including one's own outside, ordinary self."[19] Ninian Smart takes us a little further, pointing out that this sort of approach refers to:

> the procedure of getting at the meaning of a religious act or symbol or institution *for the participants*. It refers, in other words, to a kind of imaginative participation in the world of the actor.[20]

Passing over thus rejects any picture of observer and observed facing each other across the interface of method. Here method becomes more like an encircling hoop which seeks to bind them close together for the duration of any period of inquiry. Gerardus van der Leeuw, considered by many to be one of the key figures in the phenomenological tradition within religious studies, provides a further pointer towards what may be involved in this type of exercise. According to his analysis, phenomenology of religion necessitates "not only the description of what is visible from the outside, but above all the experience born of what can only become reality after it has been admitted into the life of the observer himself."[21] In other words, the phenomenological observer is not to be seen as a white-coated diagnostician standing by the patient and noting every symptom—although *part* of their work will involve such meticulous observation. Rather, the phenomenologist seeks to move close enough to the subject of study so that the religious pulse makes itself felt against, or even within, his or her own skin.

The current of thought which advocates such deliberate and disciplined use of our imagination in the attempt to understand religion, extends beyond those who actually talk about phenomenology or term themselves phenomenologists. Rudolf Otto, for example, called for "penetrative imaginative sympathy with what passes in the other person's mind,"[22] and proceeded in *The Idea of the Holy* with what some have seen as a phenomenological exercise.[23] Before Otto, James Haughton Woods suggested that the key task in the study of religion is "to reproduce, as if real to us, all the ideas which compose the mental picture present to the stranger, to repeat in our own imagination all the feelings or will-attitudes which are bound up with this experience."[24] More recently, Wilfred Cantwell Smith has cautiously suggested that by the exercise of "imaginative sympathy,"[25] cross-checked by various other methods, it may be possible to "infer what goes on in another's mind and heart."[26]

In employing this type of method—which can be referred to as "passing over" so as to avoid the various unwanted philosophical connotations which "phenomenology of religion" might suggest—Cipher will attempt to put into practice the old Native American proverb which insists that we ought not to judge someone until we have walked a mile in their moccasins. Or, to take another elucidating parallel, in a sense he will be applying to the images in the hall of mirrors Father Brown's strategy for dealing with serious crimes. For when G. K. Chesterton's famous detective is asked the secret of his success in solving apparently insoluble cases of murder, he replies: "The secret is...it was I who killed all those people."[27] This is not, of course, a literal confession of multiple homicide, nor does it mean that he embarks on anything as simple as a "psychological reconstruction," but rather, as he puts it:

> I really did see myself, and my real self, committing the murders....I mean that I thought and thought about how a man might come to be like that until I realized that I really was like that, in everything except actual final consent to the action.[28]

Such a technique was, he adds, once suggested to him by a friend as a sort of religious exercise.[29] It is a religious exercise in which he comes to share a murderer's outlook with an intimacy which some might find fearful or distasteful, for he continues the process:

> till I have bent myself into the posture of his hunched and peering hatred; till I see the world with his bloodshot and squinting eyes, looking between the blinkers of his half-willed concentration; looking up the short and sharp perspective of a strangled road to a pool of blood. Till I am really a murderer.[30]

Or, to take a third parallel, in adopting passing over, Cipher will be utilizing an expanded version of what William Golding calls "kinaesthesia," a sympathetic identification with someone else's movement—a technique which, incidentally, Golding develops to superb effect in offering a "passing over" to prehistoric religiousness in his novel *The Inheritors*.[31]

Cipher will employ passing over in the hope that it will take him to a perspective from which he may view, more closely and directly than would otherwise be possible, those points of originative and confirming experience from which the images in the hall of mirrors stem, and on which they rely for their status as legitimate bearers of peace of mind. He will, in short, use passing over to take him to—or at least *towards*—the heart of the matter.

This method is based on the assumption, perhaps voiced more often by writers and poets than by those who study religion, that no human outlook can be so alien to us that we cannot come to understand it. Such an assumption finds marvelous expression, to take just one example, in Walt Whitman's "Song of Myself," where the poet acknowledges, across a wide range of religious and historical settings, what he terms "duplicates of myself" under all the "scrape-lipped and pipe-legged concealments."[32] This assumption of accessibility is, of course, based on the belief that we all occupy the same house, however different our perception of the world may be.

Whether the process of passing over will be successful in leading him through the various religious arterial systems to the source of their pulse is not something to be decided without a careful attempt to apply its principles. This is not something which can be attempted here, although some possible consequences of success will be considered in the next chapter. Thus, to some extent, a consideration of the possible objections which might be cast in the way of passing over is better postponed until we have seen it in action. There is one objection, though, which it is, perhaps, best to mention very briefly at this stage since, if accepted, it would simply deny the possibility of the whole endeavor.

This objection, the quaintly named "if I were a horse fallacy" has been put forward by the anthropologist E. E. Evans-Pritchard in his *Theories of Primitive Religion*.[33] The objection, as its name implies, refers to, and condemns, immoderate notions of how far empathy—i.e. entering into another's personality and imaginatively re-experiencing their experiences—can actually extend. Few of us would seriously wish to claim that we could come to know what it felt like to be a horse. But is it any less ridiculous to claim that we know how it feels to occupy some distant world of religious meaning which is not our own, such as, for example, that of a devotee Krishna, or a Siberian shaman in a spirit-trance, or a Sufi mystic, or a Sikh reading the *Adi Granth*, or a Zen monk sitting in meditation, or a Quaker being "moved by the Spirit?"

Accusations of committing the "if I were a horse fallacy" are generally accompanied by the idea that the open-mindedness necessary for passing over in the first place, that is, the ability not to let our own point of view obscure the outlook we wish to examine, cannot in fact be sustained beyond a fairly limited level (even in cases where the absurdity of such a venture is not so patently obvious as it would be if it were turned in an equine direction). I would suggest, quite simply, that common sense and a study of the actual imaginative outreach displayed in works of literature could successfully refute any argument which seeks to show that imaginative re-experiencing, of the sort demanded by passing over, is simply not possible. The question of the *degree* to which it is possible remains open to research, as does the question of the extent to which it would be useful to Cipher. Obviously we would do well to eschew any thoughts of being able to perform fantastical feats of imaginative accuracy, such as, for example, claiming to know exactly what it felt like to enter a prehistoric cave sanctuary, to understand precisely all the nuances of meaning attached to the various rituals performed there, and to grasp the way in which the numinous was experienced and expressed at the very dawn of human religiousness. It would, however, be just as foolish (if not in quite so spectacular a fashion) to underrate the flexibility and accuracy of the informed and disciplined imagination. It is enough that passing over takes us closer *towards* the heart of some particular type of religiousness than we might otherwise have approached. We do not have to insist that such a process is one hundred percent successful before we can advocate it as the method by which Cipher can proceed.

Using a metaphor which is particularly apt for Cipher, I. A. Richards has outlined some of the problems facing anyone attempting to explore different religious outlooks on the world. Can the idea of passing over overcome the difficulties he suggests? Richards is looking specifically at the issues raised when it comes to trying to understand an "alien" text—but his comments go well beyond reading. The problem is this:

> Can we in attempting to understand and translate a work which belongs to a very different tradition from our own do more than read our own conceptions into it? Can we make it more than a mirror of our minds, or are we inevitably in this undertaking trying to be on both sides of the looking glass at once? Can we maintain two systems of thinking in the mind without reciprocal infection and yet in some way mediate between them? And does such mediation require yet a third system of thought general enough and comprehensive enough to include them both? And how are we to prevent this third system from being only our own familiar, established tradition of thinking rigged out in some fresh terminology or other disguise?[34]

The quotation is taken from Richards' book *Mencius on the Mind*, a volume he sub-titles "Experiments in Multiple Definition." And it is via the technique of multiple definition that we must, according to Richards, overcome the problems of trying to "translate" different outlooks into a common conceptual vocabulary. Multiple definition would involve Cipher in ensuring that any understandings he came to of key ideas within the different religions in the hall of mirrors, were arrived at only after looking at them from a range of different angles. He should be wary, in other words, of ever accepting only one interpretation of what God, Nirvana, the Tao, or Brahman means.

Let us, finally, try to anticipate what the result might be if Cipher embarked on a policy of passing over in the attempt to resolve his situation of informed neutrality. Maybe we can find a clue here by building on Ninian Smart's analogy and comparing the practitioner of such a discipline to the actor.[35] As Mircea Eliade has remarked, through the voice of Bibiscescu, one of the characters in his novel *The Forbidden Forest*, the actor:

> identifies himself in turn with innumerable human existences, and he suffers, if he is a good actor, just as the character he represents on stage suffers in his life. This means that he knows in a single

life-time the passions, the hopes, the suffering and the revelation of fifty or a hundred lives.[36]

Whether the extensive repertoire of religious roles which passing over would result in would, in fact, help Cipher towards a clear sense of his *own* identity and purpose, or if it would act simply to confuse and perplex him yet further, will, of course, depend on what actually lies at the heart of the matter and the extent to which it can be reached.

Notes

1. Quoted in Nirad C. Chaudhuri, *Scholar Extraordinary, the Life of Professor the Right Honourable Friedrich Max Müller, PC*, London, 1974, Chatto & Windus, p. 345.
2. Wilfred Cantwell Smith, *The Faith of Other Men*, New York, 1972, (1963), Harper & Row, p. 11.
3. Ibid., p. 132.
4. Langdon Gilkey, "God," in Peter Hodgson and Robert King (eds.), *Christian Theology, An Introduction to its Traditions and Tasks*, London, 1983, (1982), SPCK, p. 85.
5. Jacques Dupuis, *Towards a Christian Theology of Religious Pluralism*, New York, 1995, Orbis, p.1.
6. John Hick, *God and the Universe of Faiths*, London, 1977, (1973), Collins, p. 131.
7. This passage, from *Euripides and his Age*, inspires the title and provides the epigraph for the report from which I take it, "Heirs and Rebels, Principles and Practicalities in Christian Education," Blandford, 1982, issued by the Bloxharn Project, Chairman: Basil Mitchell.
8. Thomas Mann, *Dr. Faustus*, Harmondsworth, 1973, (1947), Penguin, p. 406.
9. Max Müller, *Thoughts on Life and Religion, An Aftermath from the Writings of Max Müller by his Wife*, London, 1906, (1905), Archibald Constable & Co., pp. 101 and 235.
10. Eugene Marais, *The Soul of the White Ant*, Harmondsworth, 1973, (1937), Penguin, p. 78.

11. Huston Smith, *The Religions of Man*, New York, 1958, Harper & Row, p. 230. A completely revised and updated edition of this book appeared in 1991 under the title *The World's Religions*. Huston Smith's work provides one of the best single volume surveys of the world's faiths. Readers interested in work of this type might also like to look at (to give only a few selected suggestions from a very wide field): T. Patrick Burke, *The Major Religions: An Introduction with Texts*, Oxford: Blackwell:1996; Ninian Smart, *The World's Religions: Old Traditions and Modern Transformations*, Cambridge, 1989, Cambridge University Press; Niels Nielsen, Norvin Hein et.al., *Religions of the World*, New York 1988, St. Martin's Press. Smart's volume has the benefit of extensive illustrations. At a more introductory level, and with by far the best illustrations of any single volume guide, one might also recommend John Bowker's *World Religions: the Great Faiths Explored and Explained*, London, 1997, Dorling Kindersley.

12. Ibid., p. 4.

13. See William James, *The Varieties of Religious Experience, A Study in Human Nature*, (The Gifford Lectures in Edinburgh for 1901-02), Lectures 4-7.

14. John Wisdom, "Gods," *Proceedings of the Aristotelian Society*, 1944-1945, p. 185f.

15. Laurence Sterne, *The Life and Opinions of Tristram Shandy*, London, 1950, (1760), Rupert Hart Davis, edited by J. A. Work, p. 151.

16. See Chapter 3 note 13.

17. See Antony Flew's contribution to the "Theology and Falsification" debate in *New Essays in Philosophical Theology*, London, 1969, (1955), SCM, especially p. 99.

18. I am using this phrase in a simplified sense. I do not intend its appearance in Cipher's methodological vocabulary to endorse as appropriate to his particular situation the full programme and procedures followed in Dunne's passing over trilogy—*The City of the Gods* (1965), a passing over to cultures; *A Search for God in Time and Memory* (1967), a passing over to lives; and *The Way of All the Earth* (1972), a passing over to religions (published in the USA by Macmillan; in the UK by Sheldon Press). In the last mentioned volume, Dunne describes passing over as "a method of entering sympathetically into another person's autobiographical standpoint, seeing the whole world anew as that person sees it," it involves the attempt "to enter sympathetically into the feelings of another person, become receptive to the images which give expression to his feelings (and) attain insight into those images" (p. 53). It is in

this straightforward sense of providing a technique for closely observing outlooks on the world other than one's own that I am using the term "passing over" here. Whether or not such passing over will provide sufficient insight to "guide one into the future" and provide "a new understanding of one's life," as Dunne suggests (*ibid.*), must, from Cipher's point of view, remain to be seen. Although, in the preface to *A Search for God in Time and Memory*, Dunne asserts unequivocally that "the method of passing over is the one I will be using in this book" (p. ix) and, in fact (as remarked above), describes his three books in terms of their being a methodological trilogy applying this technique to different areas (see *The Way of All the Earth* pp. ix-x), it is not always easy to connect the few explicit details given about passing over with the full range of its (apparent) application. Nevertheless, whatever criticisms might be voiced, it is clear that these three volumes should find a place on Cipher's bookshelf. Passing over has, perhaps, some interesting points of comparison with Henri-Frédéric Amiel's concept of "reimplication." On this see Herbert Spiegelberg, "Amiel's "New Phenomenology,"" *Archiv für Geschichte Der Philosophie*, Vol. 49 (1967) pp. 201-214, especially p. 212. A further point of clarifying comparison might be with R. G. Collingwood's concept of doing history where the historian is called upon to "re-enact the past in his own mind." See R. G. Collingwood, *The Idea of History*, Oxford, 1970, (1946), Oxford University Press, p. 282.

19. Winston L. King, "The Phenomenology of Religion," *The Drew Gateway*, Vol. 43 (1972), p. 33.

20. Ninian Smart, *The Science of Religion and the Sociology of Knowledge*, Princeton, 1973, Princeton University Press, p. 20.

21. Gerardus van der Leeuw, "Confession Scientifique," quoted in translation in Eric J. Sharpe, *Comparative Religion, A History*, London, 1975, Duckworth, p. 231.

22. Rudolf Otto, *The Idea of the Holy, an Inquiry into the Non-rational Factor in the Idea of the Divine and its Relation to the Rational*, Oxford, 1977, (1917) Oxford University Press, tr. John W. Harvey, p. 62.

23. Thus in a letter to Otto dated 5th March 1919, Edmund Husserl wrote, "Your book on the holy has affected me more powerfully than scarcely any book in years.... It is a first beginning for a phenomenology of religiousness...."Quoted in Charles Courtney, "Phenomenology and Ninian Smart's Philosophy of Religion," *International Journal for Philosophy of Religion*, vol. 9 (1978), p. 48.

24. James Haughton Woods, *The Value of Religious Facts, A Study of Some Aspects of the Science of Religion*, New York, 1899, Dutton, pp. 13-14. See also p. 52f of Woods' *Practice and Science of Religion, a Study of Method in Comparative Religion*, London, 1906, Longmans, Green & Co., where he discusses "reconstructing the inner meaning" of religious beliefs. Woods' contribution to what might be termed the proto-phenomenology of religion is extremely interesting and deserves to be more widely known.

25. Wilfred Cantwell Smith, *The Meaning and End of Religion*, p. 188.

26. Ibid.

27. G. K. Chesterton, *The Secret of Father Brown*, Harmondsworth, 1982, (1927), Penguin, *The Penguin Complete Father Brown*, p. 464.

28. Ibid. p. 465.

29. Ibid.

30. Ibid., p. 465-466.

31. William Golding talks about kinaesthesia in his *A Moving Target*, London, 1982, Faber, p. 104. On his *The Inheritors* as an exemplar for phenomenology of religion, see my "Phenomenology of Religion and the Art of Storytelling: the Relevance of William Golding's *The Inheritors* to Religious Studies," in Sumner B. Twiss & Walter H. Conser (ed), *Experience of the Sacred: Readings in the Phenomenology of Religion*, Hanover & London, 1992, Brown University Press, pp. 145-166.

32. Walt Whitman, "Song of Myself," see in particular lines 832-834 and 1096-1108.

33. E. E. Evans-Pritchard, *Theories of Primitive Religion*, Oxford, 1970, (1965), Oxford University Press, pp. 43 & 47.

34. I. A. Richards, *Mencius on the Mind: Experiments in Multiple Definition*, London 1932, Kegan Paul, Trench, Trubner & Co., pp. 86-87.

35. Smart's analogy with acting, mentioned in *The Science of Religion and the Sociology of Knowledge*, receives further attention in his *The Phenomenon of Religion*, New York, 1973, Herder & Herder, p. 75f.

36. Mircea Eliade, *The Forbidden Forest*, Indiana, 1978, (1955), University of Notre Dame Press, tr. Mac Linscott Ricketts and Mary Park Stevenson, p. 192.

CHAPTER 7

A RETURN TO BEGINNINGS

FACED WITH the many different worlds of religious meaning which
the various facets of the hall of mirrors seem to reflect, each offering an
account of his existence which, if accepted, might counter his feelings
of insignificance, mystery and meaninglessness, it was suggested in the
last chapter that Cipher should embark on a strategy of "passing over."
That is, he should attempt to investigate the reflections which perplex
him in such a way as to share as closely as possible the outlook on the
world of those whose faith constitutes the reflections in the first place.
In particular, Cipher wants to be brought close enough to the experiential
roots which seem to underlie such outlooks so that he may come to see
for himself how these are perceived by those who take them to be
sufficiently authoritative to validate the complex religious structures
stemming from them. Cipher is not interested in the straightforward
accumulation of information about religious outlooks on the world. As
we saw in Chapter 4, the information to which he already has access, as
well as constituting his dilemma and perhaps holding the means of
resolving it, constitutes a potential barrier to his arriving at any
conclusions about commitment. Rather than merely seeking to acquire
more data about religions, he is interested in arriving at a perspective
from which he may judge whether or not any particular image in the
hall of mirrors could be, for him, an effective source of peace of mind.

His focus of attention will be set primarily on the individual who
has apparently *found* peace of mind through his or her commitment to
a particular outlook. He will not be so interested in Buddhism,
Christianity, Hinduism, Judaism, Islam, Sikhism, or any other religion
per se, considered as impersonal, historical entities (although obviously

these two points of focus overlap). Cipher's aim is to share the apparently sense-giving perspectives on the world which are offered by the different varieties of religiousness. More specifically, he wants to locate within these perspectives the experience of whatever transcendent state or entity it is which, ultimately, seems to give them life and to allow that they be accepted as legitimate by those who look through them at the world.

It has been suggested that passing over could be likened to the teaching of the Native American proverb which suggests that we should not judge someone until we have walked a mile in their moccasins. In walking that mile Cipher will not wander aimlessly in circles, as if on some sort of spiritual sight-seeing trip around the new religious realm to which passing over gives access. Rather, his steps will be directed resolutely towards what he takes to be the heart of the matter, the perception of which may allow him to resolve his dilemma.

According to the French diarist Amiel, the presence of whose journal on Cipher's bookshelves we have already noted, the same process is required to understand a drama, an existence, a biography or an individual. That process, says Amiel,

> is a putting back of the bird into the egg, of the plant into its seed,
> a reconstruction of the whole genesis of the being in question.[1]

Amiel's remarks on understanding drama are useful in reminding us of the parallel which may be drawn between "passing over" and acting and for suggesting the extent to which this sort of endeavour will involve a *return to beginnings.*

The *need* to return to beginnings, to somehow start again, to discover the source, the origin, to get back to some simple, initial level where there is no confusion, doubt or falsehood, at which we may remain in, or from which we may progress to, a state of being which is clear, authentic, true—which satisfies us in some way that our existence before such a return failed to do—is, I would argue, a common human impulse.

Such a need can find expression on a variety of planes. Indeed it would make an interesting study to trace the different forms in which it has appeared in the course of history. On an intellectual level, for example, Descartes determined to rid himself of all the uncertain opinions and beliefs he had formerly held and then to start out again from a new beginning, from a foundation of incorrigible knowledge. On a more tangible level, Henry David Thoreau shed the conventional material luxuries and burdens of human society and went to live in a simple wooden hut which he had built himself in the woods at Walden, this return to simplicity being undertaken because he wished to start again, concerning himself this time only with the essentials of life as he thought they occurred in living close to nature. Combining both physical and mental aspects of this need for renewal, for a return to (or a discovery of) some absolutely real and essential source, some fundamental ground, is the Hindu figure of the *sannyasin* who divests himself of all material goods and then, hopefully aided by this practical parallel, engages in rigorous meditative exercises in an attempt to throw off all the superficial layers of personality so as, eventually, to arrive at the absolute beginning of things, the real self, the *Atman.* Doubtless parallels to such an endeavour could be found in most religions, perhaps especially in their monastic forms; for the need to return to beginnings, to be in some sense "born again," often finds expression in an overtly religious setting. (It is significant that William James—in Lectures IV and V of *The Varieties of Religious Experience*—refers to his two fundamental types of religious personality, the healthy-minded and the sick-souled, as the once-born and the twice-born.)

This type of simplifying procedure, which seeks to cut through unwanted accretions and find a new point of beginning on which to found one's way of thinking or living, suggests a prior state of dissatisfaction, confusion or complexity. With Descartes it was the realisation that his whole structure of knowledge was susceptible to radical doubt; with Thoreau it was a disenchantment with the concerns of ordinary mundane life in a middle-class urban setting, a conviction that such concerns are peripheral, of only superficial value; with the *sannyasin* it is the belief that this material world and our empirical selves are of only secondary reality.

The state of dissatisfaction, confusion and complexity which prompts Cipher towards the return to beginnings offered by the process of passing over, is constituted by his sense of lostness and his awareness of the different worlds of religious meaning contained in the hall of mirrors. Cipher is *dissatisfied* because his uncommitted stance does not provide an intellectually or emotionally satisfying response to his feelings of insignificance, mystery and meaninglessness. This does not mean that he is assuming *a priori* that such feelings will be satisfactorily countered by a religious view of things which will transform his life into something significant, meaningful, and with any mystery in it safely curbed to that of a positive wondering variety, rather than its more unnerving sibling. It *may* well be that there is simply no peace of mind to be found, in the sense of locating a positive reassuring response to his sense of lostness. Moreover, as we noted earlier, "peace of mind" may be something of a misnomer for the various world certainties offered by the religions. But as things stand, with Cipher informed about a wide range of *possible* sense-giving commitments, his attitude of neutrality towards them, of neither acceptance or rejection but simply informedness about them, is unsatisfactory, given the fact that among them may be precisely what he is looking for. He is *confused* by the number of possibilities to which he *might* commit himself, and, furthermore, uncertain of their inter-relationship. It is not, as we have seen, just a matter of deciding between a set of clearly numbered options (though that in itself would be far from easy), but also of deciding how many options there are, where the boundaries between them fall, and where any areas of overlap occur (similarly difficult tasks). Last, Cipher feels the situation is *complex,* because of the glut of information that he has at his disposal. This enables him to see the hall of mirrors in considerable detail and depth.

Dissatisfaction, confusion, complexity—Cipher's situation has exactly the characteristics that we might expect would impel him towards a new beginning, which would suggest a return to, or an establishing of, some simpler state. And in fact Cipher has already started to simplify things, his return towards beginnings has begun. Thus, having noted the potential of information to act as an inimical force, we have seen how he can adopt various common-sense strategies to cut the problem down to size. Within that reduced area he has identified a precise target, namely the experiential linchpin, the heart of the matter, the salamander, which all the various aspects of the religious images in some way express and to which they eventually refer back in asserting their sense and value. Finally, in passing over, he has located a methodological vehicle which should take him accurately towards this target. Passing over also constitutes a safeguard against misdirecting his attention. It should prevent him from focusing on refracted images of religion as seen from the sort of explanatory stances which make no real effort to see things from the point of view of the believer.

As Edward Said has remarked:

> Without at least a sense of beginning, nothing can really be done, much less ended. This is as true for the literary critic as it is for the philosopher, the scientist, or the novelist [or, we might add, for the individual in the hall of mirrors]. The more crowded or confused a field appears, the more a beginning, fictional or not, seems *imperative*.[2]

In the crowded and confused setting of the hall of mirrors, Cipher has already felt—and started to act upon—the force of this imperative. This chapter will concentrate on explaining how "passing over" may be seen as a response to it, how this technique can be viewed as a beginnings-orientated activity. I also want to anticipate something of what might happen when Cipher actually applies passing over and moves towards the point, or points, of genesis at which it is aimed.

In what sense, then, is passing over an attempt to return to beginnings? The question can be answered by comparing Cipher's quest to the famous passage in the *Chandogya Upanishad* where Uddalaka is teaching his son Svetaketu by employing a series of metaphors. At one point Svetaketu is told to bring a fruit from the banyan tree and to split it in two. He does so and is asked what he sees. "These extremely fine seeds," he replies. He is then told to split the seeds, and again asked what is there. "Nothing at all," is his reply.[3] Leaving aside the metaphysical moral which Upanishadic thinking draws from the story, we might see Svetaketu as being engaged in a search for a point of beginning from which stems the complex structure of the fully grown tree. In a somewhat similar progression, faced with the many-branched and densely-foliaged tree of religion, Cipher is seeking to find some generative seed or core which enlivens and gives rise to the whole structure.

He is *not* engaged in trying to seek out some sort of single point of *historical* origin, somewhere at the dawn of human consciousness, which might explain the genesis of all subsequent religious phenomena (just as Svetaketu is not looking for some point of vegetative genesis in prehistory which might be seen as the cause of all subsequent plant life). Nor is he engaged in reduction, in the sense of trying to dismantle religion so as to arrive at some fundamental element which might be elevated to a point of absolute importance, with everything else brushed aside as irrelevant (just as it would be similarly misguided to take the seed as qualifying the rest of the tree as somehow unnecessary). Rather, through passing over, Cipher hopes to be placed in a position of sufficient closeness to that of the believer or believers under study, so that he can feel how every element of their particular religiousness is live and significant, how it leads back to and stems from an arterial system or seedbed which gives it life, and without which it would lose much of its reason for existing.

Unlike Svetaketu, however, who approaches things from an external perspective, who plucks something from the tree and proceeds to dissect it in isolation in order to arrive at some sort of originative point, Cipher's approach will be more holistic. Accepting serious expressions of religiousness as integrated organic wholes whose vitality and viability is best gauged when they are taken as such, rather than when they are subjected to investigative dismemberment, Cipher will attempt to return to beginnings, not by lopping off some likely looking point of genesis and saying, "this is the starting point," but by feeling how such a starting point reaches out its influence even to the extremities of a religious structure. From such immediately visible extremities he will attempt to work his way back towards the source.

It is no use trying to get back to the heart of the matter if you have made a series of methodological cuts which effectively leave you with several neatly labelled piles, one of leaves, one of branches, one of bark, and so on. The temptation is, of course, to say that whilst Svetaketu studies trees *in vitro,* Cipher would seek to study them *in vivo,* but at this point the "if I were a horse fallacy" mentioned in the previous chapter might deliver a resounding—and perhaps well deserved—kick, if only to remind us of the danger which mixing or overloading metaphors may pose to the methodological credibility of passing over. The sense of beginnings which Cipher has is one which, from his point of view of informed neutrality, respects the religious person as providing the context in which is located the starting point relevant to deciding whether or not to accept some particular type of religiousness as genuinely offering peace of mind. As we shall shortly discover, however, Cipher (like Svetaketu) seems likely to be left with a similarly intangible heart of the matter to that which is visible within the innermost kernel of a banyan tree's seeds.

At this stage it may be useful to turn once again to religious studies and see where Cipher stands in relation to it. This may help us to understand more fully the nature of his intended investigative course of action. It might well be supposed that, given his beginnings-orientated approach, any relationship must now be a straightforward one of simple ostracism. At this point, perhaps more clearly than at any other, we can see how unlike are Cipher's quest and some conceptions of the academic study of religion. For in focusing on religious experience, in seeking to draw close to the originating source, the pulse, the heart of the matter, the salamander—however the transcendent element in religion may be labelled—Cipher will be very obviously breaking those strictures which many scholars insist define the only legitimate territory in which the discipline can operate.

Georg Schmid, for example, has noted how a substantial part of religious studies takes as the only legitimate object of study something which is completely secondary for religion. He writes:

Of secondary interest for religion is its own thanksgiving, hope, prayer, sensitivity, teaching and behaviour as well as all the material in which this religious experience expresses itself. These are interesting for religion only in their relation to the reality to which all religious experience refers.

On the other hand, modern religious studies (though Schmid prefers "science of religion"):

> limits itself on principle to religious data, not as referring beyond but as interesting in themselves. Instead of letting itself be directed by the data to the reality beyond the data, it becomes intensely interested in the director and the act of directing.[4]

Cipher, on the other hand, is interested precisely in that supposed reality to which religious data refer and from which they stem. He is concerned to get to the heart (or hearts) of the matter, rather than remaining mesmerized by the complex corporate bodies which it (or they) animate, and which seem to constitute the area staked out by many scholars as the territory beyond which religious studies must not go. Within this territory it may bring to bear the full range of its methodological subtlety and sophistication, but going beyond it means academic excommunication. There is a famous Zen image about pointing at the moon. Many fail to see it, focusing instead only on the pointing finger. Cipher is interested in what is being pointed at by the different religions. The "fingers" which are doing the pointing are not of any interest to him *intrinsically*. If he concludes that they are pointing at nothing, he will leave them aside and continue on his journey. Thus, while what we might dub "territorial" religious studies may focus on, and be fascinated by, all the ritual details of prayer or worship, Cipher will be interested in seeing more closely that to which such religious activities are directed. His concern is with what, ultimately, gives them sense—in terms of their being aspects of a legitimate peace-of-mind-offering outlook. Only by focusing on the experiential *beginnings* of religion, the salamander rather than the slap, to reiterate the central metaphor of Chapter 5, can he hope to arrive at a standpoint from which he may make a satisfactory decision about commitment. For, as far as Cipher can see, serious religiousness derives from and rests its weight on such experience, and holds whatever validity it can finally claim precisely by reference to this elusive locus. The only reason he should, in the end, accept an image from the hall of mirrors as compellingly authoritative, as opposed to being attractive or pragmatically acceptable, or socially sanctioned, would seem to be if he too could come to endorse the potency of these originative points. Thus, inevitably, his endeavour will be at odds with a substantial body of academic opinion. This should not come as any great surprise. As we have noted already, Cipher is not attempting to write some sort of single-handed natural history of religion, but, rather, to reach a point of personal world decision.

Not all those interested in studying religion do so in a way in which the referent of religious experience is ruled off limits. As such, it would be misleading to suppose that Cipher is now so entirely cut adrift from scholarly endeavour that he could not hope to find any points of elucidating contact with it. On the contrary, there are many engaged in this area who, at times, seem to be walking in a more or less similar direction to the one in which he is seeking to go. The study of religion is a very diverse field. Its boundaries are not clearly fixed, its methodology is not uniform. There are many voices within it (whether at what is perceived as its centre, or at its periphery).

In his translation of the Upanishads, for example, Gordon Milburn writes that the whole aim of his work is:

> to enable my readers personally to feel something of the inspiration
> which moved the original writers so that their reading may become
> a reproduction of the devotional contemplation of supreme reality
> in which this literature took its origin.[5]

For Milburn, then (after whom, incidentally, a research fellowship is named at the University of Oxford), a reading of the Upanishads is of primary concern not for any historical or linguistic points which it might raise about the writing of this type of sacred text, but because through such a reading we may somehow be brought into close proximity with that experience from which they derive. As such, Milburn accepts that as translator he must sacrifice exegesis for what he calls the transmission of inspiration.

Likewise, Lewis and Slater write of the Vedic hymns which preceded the Upanishads:

> Some of the earliest hymns have a poetic beauty and numinous quality, even in transcription, which awakens in us, as they presumably stirred in their composers and original reciters, a reaction similar to the experience of God made possible for us normally by other means today.[6]

In short, for them the slap still has a mnemonic potency which has remained unbroken, either by translation or some three and a half thousand years of history, so that it still provides an effective reminder of the salamander which Hindus would say called it into existence in the first place. Unfortunately, Lewis and Slater do not go into details of what they refer to, with such intriguing commonplaceness, as the normal present-day means of experiencing God. Clearly if such means do exist they would be of intense interest to Cipher!

Along the same lines as Milburn, and Lewis & Slater, we find in Rudolf Otto's seminal study, *The Idea of the Holy*, some similar ideas about the possibility of focusing attention on the experiential beginnings of religiousness. Of the numinous, the originative sense of the holy whose presence, he claims, lies at the innermost core of all religion, Otto writes, "It will be our endeavour to suggest this unnamed something to the reader so far as we may, so that he may himself feel it."[7] He is somewhat dubious of the power of words alone to do this, hence his call—noted in the last chapter—for "penetrative imaginative sympathy." Raimundo Panikkar sums up well the nature and value of the sort of starting point which Otto seems to reach in *The Idea of the Holy* (arguably the most influential return to beginnings in modern religious thought), when he notes that "a nonconceptual awareness allows different translations of the same transconceptual reality for different notation systems."[8] Thus Otto notes a common element underlying the sixth chapter of *Isaiah* and the eleventh chapter of the *Bhagavad Gita*,[9] and he can quite confidently assert that "Allah is mere 'numen' and is in fact precisely Yahweh in his pre-Mosaic form and upon a larger scale."[10] In reaching some sort of pre-conceptual or pre-verbal point of genesis, and in suggesting that it is possible to evoke and awaken such a sense of vital beginning in the minds of his readers, Otto clearly points in the direction in which Cipher seeks to go. He seems also to suggest, incidentally, that by returning to such a beginning we may pass below the turbulence of religions as they are perceived in all their discordant diversity by a first glance around the hall of mirrors, and find important areas of continuity underlying them.

Although he does not voice Otto's desire to take his readers towards such a point of religious beginning, it is interesting to see in R. C. Zaehner's *Hinduism,* which remains one of the best single-volume introductions to this area of religiousness, that the author himself is sensitive to the religious power of the symbols he studies, not just to their historical or mythological significance. Thus, for example, he does not simply offer us an historical analysis of the deity Shiva from his earliest primitive form in the Indus Valley civilisation, through his Vedic manifestation as Rudra, to his place as one of the three high gods of Hinduism. Rather, he comments on "the great God Rudra-Shiva, the most numinous and disturbing representation of deity that Hinduism was to produce."[11] That is, as something whose power he can apparently feel and evaluate himself.

Studying an act of prayer or worship in depth, may, Jacques Waardenburg notes with some surprise, give us a glimpse of the "intended object" of the person praying or worshipping. It may reveal something of the reality which they assume they are addressing through whatever ritual forms they use.[12] Catching sight of this reality is the explicit aim of David R. Kinsley's brilliant study of the Hindu deities Kali and Krishna. Indeed, he presents his book *The Sword and the Flute* as a deliberate attempt to "understand Krishna and Kali by trying to glimpse Kali's sword and hear Krishna's flute."[13] In other words, he is attempting to see the vital originative force which, according to Hindus, underlies their spirituality, and which is symbolised by devotees of Kali and Krishna in terms of a sword or a flute, according to whether its manifestation is perceived as malevolent or benign (this to make a simple bi-polar duality of what is, in fact, taken to be single and continuous). Kinsley is less interested in amassing historical or mythological data than in, as he puts it, discerning in the presences of these two beings "hints of the transcendentally real,"[14] as it has been perceived in Hinduism. Certainly, in his hands, we do sometimes seem to travel smoothly and easily towards the heart of an "alien" religious world. Of Kali, perhaps to Western eyes the most immediately distasteful goddess in the Hindu pantheon, since she is usually portrayed as demonic and bloodthirsty in the most lurid detail, Kinsley writes:

> Meditation on Kali, confrontation with her, even the slightest glimpse of her, restores man's hearing, thus enabling or forcing a keener perception of things around him. Confronted with the vision of Kali he begins to hear, perhaps for the first time, those sounds he has so carefully censored in the illusion of his physical immortality…He may also be able to hear, with his keener perception, the howl of laughter that mocks his pretence, the mad laugh of Kali, the mistress of time, to whom he will succumb inevitably despite his deafness or cleverness…She invites man to join in her mad dance in the cremation ground, she invites him to make of himself a cremation ground so that she may dance there, releasing him from the fetters of a bound existence. She invites man to approach the cremation ground without fear, thus releasing him to participate in his true destiny, which lies beyond this whirligig of samsara in transcendent release.[15]

This is quite a series of invitations! Where, precisely, does Kinsley stand in relation to the purported transcendent reality (of which Kali is a symbol), in order to have received them so clearly? In this sort of work we do indeed seem sometimes to catch a glimpse of something bright and enticing, but is it Kali's sword or a religious version of Macbeth's dagger? Are we brought face to face with, or unnervingly close to, some transcendent element of Hindu religiousness, or are we only encountering a creation of the "heat oppressed brain" which has reached some sort of unhealthy spiritual boiling point through too much "passing over?" It is clear that many (if not all) religious phenomena appear to point beyond themselves. As such, a focus which demands that we confine our attention to them, rather than what they point to, might be seen as setting an inappropriate and artificial limitation to inquiry in this area. At the same time, though, to what extent is it realistic to suppose that we can move towards the kind of experiences which such phenomena seem to be pointing at?

In Chapter 4 we referred to a passage from Cipher's journal where he likened his awareness of many religious outlooks on the world to being blinded by many different lights. To continue that metaphor, passing over is an attempt to return to beginnings in the sense of trying to move from the outermost, immediately visible reaches of a particular beam, ever inwards towards its source. And, as we have seen, some work within religious studies seems also to move in this direction, with results which would suggest that Cipher is not envisaging attempting the impossible. Indeed, given the number of scholars who seem to advocate some form of "passing over", with all the implications which such a methodology has, it is perhaps rather strange that some work apparently moves in the *opposite* direction, erecting some sort of crash barrier beyond which, apparently, we must not go. Thus, putting it with reference to a study of Islam, W. Brede Kristensen writes:

> We cannot become [Muslims] when we try to understand Islam,
> if we could, our study would be at an end: we should ourselves
> then directly experience the reality.[16]

Leaving aside the apparent implication that Muslims cannot study their own faith, how could such an assertion be so confidently made unless Kristensen himself had directly experienced this reality and concluded that the *only* possible response to it is an Islamic one, rather than, say, a Hindu or a Buddhist one? (In which case, had such a direct experience occurred, he would, of course, by his own criteria *be* a Muslim.) His remark assumes that a study of Islam has to do with an underlying reality which is exclusively Islamic. But many who have studied faiths other than their own have found that coming close to the transcendent reality which is apparently perceived within an "alien" tradition, in fact positively enriches their *own* religiousness, rather than encouraging some sort of apostasy. How could this be if the matter were as cut and dried as Kristensen suggests?[17] His mapping of the relationship between believer and observer, and the implied relationship between varieties of religiousness, is surely misleadingly simplistic. What of Panikkar's non-conceptual awareness allowing different translations of the same trans-conceptual reality?

Many—and Kristensen would surely be counted among them—seem to take the view of Edward Farley that:

> the actual reality-apprehendings of a determinate community (of faith) do not occur in the uncovering analyses of phenomenology, but in participating in the community itself.[18]

This may well hold for phenomenology in its guise of objective descriptive study, but "passing over," we must remember, is not simply another name for this sort of approach. If we take seriously calls for "penetrative imaginative sympathy" to see into the hearts and minds of the believers,[19] then it would surely be reasonable to put passing over as close to *participation* as it is to *observation*. Indeed, the roles of participator and observer, in terms of their being two quite separate non-overlapping functions, can only hold within an investigative situation where religious studies (to use Schmid's terms) focuses on what is of purely secondary importance for religion itself. The line between the two roles tends to blur when we see how scholars like Kinsley, Otto and Milburn apparently experience, or come very close to experiencing, the same reality as the believers.

In his study of emptiness ("*sunyata*") in the thought of the great second century Buddhist philosopher Nagarjuna, Frederick J. Streng comments:

> The aim to 'understand,' as it is conceived in this study, must be differentiated from the Buddhist disciple's aim to know the truth of 'emptiness.' While both the Buddhist disciple and the historian of religions express a desire to know the meaning of 'emptiness,' the disciple wants to realize this personally within himself and would find the historical and phenomenological distinctions that we will make here a diversion from his goal.[20]

The trouble is, exactly as it was in Wisdom's garden, Cipher is an uneasy middleman caught between two less problematic positions. In Streng's study, historian of religions and Buddhist disciple are given clearly demarcated roles (though of course that is not to say that either understanding or realising *sunyata* is easy!). What, though, of the individual like Cipher, who has been informed of the possibility of such personal realisation by the historian of religions and is uncertain where he stands in relation to such information? What of someone for whom religious studies has provided access to a variety of points of apparent contact with transcendent reality (or transcendent realities)?

The question of whether or not passing over will be successful in returning Cipher to the starting points he seeks is, I think, best postponed until he has actually attempted to put its methodology into practice. However, even if his passing over does not take him to a perspective from which he may directly observe or experience the transcendent realities which seem to animate the various forms of religiousness which interest him, his endeavours will, presumably (unless he is utterly incompetent), take him *towards* such realities. Thus, at the very least, he will be told about such points of beginning by those who feel that they do stand *directly* in their light. The problem is, such eye-witness accounts seem to have some rather special characteristics, such that their usefulness to Cipher, in terms of reaching a decision about commitment, may be highly questionable. The special characteristic on which I wish to focus in particular is that of *ineffability,* the apparent inexpressibility of religious experience, such that some have claimed it is beyond words altogether.

Of course many things *are* said about religion, even about (indeed especially about) what appear to be its most descriptively elusive originative elements. Thus there is much "talk" of one sort or another about, for example, Brahman, God, Nirvana, the Tao and so on. Indeed, whole religious structures might, perhaps, be viewed as efforts across a wide range of media—linguistic, behavioural, artistic, musical and so on—to express the nature and significance of these starting points (which are, of course, often seen as destinations too). But, sooner or later, in all such expressive instances, we come to a core of ineffability which denies any of them final sanction as being adequately expressive, and which generates yet more attempts at expression. The salamander, the originative reality, gives rise to an extensive outgrowth of tangible phenomena, at the heart of which it remains behind a mysterious opaqueness ringed with silence.

Mystics give clearest voice to this inner core of ineffability, and it is in their particular type of discourse that the live wire of originative experience, which seems to run throughout the religious realm, appears closest to the surface. In the examples which follow, then, I am taking the view that what has been so strikingly described by the mystic is, as Winston King put it, "legitimately and necessarily present in more pedestrian varieties and positive forms of religious expression,"[21] even if we may have to look more closely there to see it. That mysticism is, in Paul van Buren's words, "an extreme form of what is genuine in religion,"[22] rather than being some sort of idiosyncratic or deviant offshoot from it. In mysticism we can often see more immediately than elsewhere in religion that beginning towards which a passing over into almost any form of religiousness would eventually seem to take us.

A passage from Eckhart perhaps most clearly identifies the radical unlikeness, the complete non-comparability, which seems to characterise the ineffable starting point of religion. He writes:

> All words fail…nothing true can be spoken of God…no one can express what he actually is. We can say nothing of God *because nothing is like him*.[23]

This denial of all possible comparisons, the claimed ineffectiveness of likeness in this area of experience, is a common feature found in accounts of religious beginnings. The passage from Eckhart is, for example, clearly reminiscent of the rhetorical query posed in *Isaiah* (40.18), "To whom then will you liken God or to what likeness compare with him?" And when Muhammad was asked about the distinguishing attributes of the God he spoke of, the answer he gave (rather, the answer which, according to Islamic belief, was revealed to him) was:

> Say, God is one God; the eternal; he begetteth not, neither is he begotten and there is not anyone like unto him.[24]

But for sheer thoroughness in excluding all possible forms of comparison, the account of Brahman given by Shankara is, I think, unparalleled:

> There is no class of substance to which the Brahman belongs, no common genus. It cannot therefore be denoted by words which like "being" in the ordinary sense signify a category of things. Nor can it be denoted by quality for it is without qualities; nor yet by activity, because it is without activity; neither can it be denoted by relationship for it is without a second. Therefore it cannot be defined by word or idea, as the scripture says, it is the one before whom words recoil.[25]

Whereas Cipher *begins* his quest threatened by the sheer bulk of information about religion which is now available, it seems as if passing over, his attempt to return to beginnings, may—ironically—simply act to invert the problem. Where once information seemed to be an inimical force, it now seems that a complete *lack* of information may prevent him from making any world decision. For how is he to reach a decision about religious commitment if nothing can be said about the nature of the experiences which seem to underlie and validate its different varieties?

Assuming that Cipher *will* be led towards an encounter with what is taken by many to be the transcendent, though whether at first or second hand we leave open to research, and assuming that such a starting point exhibits the sort of ineffability found in mystical literature, then three areas of consequence for his quest are, perhaps, worth indicating.

First, it is fascinating to speculate about how Cipher might conceptualise and describe some starting point of transcendent reality, for in a sense he is religiously multilingual. How would the great figures of the various particular traditions have expressed *their* insights, had they been informed in a similarly plural religious way? Would we have seen a mutual cross-fertilisation and enrichment of the vocabularies of different faiths, or a resolute rejection of such a blending, or would the ineffability of the various starting points automatically bankrupt any apparent enrichment which might have taken place?

The question of similarity and difference is insistently posed here, for, depending on the degrees of likeness perceived between the various points of beginning—God, Brahman, Nirvana, the Tao, *etc.*, so the use of a strict mono-faith vocabulary or a more polyglot linguistic resource must be judged appropriate. Some seem to be in little doubt that the situation is one where a similar experience is *interpreted* differently, and that once this underlying similarity is recognised the subsequent interpretation can be more wide-ranging. As Ninian Smart put it:

> If religious experience is our ground of faith, then let us not be so narrow as to consider only the experiences of *our* tradition...We *interpret* our experience. We clothe our intuitions in the vestments of one tradition, sometimes quite unconsciously. Who has seen the Virgin in Banares? What Sicilian saint or Scotch divine has seen the celestial Buddha?[26]

Others seem to move towards an opposite conclusion. Thus Karl Barth remarks:

> It is unthinking to set Islam and Christianity side by side. In reality nothing separates them so radically as the different ways in which they appear to say the same thing—that there is only one God.[27]

Certainly, if ineffability is a key characteristic of religious beginnings, a state of inter-religious similarity might be given some credence simply from the fact that it is not immediately obvious how, logically speaking, two or three ineffable experiences *could*, in fact, be considered different. For, to allow any differentiation would surely be to demand some specifiable qualities on which it might be based—but this would negate the original claim to ineffability. Whatever conclusions are reached about inter-religious similarity and difference, the serious consideration of the varieties of human religiousness by a religiously multilingual individual is a phenomenon whose outcome seems likely to be of immense theological interest. This is a point to which I will return in the final chapter.

However, fascinating though it is to speculate about how an individual such as Cipher might see and describe the transcendent differently from someone located within a context of mono-faith informedness, a more pressing concern is to consider how the apprehension of religious beginnings, supposing that it did indeed come about, could help in solving his dilemma and bring him closer to a decision about commitment. For, once he has swum down to such points of beginning, it is not easy to see how he could ascend the interpretative stream again—even allowing that he knew *which* interpretative stream was appropriate. If they are ineffable, how can these beginnings bear such wordy structures as are presented in the hall of mirrors? Can such ineffable points of origin really be thought to validate anything so concrete as the Buddhist or Hindu or Christian ways of life? Or can the salamander offer peace of mind itself without anything so tangible as a slap? How is the gulf to be bridged between what is said about religion and what remains unsayable, yet apparently fundamentally originative? How, for example, could Cipher move from the starting point and destination of Hindu religiousness, Brahman, the one before whom words recoil, to an extensively conceptualised Hindu view of life—even supposing he was returned to or towards Brahman by a process of passing over which was focused on Hindu belief and practice? Or can we assume that by reaching such an originative locus the rest will somehow follow automatically?

Second, we might, perhaps, consider whether the beginnings towards which Cipher envisages a return might not be taken as possible means of accounting for continuity and diversity at least in an intra-religious, if not in an inter-religious, sense. This might go some way towards explaining why there is such a plurality of outlooks in the first place. If we compare any of the key originative terms of religion at the dawn of a particular tradition's history and at the present moment, it appears that most ancient and most recent notions of "God," for example, seem to differ in many respects. Yet, by and large, theologians firmly maintain that, in some way, it is a single and unchanging entity with which we are dealing throughout the history of a particular tradition. Unless we can point to some common element which is both specific enough to create some binding sense of tradition, of particular religious identity, yet never completely expressed by any specific attempt at expression, thus continually demanding new attempts to apprehend it, then, given the widely differing views of, for example, "God" within the Christian tradition, it is difficult to see how we could be sure that in fact they all did stem from the same source and *were* talking about the same thing. The radical unlikeness of these points of beginning, the non-comparability of such religious starting points, could be seen as providing a common element with just the required characteristics. Such an element could be what all the subsequent accounts attempt to net within the offered interpretations/descriptions. It could be what remains constant—constantly elusive, yet constantly generative of attempts to apprehend it throughout a history of consequent diversity. On this view "ineffable" acts precisely as what I. T. Ramsey termed a "qualifier,"[28] whose presence in religious language serves to "multiply models without end."[29] If we want to see the different models as belonging to a *single* interpretative stream, if any sort of continuity is to be maintained, we must surely posit some such feature as the radical unlikeness of the religious beginning. Whether this might be of use not just in explaining intra-religious diversity, but inter-religious diversity too, is uncertain—though in some ways it is tempting to think of Hinduism, Buddhism, Judaism, Christianity, Islam and so on, as being several attempted models of a persistently elusive transcendent master image.

Third, if the points of beginning are as radically unlike other experience as the quotations we considered earlier would seem to suggest, and if he succeeds in reaching them, then Cipher will be left with an interesting logical problem which will, at some stage, require attention. As J. L. Austin once pointed out, "like" is "the main flexibility device by whose aid, in spite of our limited vocabulary, we can always avoid being left completely speechless."[30] According to Austin, "like" provides the linguistic equivalent of being able to shoot round corners.[31] In other words, we can always say what something is like, even if it seems to be quite inexpressible in a more direct sense. But God, Brahman, Tao etc. seem to deny all application of likeness and leave us speechless. The problem then becomes how we can actually be *aware of* anything so entirely beyond the reach of all comparison. Whereas we can easily make sense of something which is unseeable—clearly we cannot see a child's cry or the scent of a rose—we cannot do likewise with the unsayable.

Something which is not visible may be felt or smelled or touched or heard, but something which is not sayable, which is not like anything, by what means could we ever come to be aware of such a thing? As W. T. Stace put it:

> If the mystical consciousness were absolutely ineffable, then we could not say so because we should be unconscious of such an experience.[32]

If Cipher did manage to experience the ineffable he would, one would hope, be in a better position to explain the apparent logical impossibility of having done so than is the anticipating onlooker. Indeed he would be well placed, from both a religious and logical point of view, to provide some sort of clarifying account of the varieties of religious ineffability, if we can allow that variety can exist here in the first place.

Finally, lest we think, in light of these problems, that Cipher's intended return to beginnings might be better characterised as heading nowhere, as being rather like Svetaketu's splitting of the seed from the banyan tree (in terms of being left with nothing tangible), we ought, perhaps, to stress the apparent religious fecundity of *silence,* that attitude of mind which is, arguably, most appropriate in face of the ineffable. John Bowker provides an excellent corrective to any tendency we might have to under-value religious silence, or to rate it as something negative. In *The Religious Imagination and the Sense of God,* he identifies key points in four major religious traditions—Judaism, Christianity, Islam and Buddhism—where the operative sense of the transcendent comes into crisis, but leads on from there to new ways of thinking about it. In each case, central figures are reduced to silence in some "crisis of plausibility"[33] out of which is born a new way of looking at things. The four key points are:

> Job, accepting silence before the apparent majesty of God, Jesus, choosing silence before his accusers, Muhammad in silence on Mount Hira (a silence later recapitulated by al-Ghazali when he stood in front of his university class and found himself unable to speak) and Gautama, the Buddha, electing silence after his enlightenment. Four quadrant points of silence, in each of which a transaction occurred in the prevailing characterization of God.[34]

If silence and the ineffable seem at times to be dead ends from where we cannot progress beyond logical conundrums and practical paralysis, at other times precisely such starting points seem to have acted as new beginnings of an intensely creative kind, in terms of evolving potently efficacious formulae for peace of mind. Whichever outcome lies in wait for Cipher, he might, perhaps, take to heart some advice given in the *Bhagavad Gita*. It seems strangely appropriate to his circumstances:

> With reason armed with resolution, let the seeker quietly lead the mind into the Spirit, and let all his thoughts be silence.[35]

Notes

1. Henri-Frédéric Amiel, journal entry dated 26th November 1861. See *Amiel's Journal, the Journal Intime of Henri-Frédéric Amiel*, London, 1913, (1885), Macmillan, tr. Mrs Humphrey Ward. Given Amiel's focus on drama, it is interesting to note that James Haughton Woods (whose work was highlighted in Chapter 6 note 24) also views understanding drama in terms of a process of reconstruction. In the course of advocating a similar technique in the study of religion, he points to this parallel area in which we are more accustomed to its use: "This reconstruction of another's will is a familiar process to us. Every drama we have read is an experiment of this kind." *Practice and Science of Religion, A Study of Method in Comparative Religion*, London, 1906, Longmans, Green & Co., p. 54.

2. Edward W. Said, *Beginnings, Intention and Method*, New York, 1975, Basic Books, pp. 49-50. My emphasis.

3. Chandogya Upanishad 6.1-3 and 12-14, translation taken from Wm. Theodore de Bary (ed.) *Sources of Indian Tradition*, New York, 1970, (1958), Columbia University Press, Vol. 1 p. 33.

4. Georg Schmid, *Principles of the Integral Science of Religion*, pp. 33, 34 and 35.

5. Gordon Milburn, *The Religious Mysticism of the Upanishads*, London, 1924, Theosophical Publishing House, p. 7.

6. H. D. Lewis and R. L. Slater, *World Religions,* London, 1966, Watts & Co., p. 143.
7. Rudolf Otto, *The Idea of the Holy,* p. 6.
8. Raimundo Panikkar, *The Intra-Religious Dialogue,* New York, 1978, Paulist Press, p. 43.
9. Rudolf Otto, op. cit., pp. 63-64.
10. Ibid., p. 77.
11. R. C. Zaehner, *Hinduism,* Oxford, 1977, (1962), Oxford University Press, p. 33. Zaehner's is not, of course, the only single-volume introduction to Hinduism. Also excellent are John Brockington's *The Sacred Thread: Hinduism in its Continuity and Diversity,* Edinburgh 1981, Edinburgh University Press; and Gavin Flood's *An Introduction to Hinduism,* Cambridge, 1996, Cambridge University Press.
12. J. D. J. Waardenburg, "Research on Meaning in Religion," in *Religion, Culture and Methodology* ed. Th. P. van Baaren and H. J. W. Drijvers, The Hague, 1973, Mouton, p. 122.
13. David R. Kinsley, *The Sword and the Flute, Kali and Krishna, Dark Visions of the Terrible and the Sublime in Hindu Mythology,* Berkeley, 1975, University of California Press, p. 6.
14. Ibid.
15. Ibid., p. 159.
16. W. Brede Kristensen, *The Meaning of Religion, Lectures in the Phenomenology of Religion,* The Hague, 1960, Mouton, p. 7. I have substituted "Muslims" for the "Mohammedans" given in the translation.
17. Examples of how coming close to the apparent transcendent reality perceived within an "alien" tradition may in fact enrich an *existing* religiousness, may be found in Robert A. McDermott, "Religion as an Academic Discipline," in *Cross Currents,* Vol. 18 (1968) pp. 11-33 (see especially p. 29); and in Harvey Cox, *Turning East, the Promise and Peril of the New Orientalism,* London, 1979, (1977), Allen Lane/ Penguin.
18. Edward Farley, *Ecclesial Man, a Social Phenomenology of Faith and Reality,* Philadelphia, 1975, Fortress Press, p. 23.
19. Rudolf Otto has called for "penetrative imaginative sympathy with what passes in the other person's mind." *(The Idea of the Holy,* p. 62). In similar terms, Ninian Smart has called on the student of religions to "penetrate into the hearts and minds" of the believers *(The Religious Experience of Mankind,* London, 1973, (1969), Fontana, p. 13).
20. Frederick J. Streng, *Emptiness, a Study in Religious Meaning,* New York, 1967, Abingdon, p. 24.

21. Winston L. King, "Negation as a Religious Category," *Journal of Religion,* Vol. 37 (1957), p. 108.

22. Paul van Buren, *The Edges of Language,* London, 1972, SCM, p. 157.

23. Quoted in Winston L. King's "Negation as a Religious Category," p. 107.

24. *Qur'an,* Chapter 112, Sale's translation, London, no date, Frederick Warne & Co., p. 595. Sale notes that "this chapter is held in particular veneration by the Mohammedans (sic), and declared, by a tradition of their prophet, to be equal in value to a third part of the whole Koran. It is said to have been revealed in answer to the Koreish, who asked Mohammed concerning the distinguishing attributes of the God he invited them to worship."

25. Quoted in Aldous Huxley, *The Perennial Philosophy,* London, 1950, (1946), Chatto & Windus, p. 32. The scripture to which Shankara refers is the Taittirya Upanishad, 2.4.

26. Ninian Smart, *A Dialogue of Religions,* London, 1960, SCM, p. 11.

27. Karl Barth, *Church Dogmatics,* Edinburgh, 1957, T & T Clark, Vol. 2 p. 449. Authorized English translation by T. H. L. Parker, W. B. Johnston, Harold Knight and J. L. M. Haire of *Die Kirchliche Dogmatik II: Die Lehre von Gott*

28. I. T. Ramsey, *Models and Mystery,* London, 1964, Oxford University Press, p. 60.

29. Ibid.

30. J. L. Austin, *Sense and Sensibilia,* Oxford, 1970 (1962), Clarendon Press, p. 74.

31. Ibid.

32. W. T. Stace, *Mysticism and Philosophy,* London, 1960, Macmillan, p. 291. I discuss some aspects of the logic of ineffability in, "Ineffability and Intelligibility: Towards an Understanding of the Radical Unlikeness of Religious Experience," *International Journal for Philosophy of Religion,* Vol 20 (1986), pp 109-129.

33. John Bowker, *The Religious Imagination and the Sense of God,* Oxford, 1978, Oxford University Press, p. 28. It is perhaps also worth noting here Van der Leeuw's observation that "universally, mysticism seeks silence: the strength of the Power with which it deals is so great that only silence can create a 'situation' for it" (*Religion in Essence and Manifestation: A Study in Phenomenology,* tr. J. E. Turner, London 1938 (1933), George Allen & Unwin, p.433). For some further ideas about

the importance of silence in religion, and the way in which metaphor is frequently the means used to "handle" it, see my "Silence, Metaphor and the Communication of Religious Meaning, Part I," *New Blackfriars*, Vol 74 no 865 (1993), pp 457-464, "Silence, Metaphor and the Communication of Religious Meaning, Part II," *New Blackfriars*, Vol 74 no 866 (1993), pp 486-495.

34. Ibid. The use of "God" in relation to Buddhism will doubtless sound inappropriate to many readers. Bowker provides adequate justification for his use of such shorthand terminology.

35. *Bhagavad Gita*, 6.25, Juan Mascaro's translation, Harmondsworth, 1962, Penguin Classics.

CHAPTER 8

THE SKULL ON THE MANTEL AND THE BURDEN
OF GOODNESS

THE IMAGE of the skull on the mantel, which forms the first part of this chapter's central metaphor, is taken from Thornton Wilder's description of a philosophers' club in Edinburgh. Whether Wilder's account, given in his novel *The Eighth Day*, is based on some actual club, or merely invented, does not matter. The historicity of the image does not effect its usefulness in the context of the hall of mirrors. According to Wilder, the club's members met for the purpose of discussing beliefs both past and present. Such discussions were, however, carried out in a strictly objective tone, enforced by a total prohibition on talking in the first or second person of the present tense. As a reminder of the rule, and as a punishment for those who infringed it, a skull stood grimly on the mantel and into it all offenders who inadvertently spoke of what "I" or "you" believe, were required to place a fine.[1]

The image of the burden of goodness, which completes this chapter's lead metaphor, is taken from a book by Huston Smith on, and entitled, *The Purposes of Higher Education*. According to Smith:

> If there are things that ought to be believed, this being the whole meaning of truth, there are also sides that ought to be espoused: this is the burden of goodness. To remain neutral in the face of these, or to be over-hesitant in deciding where they lie, is not wisdom but its opposite.[2]

I will use these two powerful images, *the skull on the mantel* and *the burden of goodness*, to identify the two magnetic poles of opposite attraction between which Cipher's experience in the hall of mirrors seems to hover uneasily. On the one hand, Cipher must find out what others believe and why they do so. He must explore the various worlds of religious meaning which make up the hall of mirrors. To do so effectively he must not allow his own premature evaluations to cloud the issue. Yet, on the other hand, he must try to come to some decision of his own about how he ought to view the world and, in consequence, how he ought to live his life. Given the extent of his awareness of religious outlooks and his craving for peace of mind, Cipher is placed on the horns of a dilemma. There is a risk that he may either forget about uplifting the burden of goodness in an effort to survey the different varieties of possible load, or that he might be panicked into picking up a burden prematurely, without giving due attention to its credentials or to possible alternatives. How can Cipher resolve this apparent tension between neutrality and commitment, between the need for someone in his situation to explore the hall of mirrors and his desire to reach a conclusion about what he sees there? How can he keep a proper balance between the skull on the mantel, with its insistence on maintaining an uninvolved investigative stance in which subjective feelings do not intrude, and the burden of goodness, with its insistence on personal engagement? Given the extent of possible alternatives, making any particular commitment seems threatened with indefinite postponement as each possibility is subjected to a process of investigation. Given the strength of his need for some sense-giving outlook on the world, the extended investigation of possibilities which seems to be required may be threatened with curtailment in favour of some decisive acceptance. How, in the context of the hall of mirrors, is Cipher to ensure: (a) that, whatever position of commitment he arrives at, it is not premature; and (b) that the investigative process undertaken in search of a decision is not endlessly prolonged? The aim of this chapter is to explore this tension between neutrality and commitment and to see if, from Cipher's point of view, it may be resolved constructively.

To begin with, it is important to clarify what is meant by "neutrality" in each of the two senses in which it is being used. For, without

some elaboration it is a word that is prone to spawning unhelpful interpretations.

First, it has been stressed from the outset that Cipher is "neutral" as
regards the various religious outlooks on the world with which he is
surrounded in the hall of mirrors. I have sometimes referred to his situation simply as that of "neutral informedness" or "informed neutrality."
In this sense "neutrality" refers to Cipher's formally uncommitted stance
as regards any religious position. He does not consider himself to be
Hindu, Buddhist, Muslim, Christian or Jew. At the same time, though,
he has not rejected Hinduism, Buddhism, Islam (or any other religion)
as possible sources of the peace of mind he seeks. He simply has not yet
made up his mind about them. Cipher is well-informed about the teachings of the various religions, but he has not yet reached any conclusions
about where he stands in relation to them. He is, for example *au fait*
with Hindu ideas on rebirth, with the notion of no-self in Buddhism
and with the Christian concept of a loving creator deity, to name but a
few fragments from some of the many reflections he sees in the hall of
mirrors. But he has reached no decision about how accurately these (and
a host of other images) address and reflect the nature of his existence and
provide blueprints for the way he ought to live. He does not know whether
or not to believe in the existence of God, or if he ought to think of
himself as a reincarnating entity, or if, in some sense, he has no self. He
does not know if any of the elements of his religious informedness
(whether singly or in combination) accurately reflect his situation, such
that he should live his life according to the outlook they suggest. He is
unsure, in other words, whether or not to commit himself to accepting
any religious view of things.

In his interesting study of the logic of dialogue among religions,
William Christian has remarked that, "as a generalization, it seems fair
to say that the major religions all present and teach patterns of life."[3]
The trouble is, the patterns which are suggested seem, at least at first
sight, to be very different. As he looks around the hall of mirrors, Cipher can see a whole range of proposed life-patterns. His neutrality with

regard to them means that he does not act as if any of them were true, but nor does he dismiss them as being false. He is religiously neutral in the sense of being *undecided* or *non-aligned*. Neutrality in this first sense *must not be seen as some form of covert commitment*. Cipher is not a neutralist, someone who actively favors a neutral position. On the contrary, he actively seeks an abandonment of a neutrality which is unwanted. Given his feelings of insignificance, mystery and meaninglessness, his sense of lostness in the world, he wants to arrive at a position where he may say with confidence of any offered antidote, "Yes, it's effective, I will accept it, it's true," or, "No, this particular form of religiousness is of no relevance to my life." Nor must Cipher's unwanted neutrality be seen as constituting any absence of information about, or interest in, religion. The context in which Cipher's neutrality is set, and within which he will try to end it, is one of extensive information about, and interest in, religion.

Being neutral in this first sense does not mean that Cipher will have no likes or dislikes, or that he will not have been brought up in a particular socio-geographical setting and be influenced by certain assumptions embedded in his culture and expressed by his peer group. Indeed, in the loose sense of familial background, place of birth, schooling, etc., he may even "belong" to some religion. Such "belonging" does not, however, constitute what he would see as authentic, life-defining commitment. It could not, by any stretch of the imagination, qualify as the decision towards which his energies are directed. In short, "neutrality" in this first sense is not intended to suggest that Cipher is some sort of ill-informed, opinionless zombie confronting the world with an open-mouthed and empty-minded blankness which is content to remain blank. Cipher's zero, one resonance of meaning in his name which should be stressed, refers simply to his present position *vis-a-vis* commitment to religion; it is not meant to suggest that he is some sort of hollow, history-less man.

In his Wilde Lectures of 1972, published as *The Sense of God*, John Bowker has, I think correctly, spoken of the exploration of human behaviour in ways which appear to be open to a novelist alone.[4] That

Cipher may be in danger of appearing as a "hollow man," that he has not been developed into a full-bodied fictional character, but rather has been left as a shell of ideas, has to do with his emergence on the stage of a brief academic book, not with how his character is intended. There is a definite argument to be made for suggesting that an exploration of his situation might have been better conducted via a quite different medium—as indeed there is a case for suggesting that religious studies in general might utilize the novel form much more in the course of its investigations. However, so far as this book is concerned, the reader's imagination must compensate for the lack of any narrative richness.[5]

Second, quite a different sense of "neutrality" comes into play once a method such as passing over is brought into operation. And, unless we suppose Cipher to be possessed of a full personality and an ordinary biography, it may be difficult to see some of the things to which such neutrality refers. "Neutrality" in this second sense is concerned with keeping in check and under firm control those various likes and dislikes which might prompt Cipher to an instant warming to, or cold-shouldering of, some religious outlook before he has had a chance to investigate it properly. Neutrality in this sense, far from being something unwanted, is a deliberately cultivated state of mind. Cipher will adopt it in the process of his investigation, an investigation, remember, whose goal is to end his neutrality in the first sense (that is, his indecision about commitment). This second form of neutrality is simply an attempt to ensure that Cipher does not arrive at *premature* or inaccurate judgments. He wishes to reach an evaluation of those various worlds of religious meaning which constitute the hall of mirrors, only after seeing their visions with the necessary depth and accuracy. If he is to see such visions as they appear to the eyes of those whose lives are lived according to them, who accept them as sources of peace of mind, it is essential that Cipher's own perspective does not cloud them.

In attempting to be neutral in this second sense, two main sets of potentially obscuring factors will need to be set to one side, or bracketed out. That is, they will need to be acknowledged as exerting an unwanted influence and appropriate counter-measures against them put in place.

First, various social and personal value-judgments, which are not specifically related to religion but which might, nonetheless, distort Cipher's attempted perception of other worlds of religious meaning, will need to be identified and "neutralized." For example, being a twentieth century Westerner, he will doubtless be accustomed to wearing shirt and shoes, and to eating with cutlery. Such customs may, however, extend their significance to viewing those who dress in robes, or go barefoot, or eat with their fingers, as in some way being inferior. Clearly, if such assumptions were allowed free rein they would not help Cipher to come to a close sharing of, say, the Buddhist monk's outlook on the world, dressed as he would be in saffron robes, walking in all probability barefoot and eating rice with his fingers from a wooden bowl. Similarly, Cipher may have some such personal idiosyncrasy as, say, mistrusting people whose rate of blinking is faster than his own, or finding chanting—of whatever sort—ridiculous and infantile. Again, such assumptions will have to be set to one side if his passing over is not to be thwarted by obstacles of his own making.

Second, those social or personal judgments which relate directly to religion, and which may obscure any view of this area of human experience beyond that with which they are already familiar, must, similarly, be acknowledged, and steps taken towards their neutralization during the course of passing over. In Cipher's case the methodological neutrality demanded by this sort of approach will call for the bracketing out of, the attempt to lay to one side or to see through, his neutrality as regards religious commitment (neutrality in the *first* sense described). For if Cipher is to share, say, a Buddhist vision of the world, it is unlikely that his efforts to do so would come to much if all along he was thinking to himself, "This is all very interesting, but I just don't know whether to believe it or not." It is worth stressing again that "passing over" is similar in many ways to acting. In just the same way as the actor who could not overcome an aversion to Scottish accents, or the feeling that anyone who believed in witches was feeble minded, or whose contempt for that bloody nobleman's code of conduct did not allow him to imagine just how vaulting ambition can be, might not get very far in a portrayal of

Macbeth, so Cipher's ability to stand shoulder to shoulder with Jew, Sikh, Christian, Muslim, Buddhist, or Hindu, and to look out on the world as they perceive it, may likewise be frustrated if he cannot control the intrusion of premature evaluations. To go back to that old Native American saying mentioned in Chapter 6 as summing up the ethos of passing over, namely, "do not judge someone until you have walked a mile in their moccasins," "neutrality" in the second sense in which I am using the word simply has to do with the effort to take off our own shoes before embarking on such an exercise.

In his interesting—indeed pioneering—work on methodology in the study of religion (for it was published as early as 1901) Morris Jastrow identified what he termed "the personal equation." "So strong is this factor," he wrote, "that it is perhaps impossible to eliminate it altogether, but it is possible, and indeed essential, to keep it in check and under safe control."[6] That much the same point was emphasized by many participants at the International Association for the History of Religions conference on methodology seven decades later,[7] confirms both Jastrow's status as a pioneer and the importance of this element (in particular the need to control it) when we are trying to understand religions. The attempt to impose neutrality in this second sense is simply an attempt to harness the personal equation, so that investigators may approach, with empathy rather than antipathy, outlooks different from those they already hold. Obviously it is not possible, nor indeed desirable, to neutralize the personal equation in the sense of removing it permanently. To attempt to do so would bring a new meaning to the term "character assassination." What we are referring to here is simply an attempt to hold as much of it as possible in suspense for the duration of the inquiry. In a sense, referring back to the central metaphor of Chapter 6, this sort of neutrality stresses the fact of our being in the same house, in order that we have a common basis from which to explore each other's different worlds. It brackets out temporarily our different outlooks on religion, so that we can travel beyond the boundaries of our own indigenous settings. It allows us to see visions of the world through the lenses ground by other religions, rather than seeing everything framed through a single ethnocentric perspective. It is a means of trying to ensure that we do not just render what we see in the hall of mirrors into reflections of our own mind-set, but that we try to see the religious images as they are seen by those who claim that they offer peace of mind.

The problem is that passing over, in making sure that the personal equation is not *prematurely* aligned, will stress the common denominator of the human situation, rather than any particular reading of it. This is necessary in order to investigate and evaluate a range of particular readings. Such neutrality, while necessary if we are to prevent unthinking acceptance of the status quo, or a general leaping to conclusions, would also seem to have the potential of acting against *ever* uplifting a burden of goodness. Commitment seems, paradoxically, to be postponed (seemingly indefinitely) by a neutrality which has been adopted in order to reach it.

"Neutrality" is, perhaps, an unfortunate choice of word for both the senses in which I am using it. Indeed, that I use it at all has more to do with a tradition of such usage than with any personal endorsement of its suitability. In the first sense of neutrality, "pre-commitment" might have been a less misleading label for Cipher's state of mind; while in the second sense, "non-biased" rather than "neutral" might well be preferred. "Neutral" suggests in one context something clinical, inhuman and machine-like, in another something not in gear, and in a third sense presupposes a situation of conflict from which we have decided to remain aloof. None of these connotations is particularly helpful and we would, perhaps, do better to follow Basil Mitchell's advice and instead of talking about neutrality at all, simply "register our *commitment* to conventions of free, fair and disciplined debate"[8] (for it is precisely the principles of such debate that Cipher's situation seems to require). However, rather than swim against the tide of linguistic convention by adopting a new vocabulary, I have simply qualified and explained my use of "neutrality."

Continuing with this process, it is also as well to be clear about some of the senses which "neutrality" is *not* being taken to have. In particular, it is important to avoid two possible misunderstandings of what the neutrality required in passing over involves.

First, the neutrality required in order to effect the return to beginnings which Cipher seeks does not constitute an attempt to reach some sort of presuppositionless starting point. Cipher's deliberate efforts to be neutral do not mean that he is attempting to achieve some kind of *tabula rasa* upon which may then be written the results of his explorations, uninfluenced by any extraneous factors. Anders Nygren has strongly condemned the confusion between prejudice and presupposition which lies at the heart of supposing that neutrality involves the annihilation of everything the investigator thought or believed beforehand, in the interests of a supposedly uncontaminated methodology. The desire for such antiseptic conditions of investigation overlooks the rather basic fact that the process of sterilization involved, even if it were possible to achieve, would kill off any intelligible process of inquiry as well as those germs of prejudice which might indeed threaten to influence its results. Nygren points out that "prejudice" conveniently means exactly what its etymology suggests, namely, that an opinion has been formed before (*prae*) the case has been brought to trial (*judicium*), that judgment has been reached without looking at the evidence. The common usage of "presupposition," on the other hand, tends to lose sight of the fact that presuppositions refer to those fundamental and unquestionable assumptions on which the ability to make judgments in the first place depends. To use the instances Nygren cites: we presuppose that there is a distinction between true and false and between good and evil. In *Meaning and Method*, Nygren goes so far as to suggest that the confusion between prejudice and presupposition has reached such proportions that it must be regarded as "a cultural menace."[9] He argues that:

> When the presuppositions on which all thought and cultural life rest come to be described as "prejudices" which we could well do without, this is no longer merely a harmless linguistic confusion but something with far-reaching consequences in every direction.[10]

One of those consequences would be to render quite absurd the methodological pre-requisites of passing over. For while it is one thing to seek to control potentially prejudicial aspects of one's outlook, it is quite something else to attempt to obliterate one's presuppositions in an indiscriminate jettisoning which lumps them together with prejudice. In a fascinating essay on anamnesis and belief, Jay Kim endorses Nygren's warnings. Making a presuppositionless starting point the prerequisite of an inquiry is, he says, an "inhuman obsession," a "Cartesian aberration" which has "infected Western thought for centuries."[11] Cipher wants to control possible prejudice, not attempt to eliminate inevitable presupposition. Nor is he so naïve as to imagine that complete impartiality is ever possible.

This sort of misunderstanding of what neutrality involves, which results in confusing prejudice and presupposition, can lead very easily to an interpretation of the skull on the mantel as a bleak indictment of attempts to examine religion from a neutral standpoint. As the mood in religious studies has changed from primitivism to modernism, from a dismissive judgmental approach which operated an *a priori* negative evaluation of "other" outlooks, to a non-judgmental investigative approach, the critic of such a process might point to the skull on the mantel as the death's head of neutrality, a death's head whose baleful medusa gaze, shorn of all expression of personal commitment, turns to stone each living faith it touches on and sums up graphically the lifelessness which exaggerated impartiality can lead to. Any attempt to study religion from a neutral position, so this interpretation would argue, does fatal violence to the subject matter. In such an approach, the gruesomely appropriate symbol of its own mistaken methodology simply stands for the fate which awaits the subject matter approached according to its deadening mores. If neutrality becomes an "inhuman obsession" where so much of the investigator's personality is bracketed out that, in the unlikely event of such a radical neutralization being possible, he would become a veritable zombie, then there seems to be no good reason to suppose that he would be equipped for anything except a massive misapprehension of religion (or of anything else). Perhaps it is fear of such a perversion of neutrality which fuels the idea that observer and religious believer stand on opposite sides of some great divide which all but the most minimal understanding is quite unable to cross. Although elsewhere in the same volume he has suggested that the roles of observer and believer may be starting to coalesce,[12] in a passage in *The Meaning and End of Religion,* Wilfred Cantwell Smith writes:

> Heaven and hell, to a believer, are stupendous places into one or other of which he is about to step. To an observer they are items in the believer's mind. To the believer they are parts of the universe; to the observer they are parts of religion.[13]

The neutrality which Cipher "naturally" possesses—neutrality in the first sense described above (i.e. the fact of his indecision concerning commitment), means that heaven, hell, sunyata, nirvana, the tao, and other such sacred states or loci, are *possibilities*. They are possibly stupendous phenomena, his relationship to which he has not yet decided. The neutrality which he will *deliberately* employ in passing over, in order to try to find out (i.e. neutrality in the second sense described above), does not mean that Cipher will suddenly become unconcerned, distanced and detached, in such a way that he will thereafter view such things as rather peculiar phenomena, of no particular interest to himself. All that the adoption of this sort of neutrality means is that he will attempt to see them clearly, so that he may reach a decision about them.

As Bernard E. Meland has shown, there is no such thing as a completely neutral inquiry, that is, an inquiry in which "the interested, centred existence of the inquirer plays no part."[14] Rather than aiming for something unreachable—and, indeed, undesirable—such as total neutrality, Cipher will aim for something very like the position which Meland goes on to characterize as being possible and useful, where "the biases of interest and conditioning are brought *reasonably* under control."[15] Self-awareness and self-understanding, according to Meland's analysis, are importantly contributory factors in making such a disciplined effort effective.

Cipher, like the historian, must learn to curb a self-centredness that is, as Arnold Toynbee put it, "one of the intrinsic limitations and imperfections of all life."[16] He must "consciously and deliberately (shift) his angle of vision away from the initial self-centered standpoint natural to him as a living creature,"[17] if, that is, he is to see how others see (and have seen) the world. Unless he does this, he will simply remain incapable of responding to other points of view and, as such, will see only a single reflection in the hall of mirrors. (In so doing, he would, incidentally, as Toynbee observed, be making a *moral* as well as an intellectual mistake.[18]) But such a shift in viewpoint does not involve some sort of erasure of personality so that an impersonal, camera-eye's outlook may be adopted, it simply attempts to neutralize those aspects of his existing vision which may distort what he wants to see beyond it.

Stanley A. Cook, who, along with Morris Jastrow, is one of the largely uncredited pioneers in the methodology of the study of religion, noted how the "ultra-impartial mind that drifts away from its values, that has not firm elementary principles,"[19] is, in fact, wholly unsuited for conducting an inquiry into religion. I would not want to accept Cook's views on the supposed necessity of these firm elementary principles having a religious root. The point is a more general one—just as acting requires the imaginative flexibility of a full human personality in which prejudices are carefully laid aside, so passing over requires the presence of the complete person, with certain aspects of the personality deliberately controlled, not some sort of methodological ghost.

The second possible misunderstanding of "neutrality" which it is important to correct, imagines that by adopting a methodological neutrality to render passing over effective, Cipher will lose the ability to judge and discriminate between those areas on which he will focus his passing over. "Neutrality" is taken to mean that he must accept on equal terms everyone who calls themself Christian or Hindu or Buddhist, because to do otherwise would allow in an element of obscuring judgment and evaluation. In other words, this misunderstanding of neutrality assumes that the attempt to control the personal equation will entail a loss of discernment. But in fact Cipher will choose very carefully which expressions of individual religiousness he will attempt to share. Just as it would be easy enough to dismiss music as something trite and silly if one only listened to its trivial manifestations, so it would be easy for Cipher to dismiss religion out of hand as irrelevant to his quest for peace of mind, were he to focus only on its ever-abundant mediocre or malign representatives. And just as to limit the area of music which is to be given serious consideration is not to presume that Mahler or Wagner, Beethoven or Vivaldi is best, so one can likewise limit the area of interest in an inquiry into religion, without presuming that some single particular outlook is thereby to be favoured.

For example, Cipher would not be likely to get very far with his inquiries into the Christian outlook on the world if he attempted to pass over to the perspective of the sort of Catholic described by Miguel de Unamuno. "Strictly speaking in Spain today," wrote Unamuno in 1904,

> to be a Catholic in the vast majority of cases, scarcely means more than not to be anything else. A Catholic is a man who, having been baptized, does not publicly abjure what is assumed, by a social fiction, to be his faith; he does not think about it one way or the other, either to profess it or reject it, either to take up another faith, or even to seek one.[20]

Unamuno's comment identifies a common category of nominal believer that extends religiously far beyond Catholicism and, geographically and historically, far beyond Spain in the early 1900s. Such nominal believers, unlike Cipher, are indeed neutral about religion in a somewhat zombie-like manner. Saying that Cipher would not get very far in his inquiries into the Christian outlook if his passing over were to be focused on such believers, is not, of course, to infer from their somewhat uninspiring attitude that the God of their nominal belief does not exist, or that Christianity is to be rejected lock, stock and barrel because of the unconvincing way in which they present it as being a legitimate source of peace of mind. Taking an example rather closer to home, John Bowker has shown that although the behaviour of Catholics and Protestants in Northern Ireland may suggest that "the claimed object of their belief has no specifiable reality *in effect*,"[21] i.e. that their inter-action often seems to be particularly godless, this "does not in itself provide a comment on the reality of the objects of their belief."[22] Doubtless, even from the most peripheral expressions of Christian religiousness, Cipher could eventually penetrate to the heart of the matter, unless the connections with it were so tenuous as to be indistinguishable from actual severance. It would, however, seem perverse to start off at the furthest remove from the goal which is being sought. Cipher's dilemma will be more adequately served if his passing over is directed to those examples of religiousness which offer direct access to the arterial system of a particular faith. Neutrality does not preclude the selecting for study of those cases which seem closest to the heart.

Given the importance of choosing the area to which his passing over will be directed—or, if you like, of choosing those points of entry into a religious structure which will allow him quickest access to its arterial system, Cipher might well spend some time considering what criteria to use in assessing who counts as a good Christian, a good Buddhist, a good Muslim and so on—i.e. in determining what constitutes the best examples of these sorts of religiousness at the peak of their credibility. Some guidelines will, obviously, be afforded by the religions themselves. But it is interesting to consider whether any inter-religious criteria of value might be available here. I suppose that, in a sense, what Cipher is looking for is religious *maturity*. He is looking for the image of Jewish or Islamic religiousness at the peak of its development, he is interested in finding out, as James Fowler puts it in his seminal work on *Stages of Faith*, "what developmental trajectory into mature faith is envisioned and called for by a particular faith tradition at its best."[23] If he can plot out such trajectories accurately, then clearly he will be able to direct his passing over towards those examples of religiousness where the heart of the matter beats most strongly and visibly.

Interestingly, in Fowler's analysis of faith development, the final and most mature of the six stages of faith which he identifies, what he calls "universalizing faith" (which can occur within any particular religious context), is "often experienced as subversive of the structures (including religious structures) by which we sustain our individual and corporate survival, security and significance."[24] In consequence, "many persons at this stage die at the hands of those whom they hope to change," (Gandhi and Martin Luther King being two of the modern examples which he cites).[25] The *subversiveness* which fully mature faith may display towards accepted norms of behaviour is a timely reminder that the peace of mind apparently offered by religion is something of a misnomer. Such subversiveness ties in well with what will be said in the next chapter about the way in which religions contain an important element of "nothingness, terror and risk," which can act to accentuate precisely that feeling of lostness with which Cipher is assailed.

There is no doubt that religion is subversive of many ordinary certainties and critical of many models of identity thought to be adequate, or even admirable, by society at large. As Sallie McFague has put it with regard to the Christian tradition, "every major reformation within the church has been sparked by the insight that the essence of Christianity does not support conventional standards."[26] Similarly, Thomas Merton has pointed out (in his fascinating essay, "A Devout Meditation in Memory of Adolf Eichmann") that the very concept of sanity, as it is held to in modern society, contains a fundamentally non-Christian element in its virtual exclusion of love. Thus he argues that "the worst error is to imagine that a Christian must try to be 'sane' like everyone else."[27] Far from making one a part of society and endorsing its canons of sanity unquestioningly, a Christian world decision would seem to involve condemning as fundamentally wrong much of what is regarded as socially acceptable behaviour. One is reminded of Reinhold Niebuhr's comment about "the prestige of normality which sinful forms of life periodically achieve in the world."[28] The universalizing stage of faith, the most mature taking of a world decision if we follow Fowler's analysis, strips away that prestige and is highly critical of the norms and standards we have grown used to. Pannenberg further emphasizes something of the subversive potential of Christianity when he notes that:

> The rule of God, understood in Jesus' exclusive sense, robs every political order of its absolute claim on the people living under it.[29]

Likewise Harvey Cox sees Biblical spirituality, with its vision of deity beyond the social order, as being "disruptive and subversive."[30] He suggests an example from within Judaism which clearly underscores the point that making a word decision might be seen as anti-social (or, remembering Merton's comments, perhaps even insane):

The Jewish boy who solemnly lights the candles in the ritual bar mitzvah is undoubtedly being helped to make personal sense out of adolescence. This is fine so far as it goes. What is lost in such a statement is that the boy, in some region of his being, should be dedicating himself to God; and seriously following the God of Israel can play havoc with social roles. It can bring suffering and unhappiness. It can even undermine expectations of appropriate "identity" in a given stage of the life cycle. The God to whom faith points is not the protector of the social hierarchies but the one who sometimes breaks down and overturns them. For the prophets of Israel and their successors, from Jesus of Nazareth to Baal Shem Tov, finding one's identity within any society on earth may not be salvation at all, but bondage.[31]

Thus—classically—we find each of the great sixth century seers, Zarathustra, Deutero-Isaiah, Buddha, Confucius and Pythagoras, breaking away from what Toynbee calls "his heritage of spiritual subordination to the community in which he had been born and brought up."[32] Each of them, in different ways,

> broke out of the social framework of traditional religion and made personal contact with the ultimate spiritual reality behind the phenomena.[33]

This kind of personal contact, or claimed direct sighting of what I have metaphorically dubbed the salamander, constitutes the kind of linchpin which is of such interest to Cipher. Of course such apparently direct contact, as we have seen from what the mystics say about it, seems to be *conceptually*, rather than just socially, disruptive. In short, the possible word decisions facing Cipher are far from easy or comfortable. On the contrary, they seem likely to involve quite radical re-visionings of his whole outlook. Not only is he experiencing a revolution in religious consciousness (in the sense described in Chapter 1); the different religions arrayed around him in the hall of mirrors also have the potential to exert a revolutionary impact on his life.

If passing over is an attempt to return to religious beginnings, and if it turned out to be successful in returning Cipher to a point of close proximity to whatever originative locus of transcendence lies at the source of the particular image he is investigating, then (concerns about its disruptiveness notwithstanding) surely there is little need to worry about resolving any tension which might occur between neutrality and commitment. Will the problem not be solved *automatically* if his investigations take him to (or even sufficiently *towards*) the heart of the matter? Will he not, so to speak, be pulled into its magnetic field, and his commitment follow as a matter of course? Going back to Kristensen's comments on the investigation of Islam, which were mentioned in Chapter 7, if Cipher came to perceive the reality in question, namely Allah, would he not then uplift the Islamic "burden of goodness" and be or become a Muslim? And would this not constitute a natural conclusion to his quest, such that the unwanted neutrality of his indecision about the different worlds of religious meaning would be replaced by a commitment to one particular outlook, and the neutrality required by passing over could, like the process itself, be considered redundant, having served its purpose?

This takes us back into an area of uncertainty regarding the outcome of a process of passing over, and that uncertainty is, as I have already suggested, best discussed after a serious attempt has been made actually to follow its methodological guide-lines. However, if Cipher did find himself drawn sufficiently close to the heart of Islam or Christianity or Hinduism to become a committed Muslim, Christian or Hindu, it is important to point out that although the tensions between neutrality and commitment, between the apparently conflicting imperatives issued by the skull on the mantel and the burden of goodness might then *seem* to be resolved they would, in a sense, just have been transferred to a different area. Instead of being a problem for the uncommitted Cipher, it would become a matter of *theological* concern addressed to his new religiously committed role. For could a standpoint from within any of the particular faith-territories simply close its eyes to the existence of the adjoining religious terrain? Surely as religious information intrudes into the purview of any particular faith-stance it must investigate it, if only to establish whether there is any common ground between them, to find out if the religious terrain is co-terminous across areas of different spiritual habitat, or if such habitats are, in fact, islands with no underlying connections. But if such investigation is required, then presumably neutrality will still be needed in the subsequent exploration, otherwise the whole thing could be solved in advance by juggling with a series of theological *a prioris*. Thus, even within a particular stance of commitment, the tension between neutrality and commitment seems to remain.

The opposing influences of the skull on the mantel and the burden of goodness seem likely thus to extend even into any position of commitment which Cipher's quest might reach. Does this mean that there can be no constructive resolution of the tension between them, that such a tension is simply a permanent feature of a world which is perceived to be religiously plural, so that no resting place of finally satisfactory commitment can ever be reached?

The tension will, in fact, only cause a sense of strain if neutrality and commitment are understood in what I would argue are very questionable ways. If neutrality is taken as a virtual erasure of personality such that, by adopting it, one would approach religion with indifference rather than impartiality, and if commitment is taken as a single decisive act of acceptance and allegiance which would brook no subsequent process of reflection, then, obviously, there would be considerable tension felt when any effort was made to think about religion.

But if neutrality is seen as a device for trying to ensure that we arrive at the truth, and if commitment is seen as an attempt to live according to whatever truth is perceived, then there would seem to be no particular difficulty in allowing that the two attitudes of mind, far from occupying contradictory positions, are very much part of the same continuum of moral seriousness. Northrop Frye provides us with a useful reminder of the moral dimension to the sort of neutrality required by passing over:

> The persistence in keeping the mind in a state of disciplined sanity, the courage in facing results that may deny or contradict everything that one had hoped to achieve—these are moral qualities if the phrase means anything at all.[34]

If we envisage commitment as being the adoption of a very narrow and clearly defined outlook, which acts to close the mind to any subsequent information or reflection which might amend or challenge it, then the demands of the skull on the mantel seem wholly incompatible with the rather uncomfortable, not to say crushing, burden of goodness thus uplifted. But, if commitment is envisaged as a rather more open state of mind, then it is surely more accurate to see the skull on the mantel as part of—and, indeed, an important and very weighty part of—whatever burden of goodness we decide to carry.

Joseph McClelland has suggested that this kind of open commitment involves:

> a critical attitude towards one's own commitment so that one moves between the poles of subjectivity and objectivity, or theology and religious studies, passion and apathy, or however we indicate the tension aroused by thinking about living.[35]

While I am more than a little wary of some of the implications of McClelland's list of contrasting but complementary pairs, I think his remark is quite accurate in identifying *thinking about living* as the cause of tension within any particular religious outlook. Unless it embraces the intellectual mobility facilitated by neutrality, it is hard to see how the commitment of the Sikh or Jew, the Jain, the Christian, or the Hindu or Muslim, could engage in such thought. Without neutrality, in other words, commitment risks becoming static, uncritical, unreflective, oppressive.

The idea of "open" commitment raises all kinds of interesting questions about the finality or provisionality of any particular form of religiousness, and about how becoming a Buddhist is significantly different from becoming a Christian or a Muslim and, moreover, what it means to "become" or to "be" religious in the first place. Such questions, like so many others I have identified and then side-stepped, can only be properly answered when the inter-relationship between the different religions is clearly mapped, and their similarities and differences firmly established. And such mapping also raises the fraught issue of how we should define religion in the first place, where we should think of the boundaries of the different faiths falling, what counts as being inside them, what outside, what lies on the borderlines, what religion *is*.

Although "open" commitment may involve a loss of dogmatic certainty, as this can be expressed within the confines of a single faith which never looks beyond its own boundaries, the inter-religious exploration it will encourage can, in fact, be seen as *strengthening* rather than weakening one's religious position. As Robert McDermott has put it, adapting the famous Socratic dictum:

> once it is admitted that 'the unexamined religious position is not worth living', then a critical reading of one's own religious faith and tradition, aided by the study of another position, must be considered an ideal as well as a responsibility.[36]

It is, as McDermott acknowledges, impossible to predict just what effect one's study of another religious position will have on one's own, since unlike matching it against a critical scientific or philosophical outlook which may question it at *specific* points, the value and challenge of contrasting faith with faith is that sympathetic understanding of another religious tradition "reveals an alternative for every part of one's religion."[37] Although the outcome of such a process is, as McDermott says, uncertain, it is interesting to note that, in one passing over which must, presumably, be of considerable interest to Christian and Buddhist alike, Harvey Cox has shown how it is not, apparently, impossible to strengthen and deepen a Christian religiousness by learning from, and even adopting, various Buddhist practices.[38]

James Fowler has drawn attention to the risk of precocious identity formation if children are exposed at an early age to insistent religious fundamentalism.[39] The premature voicing of adult-endorsed opinion which results in such situations is very much a case of words being parroted without any understanding of the concepts which they are meant to convey. More generally, when young people, either through choice or undue influence, take on the values and life-styles of their parents without question, they enter an identity-status which James Marcia has aptly termed "foreclosure."[40] In the context of the hall of mirrors there seems to be a risk of what we might call *religious foreclosure*, when a position of closed commitment is adopted and the role of neutrality in allowing extensive mental mobility is denied. Such a position of foreclosure, of premature commitment, might seem at first sight to solve Cipher's dilemma, but it would be a response to the many different religious lights that confuse him which had recourse merely to blinkering, rather than genuinely seeing a way through.

It is easy to run from the spectre of neutrality, conceived of as a deadening, destructive force, into the arms of a situation where closed commitment seems to offer the alternative of religious security. From Cipher's point of view, such a retreat would involve no more than a changing of valueless money from a bankrupt methodology to a bankrupt position of commitment. Given his situation of multi-religious informedness, neither indifference nor dogmatism offers an acceptable way out. Perhaps, if my metaphorical camel will stand a few more interpretative straws, the image of the skull on the mantel, *understood as an intrinsic part of each burden of goodness with which Cipher is faced*, might be taken to stand for the demise of those varieties of narrowly particularized faith whose secure singularity is afforded only by a refusal to look around them. The tide of history is surely against such religiousness. It is outmoded. Such ill-founded security as it boasts cannot survive in an era of globalization.

Finally, we might note that certain basic facts of anatomy redeem the skull from any purely funereal function which our first emotional reactions to it are likely to infer. For, quite apart from the more dramatic and imaginative aspects which have become associated with it, the skull is—quite simply—the necessary foundation for the face and the protection for the brain which gives sense to any expression which that face might make. Perhaps, in the end, any skull which Cipher places on his mantel should act as a reminder that, in order to arrive at a proper understanding of any religion, he must remember there is more to it than meets the eye, more to it than the superficiality of surface smiles and scowls, but that, to get beyond the level of the obvious, he must pass through much that may be difficult to penetrate and sometimes frightening to behold. Such a passage will not be possible if he is shackled immovably to a burden of unreflective dogmatism which he has mistaken for something more worthwhile, or if, through seeking some sort of total neutrality, he attempts to absent himself from the audience of humanity which all religions address.

Notes

1. Thornton Wilder, *The Eighth Day*, London, 1967, Longmans, Green & Co., p. 167.
2. Huston Smith, *The Purposes of Higher Education*, New York, 1955, Harper & Row, pp. 36-37.
3. William A. Christian, *Oppositions of Religious Doctrines: a Study of the Logic of Dialogue Among Religions*, London, 1972, Macmillan, p. 31.
4. John Bowker, *The Sense of God*, Oxford, 1973, Oxford University Press, p. 13.
5. For some interesting ideas on the use of fiction in the study of religion, see John Miles, "Bildungsromane and the Pedagogy of Comparative Religion," *Horizons*, Vol. 19 no. 2 (1975), pp. 75-86. I offer some ideas about the richness of literature as a resource for religious studies in "The Numinous in Modern British Fiction," *The Month*, Vol. 30 no. 11 (1997), pp. 448-452.
6. Morris Jastrow, *The Study of Religion*, London, 1901, Contemporary Science Series, p. 1.
7. See Lauri Honko (ed.), *Science of Religion: Studies in Methodology*, The Hague, 1979, Mouton. This volume consists of the proceedings of the study conference of the International Association for the History of Religions held in Turku, Finland, in 1973.
8. Basil Mitchell, *Neutrality and Commitment*, Oxford, 1968, Clarendon Press, p. 22. This booklet is the text of an inaugural lecture delivered before the University of Oxford in May, 1968. My emphasis.
9. Anders Nygren, *Meaning and Method: Prolegomena to a Scientific Philosophy of Religion and a Scientific Theology*, London, 1972, Epworth Press, authorized translation by Philip S. Watson, p. 187.
10. Ibid.

11. Jay J. Kim, "Belief or Anamnesis: is a Rapprochement between History of Religions and Theology Possible?" *Journal of Religion*, Vol. 37. (1957), p. 165.

12. Wilfred Cantwell Smith, *The Meaning and End of Religion*, p. 200.

13. Ibid., p. 131.

14. Bernard E. Meland, "Theology and the Historians of Religion," *Journal of Religion*, Vol. 41 (1961), p. 271.

15. Ibid. To further stress that, in the figure of Cipher, I am not advocating as plausible some sort of complete neutrality where an individual approaches religion in a wholly detached and inhumanly objective way, let me endorse Harvey Cox's peculiarly apt remark which emphasizes the common human interest in questions of life and death and underlines how unsatisfactory it would be to remain in a state of permanent indecision about religious commitment: "The people who study religion are not ciphers. They are faced with the same questions of life and death and right and wrong with which the various religions deal. They cannot avoid the question of truth forever. Economists who investigate rival theories of savings and inflation must decide how to invest their own money. Students of comparative religion eventually have to decide how they are going to live their lives and make their decisions. They have to ask what faith, if any, will guide their ultimate choices. This unavoidable need to choose has pushed the academic study of religion toward a frank acknowledgment that no one can study religion merely descriptively. This in turn makes the modern myths of neutrality and objectivity increasingly implausible." (*Religion in the Secular City*, New York, 1984, Simon & Schuster, p. 224). I am indebted to Professor Colin Grant, Department of Religious Studies, Mount Allison University, New Brunswick, Canada, for drawing my attention to this passage.

16. Arnold Toynbee, *An Historian's Approach to Religion*, Oxford, 1956, Oxford University Press, (based on Toynbee's Gifford Lectures for 1952-53), p. 2.

17. Ibid.

18. Arnold Toynbee, *Mankind and Mother Earth*, London, 1976, Oxford University Press, p. 3.

19. Stanley A. Cook, *The Study of Religions*, London, 1914, Adam & Charles Black, p. 26.

20. Miguel de Unamuno, *The Agony of Christianity and Essays on Faith*, London, 1974, Routledge & Kegan Paul, pp. 172-173. The quotation is taken from Unamuno's essay "What is Truth?," which was first published in 1904. Translation by Anthony Kerrigan.

21. John Bowker, *The Sense of God*, p. 18.
22. Ibid.
23. James W. Fowler, *Stages of Faith: the Psychology of Human Development and the Quest for Meaning*, San Francisco, 1980, Harper & Row, pp. 294-295.
24. James W. Fowler, Robin W. Lovin et. al., *Trajectories of Faith: Five Life Stories*, Nashville, 1980, Abingdon, p. 31.
25. Ibid.
26. Sallie McFague, "An Epilogue: the Christian Paradigm," in Peter Hodgson & Robert King (eds), *Christian Theology: An Introduction to Its Traditions and Tasks*, London, 1983, SPCK, p.332.
27. Thomas Merton, "A Devout Meditation in Memory of Adolf Eichmann," in *Raids on the Unspeakable*, London, 1977, Burns & Oates, pp. 31-32.
28. Reinhold Niebuhr, *The Nature and Destiny of Man: a Christian Interpretation*, London, 1941, Nisbet & Co., Vol 1, p.282.
29. Wolfhart Pannenberg, *The Apostles' Creed in the Light of Today's Questions*, tr. Margaret Kohl, London, 1972, SCM, p.85.
30. Harvey Cox, *Turning East: The Promise and Peril of the New Orientalism*, London 1979, Allen Lane/Penguin, p.80.
31. Ibid., pp 80-81.
32. Arnold Toynbee, *Mankind and Mother Earth*, London, 1976, Oxford University Press, p. 178.
33. Ibid., p. 287.
34. Northrop Frye, "The Knowledge of Good and Evil," in Max Black (ed.), *The Morality of Scholarship*, New York, 1967, Cornell University Press, p. 4.
35. Joseph C. McClelland, "Teacher of Religion: Professor or Guru?" *Studies in Religion/Sciences Religieuses*, Vol. 2 (1972), p. 232.
36. Robert A. McDermott, "Religion as an Academic Discipline," *Cross Currents*, Vol. 18 (1968), p. 29.
37. Ibid.
38. See Harvey Cox, *Turning East*, especially Chapter 5.
39. James W. Fowler, *Stages of Faith*, p. 132.
40. J. E. Marcia, "Development and Validation of Ego Identity Status," *Journal of Personality and Social Psychology*, Vol. 3 (1966), pp. 551-558, quoted in Helen L. Bee and Sandra K. Mitchell, *The Developing Person*, New York, 1980, p. 611.

CHAPTER 9

LESSONS FROM THREE ELEPHANTS

IN *Ascent of the Mountain, Flight of the Dove*, Michael Novak writes:

> Religion is a conversion from the ordinary, given, secure world into
> a world of nothingness, terror, risk—a world in which, neverthe-
> less, there is a strange healing joy.[1]

It is into Cipher's ordinary, given, secure world of day to day experience
that feelings of insignificance, mystery and meaninglessness intrude, so
that he feels the need for some sort of curative peace of mind, or what
Novak terms a "strange healing joy." This book has been concerned with
exploring how his quest for such a thing might best be conducted in the
context of a religiously plural world, where many *possible* senses of security are apparently available to him.

At the end of the last chapter I suggested that one interpretation of
the image of the "skull on the mantel" was to see it as a reminder of the
fact that, if we are to progress beyond a somewhat superficial view of
religion, we must pass through much that may be difficult to understand and sometimes frightening to behold. Novak's remark serves as a
useful reminder of this frightening aspect, of what we might term the
dark side of religion. All too often this is glossed over or forgotten. It
would, for example, be easy to see Cipher's intended quest as involving
a motivating sense of insecurity or unease which sends him scurrying
towards the safe havens variously offered by religions. Such a simplistic
summary risks missing the important point that although they may indeed offer such havens, religions also act to *accentuate* the sense of insecurity which desires them. The "strange healing joy" of religion, the
peace of mind which Cipher seeks, is offered in a perspective which also
involves an increase in precisely those negative senses (Novak's nothing-

ness, terror and risk) which will fuel and magnify Cipher's sense of lostness. Moreover, peace of mind, from the point of view of everyday existence, may often appear disturbingly turbulent.

To make clear the way in which religious outlooks on the world seem, with one hand, to undermine any sense of everyday security, while, with the other, they offer a purportedly deeper sense of well-being, it is necessary to draw a distinction between what we might term mundane and world aspects of certainty and uncertainty, remembering that the possibility of finding some form of religious world certainty, or peace of mind, or "strange healing joy"—call it what you choose—is the whole focus of Cipher's interest in the hall of mirrors.

In stressing the double action of religion, fostering world uncertainty and offering world certainty, we may gain further insight into what Cipher's environment is like and how it may, in fact, serve to give his quest an increasing sense of urgency. In particular, I want to develop the sense of world uncertainty given in Chapter 3, presenting it now as something intimately bound up with, if not identical to, a sense of lostness, rather than simply being a neutral position *vis-a-vis* commitment.

Mundane certainty is simply an acceptance of things as routine and everyday which does not probe beneath commonsense answers to questions of purpose, but sees them as sufficient in themselves. "What is the purpose of my life?" "What am I here for?" Mundane certainty will reply, "to get a good job, to find somewhere pleasant to live and bring up a family, to become rich and famous, to travel round the world...," or in terms of whatever else may be considered to be a worthy goal.

World certainty, on the other hand, involves accepting an account of things which sees the commonplace against the backdrop of rather wider terms of reference. "What is the purpose of my life?" "What am I here for?" World certainty will reply, "to escape from the eternal round of karma and rebirth, to follow the Eightfold Path and achieve Nirvana, to obey God's commandments, to follow the teachings of the *Qur'an*...," or in terms of whatever other world view is accepted. (I am, of course, confining myself to *religious* world certainties here; we should remember that some political, scientific, and artistic terms of reference may also provide something similar.)

We might, perhaps, define a seriously committed religious life as one in which day to day actions are performed in accordance with a view of ultimate meaning. Such a view would see some significance in them over and above their immediately observable consequences. A non-religious life, on the other hand, would be one in which day to day actions and ambitions are performed and followed without reference to any transcendent state or entity beyond themselves. And a nominal religious life would be one in which lip-service is paid to some point of transcendent reference which is then, to all intents and purposes, ignored.

Moving on to uncertainty, *mundane* uncertainty is simply that doubt or indecision which questions specific elements in our experience: what career do I want to follow, how ought I to vote, where do I wish to live? and so on. *World* uncertainty, on the other hand, questions the sense of life itself and asks in a profound and basic way, "What ought I to do?" "How ought I to lead my life?" "What should I believe about the world?" and so on. It is a state of mind where not only has no decision been reached about the overall meaning of things, but where the absence of such a decision is felt as a pressing deficiency which acts to undermine any sense of contentment.

The desire for some form of world certainty occurs when we find our lives confronted by this disturbing feeling of undermining uncertainty and indecision. This opens our eyes to how insignificant, mysterious and meaningless human life can at times appear to be, unless there are wider terms of reference to appeal to than those afforded by day to day existence. Cipher's sense of lostness is, precisely, a feeling of chronic world uncertainty. When, midway through his shopping list (to reiterate the haiku-derived image from Chapter 1) he "remembers death," Cipher moves from a mundane to a world perspective.

Clearly, for most of the time, most people are reasonably content to operate pretty much on the level of outlook offered by commonsense. We eat, sleep, read and write books, pursue whatever other business we are engaged in, without particularly worrying about issues of ultimate meaning and sense. But sometimes such a commonsense outlook simply does not seem sufficient. The mundane certainties and uncertainties which characterize so much of our existence seem suddenly overtaken and transcended by issues of an altogether different scale.

The conditions under which world uncertainty may assail us are many and varied. Although what Bourdillon and Fortes aptly term our "threshold of vulnerability"[2] to the human situation has been raised enormously, so that we can now control and understand many of those phenomena which might otherwise have aroused a sense of world uncertainty much sooner, we are still sufficiently subject to the facts of birth, suffering and death, set in the context of an unpredictable future, an irretrievable past and an awing immensity of environing space, to wonder about the ultimate nature of our existence and the way in which it ought to be conducted.

Often, a sense of world uncertainty arises out of an encounter with suffering, or with some event which stresses our transient finitude and seems to make a nonsense of any identity and rationale offered to us by considerations of occupation, intelligence, wealth, social standing and so on. Or it may be triggered through encountering information about some variety of world *certainty*, which then calls into question the adequacy of any more mundane scheme of sense.

A great deal of literature is concerned with chronicling our attempts to cope in various ways with the impingement of world uncertainty upon our lives. In *Those Barren Leaves*, for example, a novel in which mundane certainty and world uncertainty are juxtaposed with great comic effect, Aldous Huxley has summed up well the relationship between these two sides of our humanity:

> All one's daily life is a skating over thin ice, a scampering of water beetles across the invisible skin of depths. Stamp a little too hard, lean a shade too heavily and you are through, you are floundering in a dangerous and unfamiliar element.[3]

Mundane certainty and uncertainty form a thin skin over depths, and, fragile though the surface which they provide may often seem to be, it bears the bulk of the weight of human movement. Cipher seems somehow to have stamped too hard or leant too heavily, so that he is less preoccupied with surface concerns than with plotting a course through the dangerous and unfamiliar element of world uncertainty which seems to him to underlie them.

Whether or not it is approached from the standpoint of an *existing* sense of world uncertainty, such as I have made Cipher possess (to a deliberately exaggerated degree), it is important to recognize that the acquisition of information about the religions of the world is as likely to *increase* such a sense as it is to provide any antidote for it. It is one of the paradoxes of religion that it offers both fundamental certainty and uncertainty, a rich source of meaning and a formidable vision of what is meaningless. In order to set the stage upon which to present its sense-giving outlooks on the human condition, it must first stress the features of that condition which call out for its perspective in the first place. There would be no point in presenting world certainties to an audience which was unshakably satisfied with the adequacy of a mundane outlook on things. Religious perspectives rely on showing that meaninglessness, uncertainty and incompleteness characterize any life which is lived without some sort of transcendent dimension.

A neutral informedness about religious teachings might thus be expected to *increase* that awareness of our existence which sees it as something dwarfed by the immensities of time and space and perpetually threatened with disruption by the prospect of seemingly random suffering and, eventually, by the inevitability of death. At the same time, one would expect such religious knowledge to offer details of various strategies of solace which might be adopted in the face of such a daunting outlook. Religion offers peace of mind to heal those wounds which consciousness may come to feel more keenly precisely through an acquaintance with religious thinking. As Winston L. King puts it:

> One may generalize and say that religious traditions always go out of their way to paint life in its darkest colours and to stress the precariousness and evil condition of human existence. *Religion may be defined in this context as the awareness of a basic wrongness with the world and as the technique of dealing with that wrongness.*[4]

Or, as Hocking rather more concisely says (in *The Meaning of God in Human Experience*), religion may often be seen as "the healing of a breach which religion itself has made."[5] (This characteristic is, of course, closely related to the subversive aspect of making a religious world decision, to which attention was drawn in the previous chapter.)

Although there are many potent religious expressions of the "basic wrongness with the world," whether in the *Maitri Upanishad*, the *Book of Ecclesiastes*, Buddhist statements about the centrality of *dukkha*, and so on, their massive sense of something dreadfully amiss finds chillingly direct expression in Ernest Becker's *The Denial of Death*. I want to quote a passage from Becker's study because he provides a vivid picture of the kind of outlook which may result when the "evil condition" of human existence is realized without the safety net of any religious techniques for dealing with it. Becker writes:

> When you get a person to look at the sun as it bakes down on earth, the ridiculous accidents, the utter fragility of life, the power-lessness of those he thought most powerful—what comfort can you give him? What would the average man do with a full consciousness of absurdity? He has fashioned his character for the precise purpose of putting it between himself and the facts of life. It can't be over-stressed that to see the world as it really is is devastating and terrifying. I believe that those who speculate that a full apprehension of man's condition would drive him insane are, quite literally right. Anxiety is the result of the perception of the truth of one's condition. What does it mean to be a self-conscious animal? The idea is ludicrous if not monstrous. It means that one is food for worms. This is the terror: to have emerged from nothing, to have a name, consciousness of self, deep inner feelings, an excruciating yearning for life and self-expression—and with all this yet to die.[6]

Being in the hall of mirrors carries with it the potential both to increase this sense of terror and to find some solace for it.

Given his natural sense of world uncertainty, and the fact that this will, almost certainly, be strengthened and deepened by his experience of the religious outlooks found in the hall of mirrors, it is clear that Cipher's search for the possibility of peace of mind may come to be undertaken with an increasing sense of urgency, if not desperation. Let me stress again, despite its fairground connotations the hall of mirrors is not a comfortable place to be in. Its diverse images repeatedly reflect a sense of the "basic wrongness" with the world and the need to take remedial action. Of course, they also offer peace of mind (or, to use King's terms, "techniques of dealing with that wrongness"), but Cipher is unsure which, if any, of these techniques actually works. One of his key tasks must be to try to establish the extent to which the "basic wrongness," perceived by the religious consciousness as characterizing human existence, is similarly diagnosed by Hinduism, Judaism, Taoism, Buddhism, Christianity, Islam, Sikhism and so on, and if the techniques they offer for dealing with it may thus be seen as potential cures for the same ailment, or if different treatments are being offered for different aspects of the same disease or for different illnesses altogether. The completion of such a task will be one of the desired outcomes of the process of passing over.

Therefore, there appears to be (albeit perhaps only temporarily) an almost certainly *negative* outcome to Cipher's search for peace of mind in the hall of mirrors. Such an outcome is at direct variance with what he is seeking, for it entails an *increase* in precisely that which he wishes to minimize (indeed to lose altogether) namely, his sense of lostness. One conclusion it seems safe to draw is that, whatever the final outcome of his quest for peace of mind may be, his search for it in the hall of mirrors will involve a heightening of its exact opposite. For it is hard to see how, in such a context, he could avoid repeated encounter with religious senses of something wrong with the world. And these will inevitably act to erode any sense of security based on mundane certainties. Can any similarly probable conclusions be drawn on a more positive note, concerning the likelihood of Cipher's actually finding some sort of curative peace of mind? Will he discover something which might act to silence the sense of lostness which his quest may otherwise simply exaggerate? Is it reasonable to suppose that Cipher's exploration of the hall of mirrors will result in the peace of mind he is seeking, that he will find some envaluing religious integer behind which to place his zero of lostness?

Or is it more likely that his search will be inconclusive, or that he will decide that no such thing as peace of mind exists?

The attempt to draw any firm conclusions at this point, after what has, we must remember, only been a preliminary discussion about methodology, would be misguided. This book is the first part of a three-phase inquiry: the second phase would apply the technique of passing over to particular religious images, while the third would consider those critiques of religion which question the legitimacy of the peace of mind it offers. Rather than making any firm predictions about the final result of Cipher's search, I want to examine three rather negative anticipatory assessments which look forward to what seem from here to be *possible* outcomes of his quest in the hall of mirrors for peace of mind. In the remainder of the chapter, I want to say a little more about Cipher's relationship with religious studies, offer a summary of his situation by reference to Wisdom's garden, and conclude by using some metaphorical elephants to stress some key points which Cipher must carry with him as his inquiry proceeds. First, then, the three negative anticipatory assessments (and looking at these ought not to be allowed to obscure the fact that the most appropriate conclusion at this stage is, in a very real sense, "*Wait and see*").

The first negative assessment of the likely outcome of Cipher's quest sees it developing into an endless and increasingly laborious *going around in circles*, which will take him no nearer to any point of satisfactory conclusion than he was before he began. Indeed, if anything, he will be led progressively further and further away from reaching any conclusion with each additional orbit in which he turns. According to this assessment, the process of passing over will not take Cipher any closer to some point of commitment. Rather, it will simply add to the perplexing information he already has, and so serve to deepen and perpetuate the problem until he can break the circle of information/perplexity/investigation; increased information/*renewed* perplexity/further investigation, and so on. Moreover, not only will his intended quest increase his perplexity, in terms of expanding his awareness of the number of possible world certainties he might, in the end, adopt; such an awareness is, as we have seen, likely to have the effect of *increasing* his sense of lostness. Obviously, were this to be the outcome of his quest, Cipher would be likely to abandon the whole sphere of religion as being impenetrably problematic and unpleasantly disturbing. However, one slight note of encouragement might be sounded even if so apparently discouraging an outcome did, in fact, occur.

This note of encouragement simply takes the form of a reminder of the two senses in which "hall" can be understood (something which was mentioned briefly in Chapter 3). In one sense "hall" is a place of transit, somewhere you pass through on route to where you wish to go, but definitely not somewhere to envisage spending any time. It has been this sense of "hall" which has, very largely, been metaphorically dominant in our considerations so far, so that *remaining* in the hall of mirrors would be seen as unsatisfactory. But a second sense of "hall" understands it as referring to the main room in a great house, somewhere we might quite well consider to be a satisfactory destination. If this second sense is coupled to the idea of *open* commitment, suggested in Chapter 8, and if we allow that, increasingly, any particular expression of religiousness is likely to be set in the context of perceived plurality, then perhaps we ought not to view Cipher as being very much in transit, but, even if he does not feel he has reached his desired destination, more as at least occupying the proper milieu in which it will be set. Going round in circles may not be such a fruitless thing as it seems if commitment itself is viewed in orbital rather than static terms. However, this is only a *slight* note of encouragement in what might still be an emotionally, intellectually and spiritually unsatisfactory situation. Whether it could be built up into something more substantially reassuring is uncertain.

The second negative assessment of the result of Cipher's intended quest sees its likely outcome as one of coming up against a brick wall rather than going round in circles. In his thoughtful and stimulating essay on *The Purposes of Higher Education*, from which the notion of the burden of goodness was drawn, Huston Smith has argued that at the root of every subject area there are a few apparently simple questions, which regularly deflate its experts and threaten to bring their other inquiries to a halt, because such inquiries seem to be underlain, or rather *undermined*, by these simple questions, which, although they have logical priority over any subsequent inquiry, have remained substantially unanswered, and are, perhaps, unanswerable. For example, in education, according to Smith's analysis, each more specialized inquiry is underlain by the absolutely basic query which asks, "What are we trying to do when we teach?"[7] or, put another way, "What is education?"

So, too, for Cipher there seems to be a sense in which any specific inquiry into Hindu, Buddhist, Jewish or Christian religiousness will be underlain by so many unanswered fundamental questions that any conclusions he reaches must be viewed as significantly lacking in reliable foundations. To echo Smith's educational example, "What are we trying to do when we become or are religious?" or, more simply, "What is religion?"[8] Add to this questions which refer to the relationship between religions, or to the criteria for judging religious outlooks as true or false, and all Cipher's small-scale endeavors seem quite overshadowed by a handful of massively simple, but very difficult, questions. While this kind of assessment is useful for reminding us of the importance of certain fundamental questions, it would, I think, be a mistake to assume that because they have been left unanswered, all subsequent inquiry is in some way devalued. Or, more specifically, that because Cipher has not answered them they will form an impenetrable wall, upon which all his other endeavors are fated to break. It would surely be misleading to think of such questions as being initial hurdles, over which we must leap before progressing to anything else, and that once vaulted they can be forgotten about. It would seem more accurate to view them as keeping pace with whatever investigative race we run, periodically reminding us of the narrowness of our single lane. Indeed, they serve a function almost like that of the slaves who walked beside Roman generals and emperors at the head of their triumphal processions and whispered reminders of their mere mortality, lest they be carried away by the glories of present success.

The third negative assessment of the likely outcome of Cipher's quest might take as its point of departure R. S. Lee's observation that, "attitudes of belief or unbelief are never reached by processes of reasoning alone."[9] Does Cipher's intended search for peace of mind in the hall of mirrors not infringe the strictures of this truism? After all, "a correctly reasoned god," as Woods put it, "is not the object of religious devotion."[10] Thus Cipher's quest is *fated* to be unsuccessful. Trying to work out a position of religious commitment in a deliberate, rational way is akin to trying to carry water in a net. It uses the wrong tool for the job. In his autobiography, subtitled "The Story of My Experiments with Truth," Gandhi records somewhat ruefully how "it was in England that I first discovered the futility of mere religious knowledge."[11] And later, in South Africa, he records how Pearson's marvelously entitled book, *Many Infallible Proofs* had, as he put it, "no effect on me."[12] Is Cipher not risking an overestimation of the usefulness of "mere religious knowledge," if he is expecting some sort of infallible proof to emerge from his inquiry and point unambiguously in the direction of his desired commitment? Is this not to misconceive the fundamental nature of human religiousness?

Two points can be raised in reply to such an assessment. The first accepts that a position of commitment is very rarely reached by a process of reasoning alone; it is seldom the outcome of a deliberate strategy in which it was viewed as the final goal. Argument is one way of forging towards some sort of certainty, but in the religious realm it is by no means the primary *modus operandi*. As Eliade has remarked, perhaps in a religious context we must

> content ourselves with personal certitudes, with wagers based on dreams, with divinations, ecstasies, aesthetic emotions. That is also a mode of knowing, but without arguments.[13]

There is no reason why Cipher should not employ such modes of knowing. At the same time as acknowledging the possible futility of mere religious knowledge, though, we ought to remember that for someone in Cipher's position a deliberate plan of inquiry is demanded by the unsatisfactoriness of his uncommitted status—regardless of whether or not the outworking of that plan is an *ideal* strategy for the circumstances. Embarking on a quest for peace of mind in the context of the hall of mirrors is, in short, preferable to doing nothing, however inappropriate it may turn out to be.

The second point which might be raised in reply to this sort of assessment of Cipher's intended quest, an assessment which sees it as ill-suited to the goal he seeks on the grounds that religion is not reducible to reason, is to point out that the method he intends using is not strictly discursive. "Passing over" has been likened to acting rather than, say, to a process of logical reasoning. Moreover, in taking Cipher towards the heart of the matter, it would, if successful, act to take him towards a locus where words and concepts, reason's tools, seem not to work. If Cipher's intended quest is likened to an attempt to penetrate to the centre of a *yantra*, i.e. to try to reach the empty space at the heart of the complex interlocking mesh of triangles, rather than as something which focuses on the triangles themselves, then perhaps it will not seem as out of keeping with the goal which is being sought. (This point will be more readily understood by referring to the illustration of the *yantra* in Appendix A.)

Whatever outcome is reached after passing over has been attempted it is, at least, unlikely that Cipher will have to proceed alone. Although I have stressed the dangers of taking him as representative of any large-scale group, it is perhaps worth noting that the conditions necessary for the emergence of such a group are increasingly being established. This can be seen, for example, by the way in which the whole area of religion is handled in an educational context. For educationalists are increasingly intent on providing information across a wide spectrum of faiths; multi-faith religious education is in, mono-faith religious education is out. While in many respects this marks a big improvement from the old indoctrinatory confessionalist approaches, alarmingly little thought seems to have been given to the consequences for individual religiousness which stem from an exposure to the teachings of many faiths.

It has become commonplace to encounter guidebooks to the world's faiths. However, for the most part these are guidebooks in which, as R. C. Zaehner puts it in the preface to one of them, the editor may not, in the interests of objectivity, assign stars to those religious structures which seem to him the most admirable.[14]

The task of assigning stars is left to readers themselves. Such books are a staple resource of modern religious studies. But, to continue Zaehner's analogy, how much use is a guidebook if it tells us the history of a country hotel and how those who have stayed in it have viewed the world, but does not tell us that in some rooms the roof leaks?

One important off-shoot from a consideration of Cipher's problems is the question of how religious education ought to proceed in a situation of religious plurality. If, after all, as Stanley Samartha would have it, "religious pluralism, in the last analysis, means that there are fundamentally different answers to the problems of existence,"[15] then, as Edward Hulmes argues, religious education is really all about choosing sides.[16] It is about making *decisions*, not just accumulating and understanding information. What the different sides are, how they relate to each other, on what grounds any choice between them ought to be made, when it ought to be made in the course of an individual's development, and how it will affect a person's outlook, these remain critically unclear issues which constitute a twilight zone across virtually all the theological, philosophical and psychological aspects involved. In such a twilight zone it is all too easy to stumble towards quite unsound conclusions and adopt highly inappropriate educational policies.

Cipher has turned to religious studies on a number of occasions, often with little satisfaction, and doubtless will do so again. But in doing so he is, in many respects, likely to find himself in a position similar to that of the man who turns to philosophy for answers to the great questions about meaning and destiny. As William Barrett has shown, although originally philosophy was concerned with "the soul's search for salvation,"[17] and indeed in an Eastern setting is still taken up and practised in order to find such salvation, in a Western context it has become so specialized as to appear to have forgotten its original purpose. Barrett writes:

> Specialization is the price we pay for the advancement of knowledge. A price, because the path of specialization leads away from

the ordinary and concrete acts of understanding in terms of which
man actually lives his day to day life.[18]

In the study of religion too, specialization has led towards an advancement in knowledge. An individual such as Cipher may, however, be left
asking whether the price that has been paid is simply too great. Has our
knowledge not now, perhaps, advanced far enough to consider a return
to beginnings and a focusing on matters of more pressing concern than
much of that which it has become accustomed to dealing with? Perhaps
Cipher might remind those scholars who are embarrassed by what Barrett
calls the "aboriginal claims,"[19] which the non-specialist may still make
on their subject from time to time, of Collingwood's remark:

> If thought were the mere discovery of interesting facts, its indul-
> gence, in a world full of desperate evils and among men crushed
> beneath the burden of daily tasks too hard for their solitary strength,
> would be the act of a traitor. We try to understand ourselves and
> our world only in order that we may learn how to live.[20]

The extent to which some aspects of the work of religious studies contribute to such understanding is debatable. Far from offering anything
approaching the kind of life-lesson which Collingwood has in mind here
(which is precisely the sort of learning in which Cipher is interested),
such work may stand condemned by Harvey Cox's judgment, that "specialization is running amok"[21] (perhaps to the extent that "the sickness it
induces—the mastery of the minutiae and the neglect of the momentous—now imperils the existence of our species."[22]). The lesson that
Cipher needs to learn from the first elephant, which will be introduced
below, is that his quest must try to maintain its focus on the momentous
rather than the minute. Knowing increasingly more about highly specific topics is not going to solve his dilemma. He would do well to keep
in mind Marshall McLuhan's annihilating remark about the specialist.
The specialist, says McLuhan, is someone who "never makes small mis-
takes while moving toward the grand fallacy."[23] Were Cipher to lose
sight of making a world decision and become absorbed in highly detailed research, he would fall precisely under this condemnation.

Whether we assess Cipher's intended quest as likely to end up leading him round in circles, bringing him up against a brick wall, or as taking him to some quite different destination, and whether we see him as a solitary figure or one in whose steps many others may tread, we can, I think, quite usefully summarize the drama of commitment in a religiously plural world by siting it in Wisdom's garden.

In Chapter 6, I referred to John Wisdom's now famous parable, which illustrates so well the religiously ambiguous nature of the world. Wisdom imagined a situation where two people return to their long-neglected garden, and find among the weeds one or two of the old plants still surprisingly vigorous. One of them decides that a gardener must have been looking after things. The other decides that everything can be explained by chance, that no one has been looking after the garden, and that, given the overgrown state of things, it would be unreasonable to infer that any gardener came.

Wisdom's garden is not just some artificial metaphorical territory, staked out with stark precision in the abstract reaches of a philosophical consciousness. We walk through it here and now, and the need to know about its nature, and how we ought to live in it, is a pressing one. To momentarily de-analogize: the garden is the world, more particularly the human situation in the world, and Wisdom's two observers, with their different theories about the gardener, represent theistic and atheistic views. Wisdom's garden, for all its apparent story-time innocuousness, is a testing ground, if not a killing field, for religious outlooks. In this perplexingly ambiguous place (its ambiguity has led John Bowker to hold that "faith and despair are equal readings of the natural order"[24]), in this "unfriendly, friendly universe,"[25] to use the poet Edwin Muir's description, in this world where "neither a satanic or a benign vision exhausts nature's ambiguity,"[26] are there sufficient cues in one direction or the other to allow Cipher to make some sort of world decision, beyond simply accepting the existence of a pervasive ambiguity and resigning himself to puzzlement?

As we have seen, Wisdom's analysis seems to suggest that there are two basic interpretative streams (in some ways rather like William James' notions of the sick-souled and healthy-minded outlooks) whose currents act to draw every phenomenon met with in the garden into their interpretative flow. For Cipher, of course, there are not just two currents of thought. Instead, he confronts a veritable interpretative whirlpool with pressures coming from a whole spectrum of different opinions. Are there any features of the garden which would suggest unambiguously that he should navigate his course towards commitment in one particular direction?

Perhaps the best way in which to picture Cipher's situation, in the setting of Wisdom's garden, is to see him as being aware of the existence there of many different vantage points, Buddhist, Christian, Hindu, Jain, Jewish, Islamic, Sikh, Taoist, and so on in all their variety. From these vantage points, so those who have ascended their steps claim, one can catch a glimpse of the sense-giving salamander that makes the garden/world appear in a particular light. Others claim that these purported vantage points are mere castles in the sky, which look out on a perspective of pure make-believe. Cipher will be concerned, through passing over, to explore the outlooks of those who claim that religions offer an ultimately realistic outlook on the garden/life. He will be concerned to ascend the steps of whatever vantage point is offered, and to try to see from there what picture of the garden/world is suggested.

Indeed, given the setting in which Wisdom's metaphor allows us to place him, there is a sense in which we might at this point simply advise Cipher to take a walk in the garden and to make sure that he chooses some spot where its natural charms are unspoiled, perhaps the more overgrown the better; for Rudolf Otto has warned that the sense of the numinous (which he sees as lying at the core of religiousness) may be sharply affected by surroundings —forest glades being more conducive to it than, say, urban Berlin.[27] Likewise, Ninian Smart has suggested that some city environments can give rise to untypical religious assessments of things.[28] Such ideas about the importance of environment for religious experience are borne out, to some extent, by David Hay, whose book, *Exploring Inner Space*, was referred to at some length in Chapter 5. Hay notes that "the larger the city is, the less frequently is religious experience reported in it,"[29] and he concludes that the absence of religious experience could, perhaps, be like every other impoverishment, an alienation of people's natural powers.[30]

At one point in Aldous Huxley's *Brave New World*, the savage, an individual who lives outside the luxuries and comforts of this apparent utopia, asks if it is not natural to believe in God "when you're alone—quite alone, in the night, thinking about death."[31] To which the swift rejoinder from the establishment is that people in this society never *are* alone, and deliberate attempts are made to try to ensure that their thoughts never turn in this direction. One begins to wonder if there may not be a sense in which Cipher's return to beginnings should take him in the direction of a period of solitary meditation in a natural wilderness, where he may re-familiarize himself with the basic conditions of the *same house*, of the human situation, rather than focusing his attention exclusively on interpretations of it. Wisdom's suggestion of a garden as the arena in which the religious debate occurs is, perhaps, appropriate in a sense he did not intend.

Let me conclude this chapter by referring to the three elephants of its title and using them to stress some simple (but important) points which Cipher must bear in mind and carry forward with him as he continues in the hall of mirrors.

The first elephant is brought on by the question, "Can those who have examined such a creature only through a microscope claim to understand it properly?" One reply is, of course, to toss the query back and ask if those who relied solely on the unaided naked eye could claim any greatly superior understanding. Indeed, many morals could be drawn from this question and the replies which can be made to it. The lesson for Cipher, though, is quite straightforward: it is more important for him to deal with the naked-eye perspective on religion before reaching for his microscope. This is to re-emphasize the point that the urgency of his quest should not allow itself to be side-tracked or submerged beneath the specialist intricacies towards which a descriptive, phenomenological approach inevitably tends. Cipher would do well to reflect on the point made by William Paden in his excellent book *Interpreting the Sacred*. Considering the different "interpretive lenses" offered by sociologists, psychologists, anthropologists, philosophers and others when it comes to looking at religion, Paden suggests that acknowledging this range of viewpoints helps to underscore an important principle, namely that:

> there is an intimate relationship between the way we look at the world and what it is we see going on there. As an axiom has it, 'the scale creates the phenomenon.' To look through a microscope is to create a certain order of data and exclude other kinds, and the same is true for looking at the world through the characters of Shakespeare's plays. Our 'instruments' determine what will count as 'objects' in the world. Our frames are built to detect galaxies or micro-organisms, but ordinarily not both.[32]

Cipher needs to ensure that any procedures used in his exploration of the hall of mirrors are framed by the desire to reach a world decision. If his focus is to be kept on *making a decision about commitment*, then he must remember, going back to the passage about Sherlock Holmes which was quoted in Chapter 4, that much of what occurs on the microscopic level —although of considerable interest to scholars—will not make "a pennyworth of difference" to his quest for peace of mind. Although a naked-eye perspective may be accused of being too simple, or even superficial, its range of concerns seems far more appropriate to Cipher's situation in the hall of mirrors than those which would be raised by a microscopic focus.

The second elephant is introduced by an ancient Eastern story which has become quite well known in the West, particularly in theological circles, where it has percolated through one wonders what channels of inter-cultural communication to appear in the writings of Hans Küng and John Hick.[33] It is the story about the three blind men who are given the task of finding out what an elephant is like. On reporting back their various tactile sensations—for, perhaps improbably, the elephant let them touch it—one says, "It's like a snake," the second, "It's like a wall," and the third, "It's like a tree trunk." Their reports (which, incidentally, illustrate the importance of comparison in apprehending something new, highlighting again the cognitive centrality of metaphor) differ so greatly because one had caught hold of the elephant's tail, the other had placed his hands on its side, and the third had grasped one of its legs. (A recent variation of this story circulating on the Internet has three blind elephants trying to establish what a human being is. "Very flat," is their unanimous conclusion.)

One lesson which might be drawn from such a story is that any attempt which approximates to a survey of the religions of the world, undertaken with the intention of establishing which one is best, may be wholly misguided in what it is trying to do. This kind of simplistic, competition-type approach, in which a champion is thought to have emerged after all other competitors have been bludgeoned from the ring by a sustained critical onslaught, is, one hopes, a dying sport anyway; but reminders of its inappropriateness are useful, nonetheless, given that Cipher is concerned with evaluation in a religiously plural context. As we see an increasing number of points of similarity between them, the idea of making Hinduism, Buddhism, Judaism, Christianity, Islam and so on into sparring partners, let alone competitors in some sort of fight to the death, seems more and more grotesque. Such an exercise is surely based on placing too much faith in blind men's reports, assuming that there are several different elephants rather than a single beast. As it would be a bizarre endeavor to try to select which part of the elephant in the story was "best," so too it might be similarly misguided to try to elevate any single religious tradition to a position of victorious preeminence. Of course, as John Hick points out, the parable of the blind men and the elephant is only effective in conveying such a warning if we are in a position to see the whole elephant and realize that it is, in fact, a single beast. This is precisely the perspective which is lacking when it comes to our view of religions. So, any lesson drawn from the story must be a tentative and provisional one.

The third and final elephant is the one which occurs in Haribhadra's famous story of *Samaraditya*, an ancient Jain parable (though Hindu versions are also known) which has reached the Western consciousness largely via Tolstoy's *Confessions*, and William James' extensive citing of Tolstoy in *The Varieties of Religious Experience*.[34] The story tells of a man wandering lost in a forest. Suddenly a mad elephant appears out of nowhere and charges him. He flees in terror towards a huge banyan tree, but finds to his dismay that there are no branches near enough the ground to allow him to climb up to safety. At the foot of the tree, though, there is an old well, and in desperation the man jumps into it. As he falls, he reaches out and grabs hold of a clump of vegetation growing from the side of the well. As he clings to it he begins to take in his new surroundings, while above, the mad elephant charges against the tree. Looking below he sees that the well is occupied by a giant serpent, which needs only to wait for him to fall, for two mice—one white, the other black—are gnawing in turn at the stem of the plant to which he hangs. Eventually the elephant's charging dislodges a bees' nest from the overhanging branches of the tree. The nest falls into the well and the man is badly stung. However, some drops of honey trickle into his mouth and its taste of sweetness allows him, momentarily, to forget about the perils which surround him on all sides.

The story is dense with imagery and I have given a considerably simplified version. It can be read in many different ways: some see it simply as an illustration of the inevitable and unavoidable nature of pain and death, others of the way in which pleasure can cloud our vision—either mercifully or fatally, depending on whether there is any possibility of escape. One interpretation which could be offered casts both elephant and serpent as personifications of death, which no one can avoid indefinitely, while the banyan tree represents the salvific potential offered by religion (i.e. representing peace of mind, world certainty, ultimate security). The white mouse symbolizes day, the black one night. Together, as the flow of time, they eat their way through every individual's life-span. The story is a powerful statement of the massive religious sense of something wrong with the world, to which attention was drawn earlier in this chapter. It sees the fundamental elements of the *same house*, of the human situation, as something desperately in need of a curative, sense-giving, security-offering response, *not* as something which is self-sufficient in terms of meaning. To accommodate Cipher's situation of perceived religious plurality, we would have to imagine that the well was ringed with many different trees, not just overhung by a single banyan. The dilemma he faces involves deciding which, if any, offers legitimate security. Commitment would involve the difficult and strenuous process of clambering out of the well and into its branches.

At the end of the day, the most fundamental question facing Cipher is a twofold one: first, whether to accept as accurate a religious diagnosis of the precarious and unpleasant position involved in the religiously unaided human situation; second, whether there is, in fact, a genuine possibility of salvation from it. The question of choice, set amidst a variety of purported salvific resources, is very much secondary to deciding if such resources are necessary in the first place. If he rejects either the basic religious diagnosis of something wrong with the world, in the sense of its needing reference to some kind of transcendent state or entity to ensure peace of mind, or if he rejects the possibility of there being any peace of mind in this sense, then the chances are that he will just concentrate on enjoying as much honey as he can for as long as possible. If he accepts a religious reading of the human situation, seeing it as futile unless reference is made to some sense-giving transcendent entity or state such as God or Nirvana, and if he accepts that such expressions of transcendence which claim to bring the human situation into meaningful focus are more than just illusions, he might, perhaps, conclude that the well is a precarious place from which to conduct his inquiries. Maybe his first task is to get to the safety of tree level, from where he may then start to look around. Such a strategy, which might usefully have been commended to Buridan's ass (the proverbial beast of indecision which died of hunger because it could not choose between two equidistant and equally appealing sources of food[35]), would, of course, risk ascending in the wrong direction, but perhaps that is a lesser gamble than remaining uncommitted for too long. Or, to take a rather more

flattering point of comparison than an ass, Cipher's situation may perhaps be one in which he might want to put into play some sort of Pascalian
wager—arguing that making a world decision, even if it turns out to be
mistaken, may be preferable to remaining forever undecided.[36]

Jacob Needleman offers another metaphor which underlines how
unsatisfactory it would be to view all the trees from the well for too
long. It also usefully reiterates the religious sense of something wrong
with the world. His comments are made in the context of noting the
absence in many contemporary Western forms of religion of an instrumental dimension, but the image can very easily be transferred to Cipher's
situation:

> It is as though millions of people suffering from a painful disease
> were to gather together to hear someone read a textbook of medical
> treatment in which the means necessary to cure their disease were
> carefully spelled out. It is as though they were all to take great com-
> fort in that book and in what they heard, going through their lives
> knowing that their disease could be cured, quoting passages to their
> friends, preaching the wonders of this great book, and returning to
> their congregation from time to time to hear more of the inspiring
> diagnosis and treatment read to them. meanwhile, of course, the
> disease worsens and they eventually die of it, smiling in grateful
> hope as on their deathbed someone reads to them yet another pas-
> sage from the text. Perhaps for some, a troubling thought crosses
> their minds as their eyes close for the last time, "Haven't I forgotten
> something? Something important? Haven't I forgotten actually to
> undergo treatment?[37]

For Cipher, of course, it is not just a case of one curative book. In the
hall of mirrors he has access to many. At least the crazed patients in
Needleman's image know where the cure is located, even if, for whatever
bizarre reasons, they forget about actually taking it. Although Cipher's
situation is considerably more complex, he too is under pressure of time
to choose a cure and take it.

Notes

1. Michael Novak, *Ascent of the Mountain, Flight of the Dove: An Invitation to Religious Studies*, New York, 1978, (1971), Harper & Row, pp. 11-12.
2. M. F. C. Bourdillon and Meyer Fortes (eds.), *Sacrifice*, London, 1980, Academic Press, p. xviii note 2.
3. Aldous Huxley, *Those Barren Leaves*, Harmondsworth, 1967, (1925), Penguin, p. 288.
4. Winston L. King, *Introduction to Religion: a Phenomenological Approach*, New York, 1968, (this is a revised edition of King's *Introduction to Religion*, first published in 1954) Harper & Row, p. 22. My emphasis.
5. William Ernest Hocking, *The Meaning of God in Human Experience*, New Haven, 1928, (1912), Yale University Press, pp. 238-239.
6. Ernest Becker, *The Denial of Death*, New York, 1973, The Free Press, pp. 27 & 87 (see also pp. 59-60).
7. Huston Smith, *The Purposes of Higher Education*, p. 1.
8. Cipher may find some useful leads towards answering this question in Russell T. McCutcheon's, "The Category 'Religion' in Recent Publications: a Critical Survey," *Numen*, Vol. 42 (1995), pp. 284-309.
9. R. S. Lee on p. 7 of his Introduction to Paul Pruyser's *Between Belief and Unbelief*, London, 1975, (1974), Sheldon Press.
10. James Haughton Woods, *The Value of Religious Facts*, p. 109.
11. M. K. Gandhi, *An Autobiography: The Story of My Experiments with Truth*, London, 1972, (1949), Cape, tr. Mahadev Desai, p. 60.
12. Ibid., p. 102.
13. Mircea Eliade, *No Souvenirs*, p. 267.
14. R. C. Zaehner (ed.), *The Concise Encyclopedia of Living Faiths*, London, 1971, (1959), Hutchinson, p. xxi.
15. Stanley Samartha, "The Lordship of Jesus Christ and Religious Pluralism," in Gerald H. Anderson and Thomas F. Stransky (eds.), *Christ's Lordship and Religious Pluralism*, p. 35.
16. Edward Hulmes, *Commitment and Neutrality in Religious Education*, London, 1979, Geoffrey Chapman, p. 103.
17. William Barrett, *Irrational Man: A Study in Existential Philosophy*, Connecticut, 1977, (1958), Greenwood Press, p. 5.
18. Ibid., p. 6.
19. Ibid., p. 5. Mircea Eliade, in terms very similar to Barrett's, draws our attention to the way in which specialization tends to obscure the sense of vocation which draws many to the study of religions: "The present situation amounts to this: there has been a great advance in our knowl-

edge of the material, which has been won at the cost of excessive specialization, to the point of partly sacrificing our vocation." ("Psychology and Comparative Religion: A Study of the Symbolism of the Centre," in Cecily Hastings and Donald Nicholl (eds.) *Selection II*, London, Sheed & Ward, 1954, p. 19).

20. R. G. Collingwood, *Speculum Mentis, or the Map of Knowledge*, Oxford, 1956, (1924), Oxford University Press, p. 15.

21. Harvey Cox, *The Seduction of the Spirit: The Use and Misuse of People's Religion*, New York, 1973, Simon & Schuster, p.105.

22. Ibid.

23. Marshall Mcluhan, *Understanding Media: The Extensions of Man*, London, 1987 (1964), Ark, p.124.

24. John Bowker, *The Sense of God*, p. 75.

25. Edwin Muir, "The Child Dying," p. 67 in Edwin Muir, *Selected Poems*, ed. T. S. Eliot, London 1969, (1965), Faber.

26. R. W. Hepburn, *Christianity and Paradox*, London, 1966, (1953), Watts & Co., p. 200.

27. Rudolf Otto, *The Idea of the Holy*, pp. 72 and 155.

28. Ninian Smart, *Beyond Ideology*, p. 42.

29. David Hay, *Exploring Inner Space*, p. 198.

30. Ibid.

31. Aldous Huxley, *Brave New World*, Harmondsworth, 1970, (1932), Penguin, p. 183.

32. William E. Paden, *Interpreting the Sacred: Ways of Viewing Religion*, Boston, 1992, Beacon Press, p. 4. Given my use of elephants as metaphorical beasts of burden, it is perhaps also worth drawing attention to Paden's remark on p. x that, "An elephant will be seen differently by a zoologist, a conservationist, a circus manager, and another elephant. We may be interested in only its social patterns, its geographic diffusion, its commercial value, or the physiology of its liver. An elephant is an object for poachers and it is an object of wonder and beauty. Ultimately it is part of the mystery of existence itself."

33. See Hans Küng, *Does God Exist?* London, 1980, (1978), Collins, p. 607, and John Hick, "Religious Pluralism," in Frank Whaling (ed.) *The World's Religious Traditions: Current Perspectives in Religious Studies, Essays in Honour of Wilfred Cantwell Smith*, Edinburgh, 1984, T & T Clark, p. 156.

34. The relevant passage from Haribhadra's *Story of Samaraditya* (2.55-80) is reprinted in translation in Wm. Theodore de Bary (ed.), *Sources of Indian Tradition*, Vol. 1 pp. 53-55; Tolstoy recounts this "oriental fable"

in Chapter 4 of his *My Confession*; William James cites Tolstoy in *The Varieties of Religious Experience*, when he deals in lectures 6 and 7 with the "sick souled" outlook (pp. 159-161 in the 1974 Fontana paperback edition).

35. The image of an ass dying of starvation through indecision between two equally attractive sources of food, is attributed (on somewhat dubious grounds) to the 14th century French schoolman, Jean Buridan.

36. Cipher's situation is not the same as that of Pascal. However, he will surely find some interesting points of resonance in the jottings of this great French thinker. Consider the following comments (from Pascal's, *Pensées*, Harmondsworth, 1966, Penguin, translated by A.J. Krailsheimer, pp 150-151):

> If there is a God, he is infinitely beyond our comprehension, since, being indivisible and without limits, he bears no relation to us. We are therefore incapable of knowing either what he is or whether he is. That being so, who would dare to attempt to answer the question?... 'Either God is or he is not.' But to which view shall we be inclined? Reason cannot decide this question. Infinite chaos separates us. At the far end of this infinite distance a coin is being spun which will come down heads or tails. How will you wager? Reason cannot make you choose either, reason cannot prove either wrong....Yes, but you must wager. There is no choice, you are already committed. Which will you choose then? Let us see: since a choice must be made, let us see which offers the least interest. You have two things to lose: the true and the good; and two things to stake: your reason and your will, your knowledge and your happiness; and your nature has two things to avoid: error and wretchedness. Since you must necessarily choose, your reason is no more affronted by choosing one rather than the other. That is one point cleared up. But your happiness? Let us weigh up the gain and the loss involved in calling heads that God exists. Let us assess the two cases: if you win you win everything, if you lose you lose nothing. Do not hesitate then; wager that he does exist.

37. Jacob Needleman, *The New Religions*, New York 1977 (1970), E. P. Dutton & Co., pp. 16-17.

CHAPTER 10

A SENSE OF TIMING

THE FOCUS of this book has been on how an individual might respond to being aware of there being many different religious outlooks on the world. But we should not forget that this is a situation that has much wider implications too. Given the enormous social and political consequences implicit in a religiously plural setting, it is a matter for concern that education rarely seems well geared to attuning those in its charge even to the basic facts about such a setting, let alone the questions it poses. Diana Eck, assessing the level of religious literacy in America, talks about how little we "understand one another and how much our mutual perception is shaped by common stereotypes."[1] This is hardly surprising when "every high school graduate is required to dissect a frog, but every high school graduate is not required to know something about Islam—the religion of a fifth of humankind."[2] The situation in Europe is similar. Islam may be given rather more attention because of the increasingly visible presence of large Muslim communities in Britain, France, Germany and other countries, but the subject of religion is, as a rule, allowed only a minimal place on the school curriculum. And in many universities, religion does not feature as an area of academic study at all. These are curious omissions given the huge importance of religion in human affairs (a nonnegotiable fact of history, no matter what one's own religious stance may be). Buddhism is perhaps the world religion that, in a British context, tends to receive least attention in the classroom. Yet it is, like Islam, a phenomenon of planetary significance. It is a system of values and beliefs which has played, and continues to play, a hugely formative role in the way in which people have lived. Indeed in *Buddhism, a History*, Noble Ross Reat suggests, with considerable plausibility, that Buddhism "has directly or indirectly touched more human lives than any other religion or ideology in history."[3] As such, it is surely of the same order of ignorance for someone to leave school not knowing the basics of Buddhist teaching as it would be for them to leave not knowing where the Atlantic and Pacific Oceans are. This is just to point, very briefly, to the important area beyond Cipher's engagement with pluralism. Religious studies has a powerful mandate for its work. It is a pity it is not given more opportunity to put it into practice.

There are all kinds of ways of picturing our current experience of religious pluralism, and it is something of sufficient importance, both individually and socially, to make the working through of as many models and metaphors as possible a worthwhile activity. Different images have subtly different resonances and can help to cast light on the different perspectives of this complex and novel situation. In the preceding chapters I have explored it via the hall of mirrors and other metaphors, looking through the eyes of Cipher at the way in which our experience of religious pluralism can be likened to finding oneself surrounded by a multitude of reflections, each purporting to picture the way things really are and the way in which we ought to live our lives. The possibilities of these metaphors have by no means been exhausted, and I hope they will continue to suggest fruitful ways of mapping our encounter with religious pluralism. However, to conclude, I want to shift gear and consider how another metaphor might be brought into play to reiterate some of Cipher's problems and provide an opportunity to look at them through a different lens. It is a metaphor which also underscores the fact that Cipher's time is limited. His situation is not one in which endless inquiry would be an appropriate response. As we have seen, his desire for a world decision is a matter of considerable urgency (and this sense of urgency is likely to be increased the more he comes to grips with the situation).

The sense of timing metaphor is derived from a remark of the Czech poet and scientist Miroslav Holub. Commenting on translation, Holub said:

> I don't feel good about two or more translations of a single poem. It's like the man who always knew the exact time when he had just one watch, but from the moment that he had two watches he never knew what time it was.[4]

Whatever its value may be as an insight into the problems and possibilities of translating poetry, Holub's comment suggests another way of seeing some of the implications of religious pluralism. For the very different situations which he envisages for the man with one watch and the man with two, can provide a way of looking at Cipher's situation in the hall of mirrors from a slightly different angle. Time seems to be a particularly apt point of metaphorical reference given its religious significance. Religions keep their fingers firmly on the pulse of our finitude, their touch a reminder of the framing fact of death, so easily forgotten in our preoccupation with the "baked beans, bread and potato crisps" of the present moment. Religious senses of time act as correctives to mundane senses of duration, in which ultimate perspectives may be hidden beneath a preoccupation with the little urgencies of everyday life. Whether or not such religious senses of time are accurate, whether we should time our lives by the ethical, ontological, metaphysical and other chronologies they suggest, is, of course, at the root of Cipher's dilemma.[5]

As I have suggested earlier, for much of recorded history, individuals have been raised pretty much in the unchallenged singularity of one faith, and have had, in consequence, a strong tendency to believe with the same sort of unquestioning certitude which Holub allows to the man with only one watch. There are still, it should be stressed again, situations in the world today in which such singularity and certainty characterize the social, religious and educational milieu in which people grow up. As we move into the 21st century, though, such milieus seem radically out of tune with the emergent global zeitgeist. The image of the mono-religious individual enjoying unquestioning allegiance to a single outlook on the world may soon be an image only of the past. It is an image which has some claim to accuracy as a generalization, but I would not wish to advance it as an unbreakable universal rule. After all, even within apparently single faith traditions there are likely to be competing outlooks and interpretations. Individual currents of doubt, hope, speculation, rebellion, and so on, ripple through commitment, subtly altering its contours—sometimes reinforcing, sometimes challenging, officially sanctioned time-keeping. The main value of the one-watch/one-religion parallel lies not so much in its suggestion that certainty is the invariable concomitant of singularity as in its highlighting of the quite enormous differences which exist between a situation where we have access to what is essentially only one reading of the world and a situation where there is more than one alternative. The scale and nature of the differences between these two situations, as they relate to religion, is radical. We must remember that Cipher is living in a religiously revolutionary era (a point I tried to emphasize in Chapter 1). In such an era, as Martin Prozesky has remarked, "much of our traditional spiritual cartography is obsolete, of no more use in mapping the paths to heaven than Ptolemy's cosmology could guide Mariner to Mars."[6] Given the scale of change which is evident when we compare our religious consciousness with that of previous generations, it is clear that we need new ways of addressing this area of our experience. When topographies undergo significant change, it is foolish to expect traditional maps and modes of transport to retain their original usefulness. The religious landscape which Cipher inhabits would be virtually unrecognizable to those in earlier periods of history. This needs to be borne clearly in mind when we are searching for elucidating metaphors.

Just as an individual who has access to many watches may find their sense of time becoming undermined and filled with doubt and uncertainty, so someone faced with many different religious outlooks on the world may not know what sense, ultimately, to accord to their experiences. One's religion was once a given, something largely determined simply by the accident of birth. It is only comparatively recently that we have come to live in a situation where, increasingly, we are confronted by a range of different faiths. Such a situation, as Peter Berger has pointed out, "not only allows the individual a choice, it *forces* him to choose"[7] and, by the same token, "religious certainty is very hard to come by."[8] What Berger says here is tailor-made for Cipher. He does not choose to be in a situation of choice, it is, rather, dictated by his situation. And the certainty he is seeking, by which his puzzlement might be resolved, is extremely difficult to establish. That difficulty notwithstanding, the situation insistently demands that he try to find some sort of resolution.

Faced, like Cipher, with many religious "watches," each showing different "times," one could proceed in a variety of ways. Let me identify five possible responses which might be thought to resolve the situation, and then explain briefly why I think they are all inadequate.

1. One might reject them all and adopt some non-religious point of view. This is a popular strategy and it is important to recognize that its implementation is followed not just by those who consciously see themselves as atheists, agnostics, secular humanists or devotees of some other non-transcendent ideology. Many people describe themselves in such a way as to suggest that they follow some religion, that they have made a world decision of the sort which Cipher longs to make and, as a result, are Buddhists, Christians, Hindus, Jews, Muslims, Sikhs. But their lives may well suggest that their allegiance in fact lies elsewhere. Michael Warren has shown that if we want to establish what "clock" people *really* set their timing by, then we need to examine life-structure rather than verbal claim, what they *do* as well as what they say. Should we find, as he suspects, that in many cases "the images controlling the imaginations of persons who like to call themselves religious" are in fact "the irreligious images of competition or even of violent domination"[9] (which are so prevalent in society), then we will have learned an important lesson. Many people wear watches which have stopped long ago; they now pace and plot their purposes according to quite different senses of timing. Whether we deliberately reject Buddhism, Christianity, Hinduism, Islam, Judaism or Sikhism in favor of a carefully worked out position of scientific humanism, or simply turn off from the effort of

thinking about religious issues, watch TV and indulge in an unreflective consumer lifestyle, the first inadequate response to a situation of multiple outlooks involves rejecting all the religious "watches" and looking elsewhere for our sense of timing (however self-conscious or passive such a looking may be), i.e. looking exclusively to non-religious sources (of whatever degree of intellectual rigor or moral worth) for fundamental orientation and meaning, for the way in which we actually live our lives.

2. Far from rejecting all the religious watches, one could go to the other extreme and attempt to accept them all. This strategy for resolution relies on establishing some sense in which, despite their many apparent differences, all the religious "watches" are in fact saying the same thing, that their teachings can somehow be interpreted in ways which will bring them into some sort of harmonious alignment. At the end of the day, according to this kind of view, the different watches actually agree about what time it is. Any differences between them are only superficial and can be discounted by referring to their shared fundamental commonality.

3. One could elevate one's own religion to a position of primacy (on account, say, of some special revelation which is felt to establish its superiority). This strategy subordinates other senses of timing to one's own and views them as mistaken, irrelevant or inferior.

4. One might attempt to divide the world into different religious time zones and set one's life-clock according to wherever one happens to be.

5. One might deny that the different religions are in fact addressing the same questions. Far from being faced with a variety of watches, there are watches, altimeters, barometers, compasses and so on. We are not confronted with competing answers to one set of questions but with diverse responses to a whole variety of subjects.

These possible strategies for resolving a situation of pluralism might be caricatured by the following identifying slogans: "they're all wrong;" "they're all right;" "only my watch tells the right time;" "it depends on where you are;" "they are not all watches." The inadequacy of each should, I think, be clear, and for sufficiently commonsensical reasons that their refutation need not detain us for long. To assume that all the religions are wrong is to pass sweeping judgment over a staggering scale of phenomena. It is one thing to doubt the existence of an all-good, all-powerful, all-loving creator deity on the basis of the fact that evil exists, quite something else to reject religion *in toto* on account of this kind of single premise. Could we ever realistically claim to be in such a position of complete informedness and understanding that such a blanket rejection could be safely issued? Religions are sufficiently numerous, complex, diverse and extensive as to suggest that any heroic dismissal of them lock stock and barrel is, at the very least, likely to be naive. More specific, targeted rejections, focused on particular aspects of religious teaching, have a much higher order of credibility.

To assume that they are all right depends on being able to establish that essentially they are all the same, which would be extremely hard to square with appearances. Although the moral codes of Buddhism, Christianity, Hinduism, Islam, Judaism and Sikhism have very significant areas of overlap, their ontologies seem to have equally significant areas of divergence. How can the oneness of Atman and Brahman claimed by Hindus be reconciled with the otherness of God which Muslims see as of paramount importance? Is it possible to equate the centrality of *dukkha* in the Buddhist world-view with the Christian concept of a loving creator God? How can Jewish, Christian and Islamic understandings of the status of Jesus be smoothed over to make assertions of his divinity and humanity somehow "the same?" Could Hindu and Buddhist views on the authority of the Vedas ever be brought into harmony? How could the universal operation of the law of karma and the existence of an omnipotent deity be squared?

To insist that only one's own watch tells the right time involves a similarly ambitious scale of judgment as that involved in wholesale rejection. It would also need to establish why an argument for the singular correctness of any particular faith might not simply be transferred according to the allegiance of each individual. If Christians argue that their watch alone is correct, Jews that Judaism is right, Buddhists that

Buddhism is right and so on, have we really got anywhere beyond legitimating a form of indigenous favoritism whose crudely partisan nature can have little claim to theological seriousness?

Relativism might work for local religions but is immediately called into question by the universalism of the great world faiths. Moreover, given the number and diversity of religions now found in many parts of the world, such regional relativism might be hard put to know how to proceed. Most major cities now seem to contain multiple religious time zones rather than just one.

The fifth inadequate response, suggesting that the different religions are in fact concerned with different issues, would involve an ignoring of similarities which would be as difficult to justify as the "they're all the same" approach's ignoring of differences. There are clearly certain fundamental issues which all the religions address, and it is their differing outlooks on these issues that constitutes the problem.

※

In a moment, I want to sketch out some further metaphors which may help to suggest a range of more adequate responses. First, though, it is perhaps worth bringing to mind again the way in which reaching any decisions about religious pluralism may be more or less endlessly postponed. If Cipher were to make religions an area of academic inquiry, a subject to study, rather than a situation of life-changing choice, it would be relatively easy for him to ignore one of their most fundamental features, namely the fact that they are recommending particular ways of living in, and looking at, the world. Such ways invite us to join them. The great world religions are not merely an interesting collection of archaic time-pieces, but a series of deadly serious reckonings, measurements of life by reference to which people navigate their various routes through time and space. While it is, obviously, important to know something about the measurements they offer before making any decisions about their reliability, it becomes suspect if we endlessly put off making such decisions in order to gather yet more information. To do so is to imply that we are somehow uninvolved in the situation which religions address; that we are immune to time and exempt from the anxieties which its finiteness creates; that we are only interested in the varieties of watches around us, their different design, mechanism and so on, but do not want to know what the right time is. In terms of my Holub-derived metaphor, the modern study of religion, through its elevation of impartiality to a methodological norm, forbids its practitioners from offering an opinion as to which, if any, religious "watch" is accurate. While it is quite proper to bracket out evaluation in the course of conducting one's inquiry, as we have seen in looking at Cipher's passing over, if that bracketing hardens into permanence and acts to stop questions of truth and commitment from *ever* being raised, then we surely risk denying not only the nature of religion, but also the nature of our own impulses as human beings. Do we not all need some sense of timing to live by (whether it is religious or not)?

John Staudenmaier has drawn attention to the religious impact of nineteenth century standardization and uniformity. What Staudenmaier memorably describes as a "savage lust for order,"[10] far from flowing neatly in those channels of purely technological history where it had its origins, gradually became a more widespread cultural force with serious religious consequences. He observes that "while instrument makers revolutionized the world of precision measurement and quantitative analysis, religious and cultural leaders began to read the holy dark out of the Western canon."[11] Just as "factory masters tried to enforce precisely defined work rules, the church gradually turned to similarly detailed codes of law and doctrine."[12] Staudenmaier's reflections raise important questions about the extent to which assumptions about precision and detail, which control so much of modern intellectual life, are, in fact, appropriate when it comes to making a world decision. To what extent are they simply unnoticed intellectual imports which have passed from technology into more widespread currency without the quarantine of critical scrutiny? Is there not a risk that the burden of goodness has been dumped by the waysides of the ever narrower roads of specialization that we follow? His comment about the holy dark being read out of the western canon is, of course, strongly reminiscent of Rudolf Otto's concern that an overly rational approach threatens the "real innermost core"[13] of religion. Is the ambiguous, mysterious, paradoxical nature of the numinous something that can be properly evaluated by the logical analysis of an academic approach?

Particularly relevant to my use of Holub's metaphor, though, is a point which Staudenmaier makes specifically about time. "Public clocks," he reminds us, "long showed only one hand, the hour, but not the minute."[14] It was only in the eighteenth century, when improved techniques allowed much greater accuracy, that minute hands became the norm. Some aspects of the contemporary academic approach seem intent on the measurement of religious microseconds (if not nanoseconds). But do we really need to have such painstaking detail in order to make a world decision? Certainly in terms of establishing what time it is according to the great faiths and whether we should set our own life-clocks by their readings, the hour hand alone, so to speak, often seems sufficient. Taken too far, the quest for detail can become a dangerous grail which may prevent our reaching a spiritually worthwhile destination. Needless to say, this is not to advocate ignorance (which, particularly in the religious realm, exacts its own terrible price). It is merely to suggest that the balance between inquiry and evaluation, detail and decision, needs to be kept under very careful review. After all, measured on the scale of finitude, none of us has time for endless inquiry. On such a scale, much of the detail which preoccupies scholars may seem of very little relevance, and their insistence on personal non-involvement and objectivity may seem misplaced.[15] While Cipher will draw on the work of scholars who study religion, his quest and theirs, as we have seen, are attuned to different goals. It is important that he does not forget this and get drawn into becoming a "walking dictionary for others," lost in the endless information and commentation which the Zen monk's mother warned her son about (in the passage from *Zen Flesh, Zen Bones* which I quoted at the end of Chapter 4). Perhaps Cipher should keep in mind the Buddha's story about the man hit by a poisoned arrow. The scholarly approach to religion may adopt the same pace and priority as this unfortunate individual, examining the quills and wondering what sort of bird they came from, looking at the shaft and trying to work out what species of tree provided the wood, trying to get clear in his mind about the likely variety of bow from which the arrow was fired, analyzing possible identities for the assailant, and so on (needless to say, the man dies). But the imperatives of Cipher's situation demand that he should move at an altogether swifter tempo and to a different set of priorities. His primary concern is to pull the arrow out.[16]

It is perilously easy to allow ourselves to be carried along uncritically by the strong conceptual current which flows within any effective metaphor. Holub's is no exception. In this case it flows in the direction of assuming that the situation is a problematic one which requires us to come up with a clear-cut judgment about correctness, a judgment which involves deciding that one watch shows the right time, that it is synchronized properly to the way things really are, while the others are all variously in error. (Cipher has been swept along by a conceptually similar current in the hall of mirrors.) Instead of seeing a diversity of different religious outlooks as being something intractably problematic, though, could we not view it in much more positive terms, as something replete with potential? Instead of accepting the denial of diversity implied by the assumption that there is only one right answer, could we not envisage a situation where diversity would be welcomed? Must we assume that a plurality of outlooks inevitably poses the kind of question whose answer will involve most of the elements of that plurality being condemned as mistaken? Instead of following Holub and seeing the person with several translations of a poem as someone facing a problem which needs to be solved, could we not see them as experiencing a far more richly textured appreciation of the poem in question than someone with access to only a single translation? (Just as someone aware of the work of many poets would be likely to be better resourced poeti-

cally than someone with exposure to only one.) Being surrounded by
an array of watches all showing a different time may seem to be pressingly perplexing. But it might also remind us that time is viewed very
differently by different people in different situations. The way in which
a seven year old and a seventy year old view an hour, a day, a week, the
way in which time passes between lovers and between torturers and
their victims, between the joyful and the despairing, is surely indicative
of the very different senses of timing which we experience. The time
needed to read this book, time spent with friends, asleep, on holiday,
visiting a dying relative, historical time, geological time, the age of the
universe and the time it takes a mayfly to complete its life-cycle—such
diverse measurements surely caution against the imposition of some
sort of crudely clear-cut singularity. Likewise, if we are surrounded by a
range of religious world-views telling us "what time it is" (i.e. offering
various views on the nature of the human condition) it may be tempting to assume that we must find some single right answer. But does
such an imperative not invite an impoverishment quite out of keeping
with the scale and complexity of the situation that the religions address? Is it really appropriate to look for one right answer which quali-
fies all the rest as inferior to it? Might this not offer constraint rather
than certainty?

In the history of any religion there are many things which are highly
negative, wholly mistaken, tragically unfortunate, in terms of the way
in which they have blighted people's lives. This is a continuing and
current problem. But such criticisms notwithstanding, would we hon-
estly wish to argue that, at this juncture in history, from a spiritual
point of view, we would be better served if, instead of the diverse wealth
of faiths which have existed and which continue to thrive, everyone had
access to only one type? To continue the logic of such a position, this
would mean only one variety of faith within each of the great religions,
only one scripture, only one interpretation of its meaning. Cipher may
feel perplexed and lost, eager to find the sort of peace of mind which
religions seem to offer, but no matter how troubled he may feel as he
wanders the hall of mirrors looking for world certainty, would he prefer

to have opted for the kind of radical singularity which this kind of monistic reduction would inevitably result in? If he is "one of those men who torment themselves trying to discover the meaning of existence," to go back to the description of him which I borrowed from P. D. James' philosophical policemen, if he is someone who thinks deeply about life, who has "remembered death" amidst the baked beans, bread and potato crisps, then the answer would surely be a resounding no. Even though pluralism may be problematic, it carries with it an enormous resonance of richness. To have Cipher choose the relative impoverishment of a mono-religious situation in preference to it would seem entirely out of character. (This would be rather like his preferring monochrome to color vision.)

Whatever our sense of timing may be, does the manner of our allegiance to it doom other such senses to extinction? If we advocate a singular point of view which responds to pluralism by demanding a simple right answer, do we not risk subscribing to a triumphalist (if not genocidal) theology, which would consign the faith of millions of our fellows to oblivion (and which would ignore the point made in Chapter 1 about the importance of recognizing how differently different people see the world)? Trying to unravel the rich tapestry of human religiousness in order to find one single veridical thread seems likely to leave us perilously exposed to the kind of intolerance that has fueled bigotry and persecution throughout history. Such singularity is surely out of keeping with the globalizing trends which have done (and are still doing) so much to shape our world. Just as the diversity of life within a jungle includes particular organisms that we might prefer not to encounter, so the diversity of religion may likewise encompass points of view which we consider predatory, parasitic or poisonous. Cipher will, alas, have to encounter all of these in his search, otherwise the hall of mirrors would take on a fairy tale quality where everything was dusted with a kind of sugared goodness and happy-ever-after endings. Indeed, to be a realistic reflection of the story of religious difference and diversity, the hall of mirrors would have to, more than occasionally, echo to the sound of breaking glass. And there would be bloodstains and tears on many of the images held by its reflective surfaces. But is it possible, through advocating a policy of unsqueamish tolerance, coupled with respect for individual choice, to allow a place even for what we consider to be mistaken? This is not to advocate the acceptance of error; merely to point out that within any diversity of religious outlooks there are likely to be points of view which will offend us, but that (like bio-diversity) religious diversity offers more potential for spiritual well-being than any mono-religious situation could claim.

I am suggesting, then, that the metaphor derived from Miroslav Holub's image of the man with two watches is, in fact, inappropriate when applied to a situation of religious pluralism. Why introduce a misleading metaphor at such length into a book's final chapter? At one level justification can come simply from stressing a basic feature of metaphors. Namely, the fact that they offer creatively tangential perspectives by looking at one thing in terms of another. But this does not mean that the two things in question are identical. Metaphorical likeness is always off-center, it is never a perfect match. While someone's laughter can be compared to the sound of silver bells, we will soon get into difficulties if we take such an image literally and press the fruitful web of likeness which it offers too hard. All metaphors are to some extent misleading; this does not discredit their educational value (indeed it is what makes them valuable).

The watches/religions metaphor has two main limitations. These can be highly misleading if we fail to see them and highly instructive once we have clearly marked them on our conceptual navigation charts. First, the metaphor automatically builds into the picture it offers the assumption of singular correctness. Choose another metaphor and that assumption disappears. If, for example, we likened the different religions to different gems—the emerald of Islam, the diamond of Buddhism, the ruby of Christianity and so on—the emphasis would be more on personal preference than on any one pre-eminent source of wealth, or on acquiring a range of such precious gemstones to match a range of moods, colors, occasions. Or, if we likened the different religions to an alphabet, the different letters offering a range of combinations with an expressive depth which no single letter could equal, then, again, the current changes and the idea of singular correctness disappears.

Secondly, the watch metaphor makes the assumption that each of the faiths offers a single, simple "time"—that the watch of Buddhism says it's 1015, the watch of Islam says 2300, the watch of Judaism 0714 and so on. But this is to foist on what are massive and diverse systems a singularity which they simply do not possess. Within each faith there may be a measure of agreement about some underlying questions of tempo and duration, but the careful listener will hear a whole range of tickings. The internal pluralism of the world's religions is a feature sometimes overlooked when we start to examine different faith traditions side by side. Yet, according to which aspect of each faith we decide to stress, their senses of timing can appear radically different or almost wholly synchronized.

❧

As Sallie McFague puts it, "human thought and language grow and change by seeing one thing in terms of another: they are intrinsically metaphorical."[17] If we want to understand the revolution in religious consciousness which I outlined in Chapter 1, a revolution which is very much rooted in our new-found awareness of religious pluralism, our thought and language needs to grow. If it is to do so successfully, it will need to find metaphors which fit the situation. What is a situation of being aware of many different religious outlooks actually like? In terms of what parallels should we envisage it? What sorts of comparisons are useful to pursue in order to understand all the different nuances which stem from this complex situation? Is it more like being in a hall of mirrors, or wearing a score of different watches, each showing a different time? Is it like having access to the contents of a vastly varied spiritual wardrobe, or being in a supermarket of beliefs and practices, so that we may put on and take off various garments, fill our spiritual trolleys, at will, as it suits our whim? Are we looking at a rainbow of faiths, the spectrum of colors a fractured part of one ultimately integrated phenomenon, or is it more a case of witnessing not one picture, but a chaos of unrelated brush strokes across the canvas of space and time which seek to color our existence in quite different ways? Does God (if God exists) have many names or only one? And, if many, can they all be called upon with equal hope?[18] Are we, in the hall of mirrors, provided with reflective surfaces at all kinds of heights and angles, so that we can get a series of perspectives on some one thing which no single mirror could provide, or are we looking at reflections of what are essentially different vistas? Has the glass of the different religious mirrors been forged and blown and ground in so many different ways that even the simplest scene will appear radically differently according to which mirror we look in? Are we listening to a whole series of stories which, cumulatively, act to enrich our imagination and insight, which contain many truths which may be useful to us, and where it would be inappropriate to seek to cull everything in this rich narrative hoard except for some one preferred story line, or are we listening to a confused babble of crazed and competing voices which threaten to make inaudible a single truth-telling?[19]

Or might we think of an awareness of religious pluralism as being similar to the situation which the composer Karlheinz Stockhausen describes in his fascinating essay on "world music."[20] Instead of, as in previous periods of history, being confined to a single culture's musical tradition, are we not now in a situation where we have access to a far wider range? As Stockhausen puts it:

> for the first time an earthling can literally encompass the globe
> and become conscious of the simultaneity of all levels of culture,
> the fantastic variety of musical expression and ceremony.[21]

It would be naively optimistic to assume that such a situation would automatically issue in fantastic new music attuned to the ear of the globalization which spawned it. Stockhausen is well aware that musical specialization could be fundamentally undermined by this new consciousness and that this could have a highly detrimental impact on creativity. However, he also points to the possibility that henceforth "the most creative spirits" will "attempt to play in all the registers."[22] This is surely an exciting possibility, both intellectually and spiritually. Cipher is experiencing a situation of cacophony and longs to resolve the confusing din of pluralism into the harmony which a world decision seems to offer. Listening to the music of the different faiths is likely to leave the listener somewhat dazed. But might it not also provide them with a musical resource of astonishing richness in terms of creating new compositions? There is, naturally, the risk of discord, and we should not expect the massively extended repertoire to instantly or easily issue in masterpieces. But it would surely be obtuse not to see the new possibilities which this situation creates.

A similar metaphorical thread to that of Stockhausen's "world music" can be teased out of George Orwell's idea of "Newspeak," as outlined in his novel *Nineteen Eighty Four*.[23] Briefly, Orwell's novel, first published in 1949, envisages a future totalitarian state in which individual freedom is crushed. One of the tactics of the ruling regime in seeking to further tighten their stranglehold on society, comes in the shape of Newspeak. This is publicly presented as an entirely practical, indeed benign phenomenon. Given the unscientific nature of English, why not make it more user-friendly and concise by the introduction of some rules designed to make it more logical? So, instead of the wasteful plethora of words which could be used to describe what is fundamentally a good experience (wonderful, fantastic, amazing, enthralling, *etc.*) why not just build on one root concept? Thus something would be good, plus-good, or double-plus good. Beneath this apparently harmless attempt to make language easier to use, there is a much more sinister purpose. The end goal is to control the vocabulary, and thus the thought, of every citizen. Eventually people will not be able to voice dissent from the government because there will be no words in which that dissent might be expressed. Newspeak, far from being designed just to streamline verbal communication, is designed to control it. The intention is to narrow the range of concepts which people have names for and so to channel and confine the intellect and the imagination. Orwell explains the sinister goal of Newspeak in an appendix to Nineteen Eighty Four:

> The purpose of Newspeak was not only to provide a medium of expression for the world-view and mental habits proper to the devotees of Ingsoc [the Newspeak name for English Socialism], but to make all other modes of thought impossible. It was intended that when Newspeak had been adopted once and for all, a heretical thought—that is, a thought diverging from the principles of Ingsoc—should be literally unthinkable, at least so far as thought is dependent on words.[24]

Far from subtracting from our vocabulary and systematically eroding our range of thought, the experience of the hall of mirrors moves us in the other direction. It could be seen as constituting a kind of Newspeak-in-reverse, offering the potential to think more widely and deeply about religious matters, and to express ourselves in ways that have not hitherto been possible. And just as Orwell's Newspeak is imprisoning, such religious Newspeak-in-reverse might be seen as having an equal and opposite potential for liberation. Of course this is an optimistic simplification which, for Cipher, may well turn out to be more of an unrealizable dream than a present reality. It is, however, a picture which offers a way of looking at the hall of mirrors which does not so much assume that it is a problematic environment which needs to be changed, that it constitutes a question which must be answered, as that it is a situation of much promise, offering the possibility of new ways of thinking altogether. That is not to say that its promise will be easy to realize or comfortable to accept.

This kind of metaphor suggests that the religions of the world might be seen as repositories of ideas, images, insights as rich and varied as the life in a rain forest. As such, perhaps the conservation of religious thinking across a whole spectrum of possibilities—ancient, modern, Eastern, Western, polytheistic, atheistic, Buddhist, Christian, Hindu, Jew, Muslim, Sikh and so on—is as important for the ecology of our spiritual landscapes as the maintenance of species diversity is for the biological environment. As the geneticist Bryan Clarke has proposed, perhaps the existence and importance of biological diversity should prompt us to search "not for the ideal social or political system but for the ideal array of social and political systems."[25] A "polymorphism in our institutions," argues Clarke, would "match the polymorphism in ourselves."[26] Might the extension of diversity into the social and political realms, which Clarke proposes, be extended to include religion too? Rather than thinking of religious pluralism in terms of finding one true faith, might we not see the hall of mirrors situation as something bearing similar value to the biological diversity on which we depend for our well being? Just as the diversity of the natural world offers us enormous potential (aesthetic, technological, medical, *etc.*) is there any reason to suppose that the plurality of religions will not offer a similarly fecund potential for enriching and vivifying the religious imagination? Of course the selection and use of a range of ideas from various points in the history and geography of human religiousness is not something which can be engaged in without encountering some profound and disturbing questions, about ourselves, about the adequacy of our forms of discourse about religion, about the nature of truth. But such questions should not be allowed to abort the search for new ways of understanding our ultimate nature and purpose. Why should Cipher's search for a world decision confine itself to drawing on only one of the many reflective surfaces with which he is surrounded? If that surface itself contains an injunction to look no further than what it offers, or to reject other outlooks as mistaken, perhaps Cipher needs to query the extent to which such exclusive theologies are rooted to an age that is gone and whose insights may therefore be of limited use to him. Their suggested limitations sound rather like trying to deny the permeability of boundaries, even as the diverse waters of influence from other cultures, religions, ideologies, languages, seep into the water-table of our discourse and intermingle inseparably with whatever flows from our own indigenous springs.

Or, as a final suggestion, we could develop John Hick's ideas about utilizing the Buddhist concept of *upaya*, or skilful means, to picture religious pluralism in general.[27] This offers some interesting possibilities (though one would have to be sure that it was not reduced to the fatuous level of saying that the religions are really all the same). Skilful means is "a provisional expedient designed to draw people into the Buddha's dharma."[28] That is, it is a means of teaching in which the message is geared for the particular situation of the audience. The Buddha, or a Bodhisattva, assesses the spiritual condition of the person to whom they are speaking and pitch their message accordingly. As such, skilful means relies on levels of truth. The ultimate truth of the Buddha's insight will not be communicated immediately or directly. Rather, people will be led to it by a series of devices. Anything other than enlightenment itself (which is what, ultimately, is being pointed at) may be seen as being skilful means. The idea behind this concept is epitomized by a story in the third chapter of the Lotus Sutra. This tells of how, to his horrified surprise, a father notices that the house in which his three small children are playing, is on fire. They are so absorbed in their play that they are deaf to warnings and appeals to leave. So the father resorts to other tactics. He promises each child what he knows to be its most desired toy if they will only come out of the house to get it. The children respond to this skilful subterfuge but find when they come out that instead of the promised toy there is something much finer and more valuable waiting for them. The story is taken to represent the way in which the Buddha saves suffering humanity from the burning house of *samsara*. A variety of distinct "Ways" are offered, though in fact, ultimately, there is only one path. Stories like this illustrate "how certain elements in the teachings as a whole are less than ultimately true. However, they are supposed not to be fraudulent, because they are psychologically necessary in the initial stages."[29] Skilful means offers a way of explaining the diversity within Buddhism that is analogous to I. T. Ramsey's ideas about qualifiers (to which reference was made in Chapter 7). Both explanations involve the idea that, ultimately, religion is dealing with something which eludes ordinary expression, in the attempted elucidation of which many models, of various degrees of accuracy and usefulness, are generated. These can be discarded once one gains access to the experiential reality itself (and it is precisely such access that Cipher is seeking). As Hick puts it:

> The notion of *upaya* is, then, the notion that the cosmic signifi-
> cance of the nirvanic experience can be conceptualized in a variety
> of ways all of which communicate the importance and availability
> of the experience, but none of which constitutes the one and only
> correct way of conceptualizing it. These schemes of thought are
> provisional and instrumental, and are to be discarded like the raft
> in the Buddha's parable once they have fulfilled their function.
> Further, there are a number of different conceptual rafts, each of
> which may serve the same purpose, perhaps equally well, for dif-
> ferent people, or even for the same person at different times.[30]

Hick sees skilful means as expressing "a profound insight, excitingly illuminating or deeply disturbing according to one's presuppositions, into the nature of Buddhism, and perhaps also into the nature of religion generally."[31] He develops it into a possible way of picturing religious pluralism, such that:

> the great world traditions constitute different ways of conceiving,
> and therefore of experiencing, and therefore of responding in life
> to the Ultimate. They are thus different forms (each including
> many sub-forms) of *upaya*, skilful means to draw men and women
> from a consuming natural self-concern, with all its attendant sins
> and woes, to a radically different orientation in which they have
> become "transparent" to the universal presence of the ultimate.[32]

Skilful means raises many difficult questions about truth. It is certainly a key concept within Buddhism and provides a way of understanding the huge importance accorded to metaphor and story within this tradition. Whether it can usefully be transferred to a wider setting is less certain, but Hick has certainly provided some interesting leads for further reflection. (And the fact that Hick, a Christian theologian, makes use of this Buddhist concept is, in itself, highly significant.)

In testing these and other metaphors for fit we need to try to ensure that we do not smuggle into our picture of the situation features which are in fact located only in the metaphor. According to which metaphor we choose, the situation in the hall of mirrors can appear competitive, problematic or creative. If we are to reach any kind of understanding of their different dynamics and inevitable limitations, we will have to test them out carefully for fit. But whatever sense (or senses) of timing we may opt for, it is vital to keep in mind the overarching fact that we live at a time of pluralism. Any particular sense of time we wish to set our lives by has to take this fundamental fact into account.

⚭⚮

Finally, it seems appropriate to remember that Cipher is attempting to make headway in a situation in which metaphor ultimately has no purchase. In the end it breaks down and fails. As such, I would like to bring this metaphorical meditation on his plight to a close by highlighting this crucial aspect of religion. It is one which we have already touched on in looking at the way in which Cipher's return to beginnings, his attempt to get to the salamandric heart of the matter, may well bring him face to face with something which defies expression. An incident in Wu Ch'eng-en's *Monkey* underlines the fact that in dealing with religion we seem fundamentally to be dealing with something of this nature. Described by one of its English translators as a blend of "folklore, allegory, religion, history, anti-bureaucratic satire and pure poetry, unique in its combination of beauty with absurdity and profundity with nonsense,"[33] *Monkey* relates the fantastic adventures which befell Tripitaka and his three companions during a pilgrimage to India, an epic journey undertaken to acquire copies of Buddhist scripture. Their journey, like Cipher's, was undertaken in search of a source of religious certainty. Unlike Cipher, though, Tripitaka is based on a real individual, for beneath the richly colorful mythological embellishments, the story draws on the life of Hsuan Tang (600–664), one of the most important of the Chinese pilgrim monks.

After many incredible incidents, Tripitaka, Hsuan Tang's fictional alter ego, finally secures the scrolls of scripture he had set out to find. But, on examination, it turns out that they are completely blank. There "was not a trace of so much as half a letter" on them, they were "snowy white and quite unmarked."[34] Understandably dismayed, Tripitaka appeals to the Buddha for help and is promptly told that "as a matter of fact, it is such blank scrolls as these that are the *true* scriptures."[35] Then, making a somewhat barbed concession to human frailty, the Buddha adds that since the people of China are evidently too ignorant to appreciate this, there is nothing for it but to give Tripitaka some inferior copies covered in writing.[36]

The story provides a good illustration of two powerful currents in human religiousness which flow in opposite conceptual directions. The resulting tension between them has important implications for anyone searching for a way in the hall of mirrors. It shows, first, the common tendency within religions towards silence; the way in which matters of primary importance—God, Brahman, Nirvana, the Tao—tend to be viewed as very difficult, if not impossible, to express in any direct manner, verbal or otherwise. And, secondly, the story illustrates how people usually react against such a tendency, finding it highly unsatisfactory. Most of us are loathe to accept nothingness, emptiness, silence. Like Tripitaka, few would rest content with a blank version of a long sought-for book. The tension between the mysterious silence implicit at the heart of religion and the irrepressible human urge towards communication, is handled differently in different faith-traditions and pulls different cultures and individuals in different directions. The history of religious art and literature tells the complex and unfinished story of its attempted resolution. In whatever way one pictures the relationship between these two aspects of religion, symbolized by blank scrolls on the one hand and written versions on the other, it is at this interface that Cipher is likely to make any world decision he arrives at. What that decision will be, will, however, have to await his putting into practice the principles and procedures which I have tried to outline in the preceding chapters.

Notes

1. Diana Eck, "Challenge of Pluralism," *Nieman Reports*, Vol. XLVII, no. 2 (1993). Quoted from p.9 of the Internet version, at: http://www.fas.harvard.edu/~pluralsm/html/article-cop.html
2. Ibid.
3. Noble Ross Reat, *Buddhism, a History*, Berkeley, 1994, Asian Humanities Press, p.xi.
4. Miroslav Holub, *Poets and Writers*, November/December 1992. As quoted by Dennis O"Driscoll, "Findings," *Poetry Ireland Review*, 37 (1992/3), p.140. I am using Holub's metaphor in a sense he never intended. Criticism of it should therefore not be read as criticism of Holub, a writer for whose work I have a high regard.
5. For a study of different religious senses of time, see Anindita Niyogi Balslev & J. N. Mohanty (ed.), *Religion and Time*, Leiden, 1993, E. J. Brill (Vol. LIV in the Studies in the History of Religions series).
6. Martin Prozesky, *Religion and Ultimate Well-Being: An Explanatory Theory*, London, 1984, Macmillan, p.64.
7. Peter Berger, *The Heretical Imperative*, p.62, my emphasis.
8. Ibid.
9. Michael Warren, *Communications and Cultural Analysis: A Religious View*, London, 1992, Bergin & Garvey, p.18.
10. John Staudenmaier, "The Media: Technique and Culture," in John Coleman and Miklos Tomka (Ed), *Concilium* 1993/6, p.16.
11. Ibid., p.17.
12. Ibid.
13. Rudolf Otto, *The Idea of the Holy*, p. 6.
14. Staudenmaier, op.cit., p.16.
15. Going beyond a critique of neutrality in the study of religion alone, it could be argued that this kind of stance, so prevalent within the Western academic tradition in general, ought not to be considered as the unquestionable *sine qua non* which it is often presented as. For instance, Mark Taylor and Esa Saarinen have argued that "in a culture of potential ecocatastrophe, academic neutrality paves the way for polite, silent rape." Likewise, they suggest that reason which is "emotionally detached and socially indifferent" is irresponsible and immoral in "an era of global agony." See their *Imagologies*, London, 1994, Routledge, pp. 38 & 60. Though I think this is an important point, which needs to be high on the academic agenda for debate, this should not be seen

as general approval of Taylor & Saarinen's very flawed volume. For a critical review see *Media Development*, Vol. 42 no 2 (1995), pp.42-44.

16. An English translation of the parable of the poisoned arrow is given in Whitfield Foy (Ed), *Man's Religious Quest*, London, 1978, Croom Helm, pp.216-219. The story is taken from the *Majjhima Nikaya* I: 427-432. The Buddha used it to stress the foolishness of asking metaphysical questions instead of concentrating on finding enlightenment.

17. Sallie McFague, *Metaphorical Theology: Models of God in Religious Language*, London, 1983, SCM Press, p.42.

18. I am taking the rainbow and many names metaphors from John Hick's work. See his *God has Many Names*, London, 1980, Macmillan; and *The Rainbow of Faiths*, London, 1995, SCM.

19. I am taking the story metaphor from James Wiggins. Wiggins suggests: "We simply have an abundance of stories available to us, and unless we willfully refuse to listen to any but those we accept as our own, we may find their differences quite unsettling. But only if one confuses the telling of a story with the aspiration to engage in truth-telling in an absolute and singular way will a diversity of narratives be confounding." (*In Praise of Religious Diversity*, New York & London, 1996, Routledge, p.119).

20. Karlheinz Stockausen, "Weltmusik," in *Texte zur Musik: 1970-1977*, Koln, 1978, pp. 468-476. An English translation by Bernhard Radloff appears in the *Dalhousie Review*, Vol. 69 no. 3 (1989), pp.318-326.

21. Ibid., p.322.

22. Ibid.

23. Bernard Crick relates Newspeak to the modern media situation in the edition of *Nineteen Eighty Four* published in 1984 by the Clarendon Press, Oxford, which contains his excellent critical introduction and annotations. See, in particular, pp.59-60.

24. George Orwell, *Nineteen Eighty Four*, p.241. Orwell's chilling concept of Newspeak is worked out in considerable detail and complexity in *Nineteen Eighty Four*. I am giving a very simplified picture of it here.

25. Bryan Clarke, "The Causes of Biological Diversity," *Scientific American*, Vol. 233 no. 2 (1975), p.60.

26. Ibid.

27. John Hick, "Religion as 'skilful means': A Hint from Buddhism," *International Journal for Philosophy of Religion*, Vol. 30 no. 3 (1991), p.157.

28. Michael Pye, in Mircea Eliade (ed.), *The Encyclopedia of Religion*, New York/London, 1987, Macmillan/Collier Macmillan, Vol. 15, p.153.

29. Michael Pye, *Skilful Means: a Concept in Mahayana Buddhism*, London, 1978, Duckworth, p.43

30. Hick, "Religion as Skilful Means," p.152. The raft parable refers to the Buddha's likening his teaching to a raft. Once it has accomplished its end, it should be discarded. It would be as inappropriate to cling to it as it would be to keep carrying a raft after one had used it to cross a river.

31. Ibid., p.142.

32. Ibid., p.157.

33. Wu Ch'eng-en, *Monkey*, tr. Arthur Waley, London, 1961 (1942), Penguin, p. 7

34. Ibid., p.329.

35. Ibid., p.330. My emphasis.

36. Wu Ch'eng-en's *Hsi-yu Chi* is monumental, both in scale and mythological detail. The incident of the blank scriptures given here follows Arthur Waley's fairly simple rendition. Anthony Yu's four volume translation, *The Journey to the West*, Chicago, 1977-1983, University of Chicago Press, gives a rather more complex account.

APPENDIX A

THE SHRI YANTRA

"IF CIPHER'S intended quest is likened to an attempt to penetrate to the centre of a *yantra,* i.e. to try to reach the empty space at the heart of the complex interlocking mesh of triangles, rather than as something which focuses on the triangles themselves, then perhaps it will not seem as out of keeping with the goal which is being sought (p. 208)"

An illustration of the *Shri Yantra,* the most highly regarded of all the linear *yantras,* follows below.

I am taking the *yantra* out of context here and using it in a very simplified sense to illustrate a point. A good introduction to the rich symbolic significance of *yantras* can be found in Heinrich Zimmer's *Artistic Form and Yoga in the Sacred Images of India,* Princeton, 1984, Princeton University Press, pp. 122-180 (translated from *Kunstform und Yoga im indischen Kultbild,* Berlin, 1926). Gerald Chapple and James Lawson, Zimmer's translators, suggest that "*yantras* can properly be viewed as utensils of consciousness transformation that enable the meditating devotee to realize unity with the object of devotion" (p. xxii). In likening Cipher's quest to an attempt to focus on the intangible centre of the *yantra*, I am trying to stress his interest in that to which religious phenomena seem to point, and from which they derive any legitimacy they claim. I am not suggesting that he engage in some kind of devotional exercise (though of course passing over does seek proximity to, if not union with, the heart of religious experience).

Comparing Cipher's quest with trying to reach the empty space framed by the *yantra* can also be usefully linked to the story of Svetaketu and the banyan tree seeds (referred to in Chapter 7) and to the story of Tripitaka and the blank scriptures (referred to in Chapter 10).

APPENDIX B

AN EARNEST INQUIRER AFTER TRUTH:
LORD GIFFORD AND THE GIFFORD BEQUEST

IN THE *Trust Disposition and Settlement of the Late Lord Gifford,* dated August 21, 1885, Adam Gifford, one of the senators of the College of Justice in Scotland, laid down the terms under which a series of lectures in natural theology were to be founded. Such was the nature of his bequest that it was to establish a tradition of first class scholarship in the study of religion, a tradition which, more than a century later, shows no sign of flagging. The lectureships quickly acquired world-wide renown and they continue to attract scholars of international reputation to the unique forum which was created posthumously by Lord Gifford.

From a residual sum of £80,000, the four ancient universities of Scotland were given funds to establish lectureships for "promoting advancing, teaching and diffusing the study of natural theology."[1] Edinburgh received £25,000, Glasgow and Aberdeen £20,000 each and St Andrews £15,000. These were colossal sums at the time. A contemporary equivalent for the total amount, in terms of actual purchasing power, would, according to Stanley L. Jaki, be in the region of £3 million, or $5 million.[2]

Today one reads with admiration and no little amazement the terms which accompanied this generous legacy, for they suggest an open-mindedness about religion uncommon in any age. In consequence, what might well have become a stultifying theological cul-de-sac became instead a potent vehicle for the advancement of learning about religion across many of its different facets. How did Lord Gifford ensure so effectively that the lectures did not become moribund?

To begin with, rather than limiting their terms of reference by the strict demarcation of a narrow subject area, he stressed that natural theology was to be understood in "the widest sense of that term," an understanding which has allowed lecturers to adopt diverse philosophical, theological, psychological, historical and scientific standpoints. Apart from the stipulation that their lectures were to be addressed to the community at large, not just to a purely university audience, and that they were to approach their chosen topic in the same manner as one would approach any other academic subject, "without special reference to or reliance upon any special exceptional or so-called miraculous revelation," the lecturers were put under "no restraint whatever in the treatment of their theme."

The openness of these stipulations and the leeway they have allowed incumbents to take has occasionally led to murmurs of complaint that some of the lecture series have, in fact, no claim to be—indeed no bearing on—natural theology, and that far from being "public and popular" in the sense which Lord Gifford intended, they are quite abstruse and meant for purely academic consumption. Stanley L. Jaki is quite correct in identifying two factors which have militated against the lectures becoming truly popular. First, their specialist subject matter is hardly an area in which most people feel at home; and, second, the "eminent academic standing" of the lecturers tends to be reached "by qualifications other than the skill to hold audiences spellbound."[3] The exception to his generalization, and an exception that has done a great deal to advance the name and reputation of the Gifford Lectures, was William James' *Varieties of Religious Experience*, which, despite its subject matter, scale and sophistication, became a "runaway bestseller."[4]

In the choice of lecturer, as in the stipulation of the subject matter, Lord Gifford took pains to ensure that no religious prejudice which might channel things into its own brand of narrow dogmatism would be allowed expression. Indeed, what he has to say about choosing a lecturer would provide admirable guidelines for selecting a candidate for any non-partisan teaching post in the whole area of religious studies. The relevant passage from the *Trust Disposition* is worth quoting in full:

> The lecturers appointed shall be subjected to no test of any kind, and shall not be required to take any oath, or to emit or subscribe to any declaration of belief or to make any promise of any kind, they may be of any denomination whatever, or of no denomination at all...they may be of any religion or way of thinking, or as is sometimes said, they may be of no religion, or they may be so-called agnostics or free-thinkers, provided only that the patrons will use diligence to secure that they be able reverent men, true thinkers, sincere lovers of and earnest inquirers after truth.

That Adam Gifford might himself be fairly described as a sincere lover of, and earnest inquirer after, truth seems clear. Even as a boy he was nicknamed "the Philosopher" by his playmates—an early indication of the passion which was to shape his life and which would lead him eventually to set up the lectureships which bear his name.

Given his passion for inquiring after truth, it is perhaps not surprising that he chose the law as his profession, becoming a judge before he was fifty. The terms which he lay down for the lectures betray a fascinating mixture of idealism, legal acuity and a down-to-earth awareness of how an open approach to the emotive area of religion must protect itself from all the closures which some varieties of faith might seek to impose, by laying down ground rules of incontrovertible fairness. Born in Edinburgh in 1820, Lord Gifford was very much the child of a scientifically optimistic age, an optimism which led him and many others to think that the objective investigative method found in the natural sciences could be extended to what he saw as "the greatest of all possible sciences," that is, to the realm of religion.

For him, theism depended on evidence which was accessible to reason, and it did not rely on appeal to events or experiences which claim special exemption from well reasoned evaluations. As well as pursuing truth in the course of his professional legal duties, Lord Gifford seems to have spent much of his free time reading and studying what pertained to "the knowledge of God, the infinite, the All."[5] Plato and Spinoza seem to have been among his favourite thinkers. The lectureships which he founded were intended for more than a small specialist audience because, in his eyes, a "true knowledge of God" is the "means of man's highest well-being." Thus, the lectures were designed to promote thinking about such important matters "among the whole population of Scotland." They have, of course, had a much wider audience and relevance than that.

Before the progressive paralysis which confined him to his sick-bed for the last seven years of his life (he died in 1887), Gifford himself undertook many engagements as a public lecturer in his desire to disseminate among the general public what we might call (to use a particularly apt Buddhist phrase) "right thought" about religion and metaphysics. His topics ranged from "The Ten Avatars of Vishnu" to "Ralph Waldo Emerson," but the underlying concerns were the same and can, perhaps, be summed up in a comment he made during an address to the Edinburgh YMCA in 1878. "No truth of the smallest value can be attained without thought, without thought often painfully earnest and protracted."[6]. The way in which he disposed of so large a fortune stands at the other extreme of generosity from those more common legacies of smaller amounts left to academic use, where the memory of the benefactor, or the propagation of his particular faith, seems to be the guiding intention behind the bequest, rather than any genuine desire to foster free inquiry.

The Gifford bequest has so few strings attached that through the work it has fostered it has risen high into the upper reaches of the academic atmosphere. Niels Bohr, Alfred North Whitehead, Arnold Toynbee, Paul Tillich, Werner Heisenberg, William James, Max Müller, J.G. Frazer, Karl Barth and Rudolf Bultmann are some of the brighter stars from the galaxy of academic celebrities who have been Gifford lecturers. The tradition continues today with contemporary thinkers of the stature of George Steiner, Iris Murdoch, Paul Ricoeur, Mary Douglas, Ninian Smart, John Hick and others lecturing. Small wonder, then, that Stanley L. Jaki (himself a Gifford lecturer) gives the lectures such a high value:

> In a world increasingly bogged down in technological pursuits and
> at a loss with how to cope with the problems—psychological, social,

moral and ideological—they create, no academic organ has kept
so alive some higher perspectives as have the lectureships which
Lord Gifford decided to establish a hundred years ago.[7]

Although a much more recent development, designed to encourage
the work of those at a much less exalted level than customarily occupied
by the Gifford lecturers, the Gifford Research Fellowship is also governed
by the terms which Lord Gifford laid down in 1885. In particular, the
Fellow is required to give a series of public lectures which will be "public
and popular," accessible to the interested lay person, not just a specialist
audience. The designated subject matter follows the same specification
as for the Gifford Lectures. In October 1984 I was appointed Gifford
Fellow at the University of St Andrews. This was a new position,
establishing for the first time at a junior level, a post funded by the
Gifford Bequest. This book had its origin in the first series of lectures
which I gave at St. Andrews (which were the first ever to be given under
the auspices of the Gifford Research Fellowship).

It is daunting and inspiring to have stood at the beginning of what
may become a (minor) tradition. It is pleasing to note that, following
the St. Andrews lead, Aberdeen and Glasgow have also instituted Gifford
Fellowship schemes. One hopes that Edinburgh may, in due course, do
likewise. The Fellowship scheme has hosted a range of fascinating
lectures. Among topics covered at St. Andrews have been, "Philosophical
Aspects of Probability" (Paul Castell, 1993); "Perichoresis: Dancing
Round the Doctrine of the Trinity" (Karen Kilby, 1996); "God and
Ultimate Explanation" (Timothy O'Connor, 1997) and "The Structure
of Reality" (Fraser Macbride, 1998). At Glasgow the Fellows have looked
at "Machine Consciousness (Euan Thompson, 1986); "Michael Faraday
and the Sandemanians" (Geoffrey Cantor, 1988); "Persons and Human
Fellowship" (Daniel Rashid, 1991); "Spinoza and Heidegger as
Philosophers of the Natural World" (Clare Palmer, 1992); "Searching
for Consciousness in the Material World" (Greg Mulhauser, 1995) and
"Divine Nature and Human Reason" (Mark Wynn, 1997). I am assured
that Aberdeen has followed St. Andrews and Glasgow and instituted a

fellowship scheme, but at the time of writing the University was unable to supply details of incumbents or their topics.

In looking back at my time in St Andrews, I am often reminded of Miguel de Unamuno's remark, that "it is not the shilling that I give you that counts, but the warmth that it carries with it from my hand." The Gifford Fellowship funded two years of well-paid work at a crucial point in my professional life, and I remain grateful for it. But there is an additional feeling beyond mere financial well-being. In an age where the study of religion seems so often to be under-valued, where it is increasingly difficult to get funding to pursue one's inquiries into what Lord Gifford saw as "the greatest of all possible sciences," where government policy and public opinion have made education in matters pertaining to religion the poor (or absent) relation in far too many educational establishments, it is refreshing and inspiring to have stood, albeit temporarily, in the warmth of Lord Gifford's passion for the subject. Had I not had the privilege of doing so, I doubt if I would have continued as a university teacher. I hope that, were he to have read these pages, Adam Gifford would not have been too displeased by what he found. Given his views on the importance of religion, one suspects that he would at least have identified with Cipher's priorities. As Herbert Paton put it (Paton was Gifford Lecturer at St. Andrews in 1949-50), "The question of religion, like that of morality, is not one of theory: it is a question of the life a man is going to lead."[8] That, in the end, was Gifford's concern. It is likewise Cipher's.

Notes

1. From the *Trust Disposition and Settlement of the Late Lord Gifford*, dated 21 August 1885. This, and all subsequent quotes not otherwise attributed, is/are from the *Extracts from the Trust Disposition and Settlement*, published by the University of St Andrews (undated and unpaginated).
2. Stanley L. Jaki, *Lord Gifford and His Lectures: A Centenary Retrospect*, Edinburgh 1986, Scottish Academic Press, pp. 2-3. Jaki's study reprints some of Lord Gifford's own writings, provides some biographical background about him and provides a full listing of the lectures that have been given to date. (A second, updated, version was published in 1995.) Jaki's books, together with Bernard Jones' anthology, listed in note 6 below, provide an excellent starting point for anyone wishing to get a feel for the nature of the Bequest and the richness and variety of the work which it has fostered.
3. Jaki, op. cit., p. 9.
4. Ibid., p. 10.
5. Ibid.
6. As quoted in Bernard E. Jones, *Earnest Enquirers After Truth: A Gifford Anthology* (Excerpts from the Gifford Lectures 1888-1968), London, 1970, George Allen & Unwin, p. 12.
7. Jaki, op. cit, p. vii. Jaki's own Gifford Lectures, given in Edinburgh in 1974-5 and 1975-6, are published as *The Road of Science and the Ways to God*, Edinburgh, 1978, Scottish Academic Press.
8. I am quoting from the extract from Paton's lectures included in Bernard E. Jones' anthology, p.208.

APPENDIX C

Acknowledgments

LIKE ANY author, I am deeply indebted to a range of individuals and institutions. In writing this book I drew heavily on the resources of the National Library of Scotland, and of the University Libraries at Edinburgh, St. Andrews and Lampeter. The efficiency and pleasantness of staff at each of these very different places was much appreciated. I am grateful to those who chaired the public lectures in which this book had its genesis, and to the appointing committee at the University of St. Andrews for entrusting me with the first fellowship under the Gifford scheme. Students and colleagues at St. Andrews, Edinburgh, and Lampeter, the three universities at which I have been based since 1984, have helped to refine the ideas whose first voicings were sometimes less than adequate. Family and friends have done likewise, while also patiently tolerating the demands which writing has made on my time.

Religious Pluralism: a Metaphorical Approach would not have come into being without the unfailing dynamism, enthusiasm and efficiency of its publisher. As such, I am particularly indebted to Keith Davies of the Davies Group Publishers.

Finally, it seems apt to remember Lord Gifford himself, that earnest inquirer after truth without whose generosity Cipher and all his works might never have been conceived.

While others have been instrumental in shaping my thinking, the responsibility for any shortcomings or errors is mine alone.

The book's epigraph is taken from Sallie McFague TeSelle's excellent book, *Speaking in Parables: a Study in Metaphor and Theology*, London, 1975, SCM Press, p. 56

For permission to reproduce material from works under copyright, grateful acknowledgement and thanks are extended to the following individuals and organizations:

The Society for Promoting Christian Knowledge for extracts from *The Meaning and End of Religion* (1978) by Wilfred Cantwell Smith.

Collins Publishers for an extract from *Beyond Ideology: Religion and the Future of Western Civilization* (1981) by Ninian Smart.

Oxford University Press for extracts from *The Sense of God* (1973) and *The Religious Imagination and the Sense of God* (1978) by John Bowker, *Speculum Mentis* (1924) by R. G. Collingwood, *Beyond Existentialism and Zen* (1979) by George Rupp, *Mankind and Mother Earth* (1976) by Arnold Toynbee, and *The Idea of the Holy* (1977) by Rudolf Otto, translated by John W. Harvey.

University of California Press for extracts from *The Sword and the Flute: Kali and Krishna: Dark Visions of the Terrible and the Sublime in Hindu Mythology* (1975) by David R. Kinsley.

Random House, Inc. for an extract from *The Autobiography of Benvenuto Cellini*, translated by John Addington Symonds.

Mrs Laura Huxley and Chatto & Windus Ltd for extracts from *Those Barren Leaves* (1925) and *The Perennial Philosophy* (1946) by Aldous Huxley.

Falmer Press Ltd for an extract from Lesslie Newbigin's "Teaching Religion in a Secular Plural Society" from *New Directions in Religious Education* (1982), ed. by John Hull.

The Revd. Master Daishin Morgan for an extract from "Choosing your Way" in the *Journal of Throssel Hole Priory* Vol. X, No. 1.

Penguin Books Ltd for extracts from *Exploring Inner Space* (1982) by David Hay, copyright © David Hay, 1982.

Muller, Blond & White Ltd for an extract from *The Soul of the White Ant* (1937) by Eugene Marais.

University of Notre Dame Press for an extract from *The Forbidden Forest* by Mircea Eliade, © 1978 by University of Notre Dame Press.

APPENDIX D

WORKS CITED

Adams, Douglas, *The Hitch Hiker's Guide to the Galaxy*, London 1979, Pan Books.

Amiel, Henri-Frédéric, *Amiel's Journal: the Journal Intime of Henri-Frédéric Amiel*, tr. and with an introduction and notes by Mrs Humphrey Ward, London, 1913, (1882), Macmillan.

Arthur, C. J., *In the Hall of Mirrors: Some Problems of Commitment in a Religiously Plural World*, London & Oxford, 1986, Mowbray.

Arthur, C.J., "Ineffability and Intelligibility: Towards an Understanding of the Radical Unlikeness of Religious Experience," *International Journal for Philosophy of Religion*, Vol. 20 (1986), pp. 109-129.

Arthur, Chris, "Phenomenology of Religion and the Art of Storytelling," in Sumner B. Twiss and Walter H. Conser (eds), *Experience of the Sacred: Readings in the Phenomenology of Religion*, New England, 1992, Brown University Press, pp. 145-166.

Arthur, Chris, "Silence, Metaphor and the Communication of Religious Meaning, Part I," *New Blackfriars*, vol. 74 no. 865 (1993), pp 457-464; "Silence, Metaphor and the Communication of Religious Meaning, Part II," *New Blackfriars*, vol. 74 no. 866 (1993), pp. 486-495.

Arthur, Chris, "Media, Meaning and Method in the Study of Religion," *British Association for the Study of Religion, Occasional Paper* no. 16 (1996).

Arthur, Chris, "The Numinous in Modern British Fiction," *The Month*, Vol. 30 no. 11 (1997), pp. 448-452.

Austin, J. L., *Sense and Sensibilia*, Oxford, 1970 (1962), Clarendon Press.

Babin, Pierre, *The New Era in Religious Communication*, tr. David Smith, Minneapolis, 1993, Fortress Press.

Bagdikian, Ben, *The Media Monopoly*, Boston, 1992 (1983), Beacon Press.

Barrett, William, *Irrational Man, A Study in Existential Philosophy*, Connecticut, 1977, (1958), Greenwood Press.

Barth, Karl, *Church Dogmatics*, Edinburgh, 1957, T & T Clark, Vol. 2. Authorized English translation by T. H. L. Parker, W. B. Johnston, Harold Knight and J. L. M. Haire of *Die Kirchliche Dogmatik II: Die Lehre von Gott*.

Batchelor, Stephen, *The Awakening of the West: the Encounter of Buddhism and Western Culture*, London, 1994, Aquarian.

Becker, Ernest, *The Denial of Death*, New York, 1973, The Free Press.

Bee, Helen L. and Sandra K. Mitchell, *The Developing Person: a Life-Span Approach*, San Francisco, 1980, Harper & Row.

Berger, Peter, *A Rumour of Angels, Modern Society and the Rediscovery of the Supernatural*, Harmondsworth, 1970, (1969), Penguin.

Berger, Peter L, *The Heretical Imperative, Contemporary Possibilities of Religious Affirmation*, London, 1980, Collins.

Beveridge, William, *Private Thoughts Upon Religion*, Glasgow, 1753, (1709), William Duncan Junior.

Beyer, Peter, *Religion and Globalization*, London, 1994, Sage.

Bhagavad Gita, Juan Mascaro's translation, Harmondsworth, 1962, Penguin Classics.

Black, Max, *Models and Metaphors: Studies in Language and Philosophy*, New York, 1962, Cornell University Press.

Bleeker, C J, *The Sacred Bridge: Researches into the Nature and Structure of Religion*, Leiden 1963, E. J. Brill.

Bourdillon, M. F. C., and Meyer Fortes (eds.), *Sacrifice*, London, 1980, Academic Press.

Bowker, John, *The Sense of God*, Oxford, 1973, Oxford University Press.

Bowker, John, *The Religious Imagination and the Sense of God*, Oxford, 1978, Oxford University Press.

Britton, Karl, *Philosophy and the Meaning of Life*, Cambridge, 1969, Cambridge University Press.

Burhoe, Ralph Wendell, "The Phenomenon of Religion seen Scientifically," in Allan W. Eister (ed.), *Changing Perspectives in the Scientific study of Religion*, New York, 1974, Wiley Interscience.

Burnouf, Emile, *The Science of Religions*, London, 1888, (1870), Swan, Sonnenschein, Lowrey & Co.

Byrne, Peter, *Prolegomena to Religious Pluralism: Reference and Realism in Religion*, London, 1995, Macmillan.

Capps, Walter H., *Religious Studies: the Making of a Discipline*, Minneapolis, 1995, Fortress Press.

Cellini, Benvenuto, *Autobiography*, New York, undated, Random House Modern Library, tr. John Addington Symonds, (1728).

Chaudhuri, Nirad C., *Scholar Extraordinary: the Life of Professor the Right Honourable Friedrich Max Müller*, PC, London, 1974, Chatto & Windus.

Cheng-en, Wu, *Hsi-yu Chi*, translated as *Monkey*, by Arthur Waley, Harmondsworth, 1961 (1942), Penguin, and as *The Journey to the West* by Anthony Yu, Chicago, 1977-1983 (4 vols.), Chicago University Press.

Chesterton, G.K., *The Penguin Complete Father Brown*, Harmondsworth, 1982, (1927), Penguin.

Christian, William A., *Oppositions of Religious Doctrines: a Study of the Logic of Dialogue among Religions*, London, 1972, Macmillan.

Clarke, Bryan, "The Causes of Biological Diversity," Scientific American, vol. 233, no. 2 (1975), pp.50-60.

Collingwood, R. G., *Speculum Mentis, or the Map of Knowledge*, Oxford, 1956, (1924), Oxford University Press.

Collingwood, R. G., *The Idea of History*, Oxford, 1970, (1946), Oxford University Press.

Cook, Stanley A., *The Study of Religions*, London, 1914, Adam & Charles Black.

Courtney, Charles, "Phenomenology and Ninian Smart's Philosophy of Religion," *International Journal for Philosophy of Religion*, vol. 9 (1978), pp. 41-52.

Coward, Harold, *Religious Pluralism: Challenge to World Religions*, New York, 1985, Orbis Books.

Cox, Harvey, *The Seduction of the Spirit: The Use and Misuse of People's Religion*, New York, 1973, Simon & Schuster.

Cox, Harvey, *Turning East: the Promise and Peril of the New Orientalism*, London, 1979, (1977), Allen Lane/Penguin.

Cox, Harvey *Religion in the Secular City*, New York, 1984, Simon & Schuster.

Cragg, Kenneth, *The Christian and Other Religion*, London, 1977, Mowbray.

Dalai Lama, The, *My Land and My People: the Autobiography of His Holiness the Dalai Lama*, edited by David Howarth, London, 1962, Weidenfeld & Nicolson.

D'Costa, Gavin, *Theology and Religious Pluralism: The Challenge of Other Religions*, Oxford 1986, Basil Blackwell.

de Bary, Wm. Theodore, (ed.) *Sources of Indian Tradition*, New York, 1970, (1958), Columbia University Press.

Descartes, René, *Philosophical Works*, Vol. 1, Cambridge, 1973, (this edition 1911), Cambridge University Press, tr. Haldane and Ross.

de Unamuno, Miguel, *The Agony of Christianity and Essays on Faith*, London, 1974 (1906), Routledge & Kegan Paul, tr by Anthony Kerrigan.

de Vries, Jan, *The Study of Religion: a Historical Approach*, tr. Kees Bolle, New York, 1967, Harcourt, Brace & World.

Doyle, Arthur Conan, *The Penguin Complete Sherlock Holmes*, Harmondsworth, 1981, (1887), Penguin.

Dunne, John S., *The City of the Gods*, London, 1965, Sheldon Press .

Dunne, John S., *A Search for God in Time and Memory*, London, 1967, Sheldon Press.

Dunne, John S., *The Way of All the Earth*, London, 1972, Sheldon Press.

Dupuis, Jacques, *Toward a Christian Theology of Religious Pluralism*, New York, 1997, Orbis Books.

Eck, Diana L., "Challenge of Pluralism," *Niemann Reports,* "God in the Newsroom" issue, Vol. XLVII no.2, Summer 1997.
        http://www.fas.harvard.edu/pluralism/html/article-cop.html

Eliade, Mircea, "Psychology and Comparative Religion: A Study of the Symbolism of the Centre," in Cecily Hastings and Donald Nicholl (eds.) *Selection II*, London, Sheed & Ward, 1954.

Eliade, Mircea, *The Forbidden Forest*, Indiana, 1978, (1955), tr. Mac Linscott Ricketts and Mary Park Stevenson, University of Notre Dame Press .

Eliade, Mircea, *The Sacred and Profane: the Nature of Religion*, New York, 1959, (1957), Harcourt Brace & World.

Eliade, Mircea, *Patterns in Comparative Religion*, London, 1976, (1958), Sheed & Ward.

Eliade, Mircea, *From Primitives to Zen: A Thematic Sourcebook of the History of Religions*, London, 1979, (1967), Collins.

Eliade, Mircea, *No Souvenirs: Journal 1957-1969*, London, 1978, (1973), Routledge & Kegan Paul.

Eliade, Mircea, *A History of Religious Ideas, Vol. 1: From the Stone Age to the Eleusinian Mysteries*, London, 1979, (1976), Collins.

Evans-Pritchard, E. E., *Theories of Primitive Religion*, Oxford, 1970, (1965), Oxford University Press.

Evans-Wentz, W. Y. (ed.), *The Tibetan Book of the Dead*, London & New York, 1977, Oxford University Press (this edition first published 1927).

Farley, Edward, *Ecclesial Man, a Social Phenomenology of Faith and Reality*, Philadelphia, 1975, Fortress Press.

Flew, Antony, "Theology and Falsification," in Antony Flew and Alasdair MacIntyre (eds.), *New Essays in Philosophical Theology*, London, 1969 (1955), SCM, pp.96-99 & 106-108.

Fore, William, *Television and Religion: the Shaping of Faith, Values and Culture*, Minneapolis, 1987, Augsburg.

Fowler, James W., *Stages of Faith: the Psychology of Human Development and the Quest for Meaning*, San Francisco, 1980, Harper & Row.

Fowler, James W., Robin W. Lovin et. al., *Trajectories of Faith: Five Life Stories*, Nashville, 1980, Abingdon.

Frye, Northrop, "The Knowledge of Good and Evil," in Max Black (ed.), *The Morality of Scholarship*, New York, 1967, Cornell University Press.

Gandhi, M. K., *An Autobiography: The Story of My Experiments with Truth*, London, 1972, (1949), Cape, tr. Mahadev Desai.

Gaskin, J C A, *The Quest for Eternity: An Outline of the Philosophy of Religion*, Harmondsworth, 1984, Penguin.

Gilkey, Langdon, "God," in Peter Hodgson and Robert King (eds.), *Christian Theology: An Introduction to its Traditions and Tasks*, London, 1983, (1982), SPCK, pp. 62-87.

Goethals, Gregor, *The Electronic Golden Calf: Images, Religion and the Making of Meaning*, Cambridge,1990, Cowley.

Golding, William, *The Inheritors*, London, 1970 [1955], Faber.

Golding, William, *A Moving Target*, London, 1982, Faber.

Goody, Jack & Watt, Ian, "The Consequences of Literacy," in Jack Goody (ed.), *Literacy in Traditional Societies*, Cambridge, 1968, Cambridge University Press.

Goody, Jack, *The Logic of Writing and the Organization of Society*, Cambridge, 1986, Cambridge University Press.

Hamnet, Ian (ed), *Religious Pluralism and Unbelief: Studies Critical and Comparative*, London, 1990, Routledge.

Hardy, Alister, *The Biology of God, a Scientist's Study of Man the Religious Animal*, London, 1975, Cape.

Hay, David, *Exploring Inner Space: Scientists and Religious Experience*, Harmondsworth, 1982, Penguin.

Heirs and Rebels: Principles and Practicalities in Christian Education, Blandford, 1982, issued by the Bloxham Project, Chairman: Basil Mitchell.

Hepburn, R. W., *Christianity and Paradox*, London, 1966, (1953), Watts & Co.

Hick, John, *God and the Universe of Faiths*, London, 1977, (1973), Collins.

Hick, John, *Death and Eternal Life*, London, 1976, Collins.

Hick, John, *God Has Many Names*, London, 1980, Macmillan.

Hick, John, "Religious Pluralism," in Frank Whaling (ed.) *The World's Religious Traditions, Current Perspectives in Religious Studies, Essays in Honour of Wilfred Cantwell Smith*, Edinburgh, 1984, T & T Clark.

Hick, John, *Problems of Religious Pluralism*, London/New York, 1985, Macmillan/St. Martin's Press.

Hick, John & Askari, Hasan (ed.), *The Experience of Religious Diversity*, Aldershot, 1985, Gower.

Hick, John, "Religious Pluralism", in Mircea Eliade (ed.), *The Encyclopedia of Religion*, New York/London, 1987, Macmillan/Collier Macmillan, Vol. 12 pp. 331-333.

Hick, John, *An Interpretation of Religion*, London/New Haven, 1989, Macmillan/ Princeton University Press (an expanded edition of the Gifford Lectures, delivered at the University of Edinburgh, 1986-7).

Hick, John, "Religion as Skilful Means: a Hint From Buddhism," *International Journal for Philosophy of Religion*, Vol. 30 no. 3 (1991), pp. 141-148.

Hick, John, *The Rainbow of Faiths*, London, 1995, SCM.

Hocking, William Ernest, *The Meaning of God in Human Experience*, New Haven, 1928, (1912), Yale University Press.

Hollis, Martin, *Models of Man, Philosophical Thoughts on Social Action*, Cambridge, 1977, Cambridge University Press.

Honko, Lauri (ed.), *Science of Religion: Studies in Methodology*, The Hague, 1979, Mouton.

Hulmes, Edward, *Commitment and Neutrality in Religious Education*, London, 1979, Geoffrey Chapman.

Hume, David, *An Enquiry Concerning Human Understanding*, Oxford, 1894, (1748), Oxford University Press, Selby-Bigge edition.

Hurley, Neil P., *Theology Through Film*, New York, 1970, Harper & Row.

Huxley, Aldous, *Those Barren Leaves*, Harmondsworth, 1967 (1925), Penguin.

Huxley, Aldous, *Brave New World*, Harmondsworth, 1970 (1932), Penguin.

Huxley, Aldous, *Eyeless in Gaza*, Harmondsworth, 1974 (1936), Penguin.

Huxley, Aldous, *The Perennial Philosophy*, London, 1950, (1946), Chatto & Windus.

Jaki, Stanley L., *The Road of Science and the Ways to God*, Edinburgh, 1978 (the Gifford Lectures for 1974-5 & 1975-6), Scottish Academic Press.

Jaki, Stanley L., *Lord Gifford and His Lectures: a Centenary Retrospect*, Edinburgh, 2nd enlarged edition, 1995 (1986), Scottish Academic Press.

James, P. D. *Death of an Expert Witness*, London, 1983 (1977), Sphere Books.

James, William, *The Varieties of Religious Experience: A Study in Human Nature*, (The Gifford Lectures in Edinburgh for 1901-02), London, 1928, Longmans, Green & Co.

Jastrow, Morris, *The Study of Religion*, London, 1901, Contemporary Science Series.

Jones, Bernard E., *Earnest Enquirers After Truth: A Gifford Anthology*, London, 1970, George Allen & Unwin.

Jordan, Louis Henry, *Comparative Religion, its Genesis and Growth*, Edinburgh, 1905, T & T Clark.

Kim, Jay J., "Belief or Anamnesis: is a Rapprochement between History of Religions and Theology Possible?" *Journal of Religion*, Vol. 52. (1972), pp. 150-169.

King, Winston L., "Negation as a Religious Category," *Journal of Religion*, Vol. 37 (1957), pp. 105-118.

King, Winston L., *Introduction to Religion: a Phenomenological Approach*, New York, 1968 (this is a revised edition of King's *Introduction to Religion*, first published in 1954), Harper & Row.

King, Winston, L., "The Phenomenology of Religion," *The Drew Gateway*, Vol. 43 (1972), pp. 27-41.

Kinsley, David R., *The Sword and the Flute, Kali and Krishna, Dark Visions of the Terrible and the Sublime in Hindu Mythology*, Berkeley, 1975, University of California Press.

Knitter, Paul, *No Other Name? A Critical Study of Christian Attitudes Towards the World Religions*, London 1985, SCM.

Kolakowski, Leszek, *Religion, If There is no God.... On God, the Devil, Sin and other worries of the so called Philosophy of Religion*, Glasgow, 1982, Fontana Books.

Kraemer, Heinrick, *Religion and the Christian Faith*, London, 1956, Lutterworth Press.

Kristensen, W. Brede, *The Meaning of Religion: Lectures in the Phenomenology of Religion*, The Hague, 1960, Mouton.

Kuhn, Thomas S., *The Structure of Scientific Revolutions*, Chicago, second [enlarged] edition 1970 (1962), University of Chicago Press.

Küng, Hans, *Does God Exist?*, London, 1980, (1978) Collins.

Kurtz, Lester R., *Gods in the Global Village: the World's Religions in Sociological Perspective*, Thousand Oaks, 1995, Sage.

Lakoff, George and Mark Johnson, *Metaphors We Live By*, Chicago, 1980, Chicago University Press.

Lewis, H.D., and R. L. Slater, *World Religions*, London, 1966, Watts & Co. London, 1970, 2nd edition (1961), Oxford University Press.

Luckmann, Thomas, *The Invisible Religion: the Problem of Religion in Modern Society*, New York,1967, Macmillan.

MacCormac, Earl R., "Religious Metaphors: Mediators Between Biological and Cultural Evolution that Generate Transcendent Meaning," *Zygon*, Vol 18 (1983), pp.45-65.

Mann, Thomas, *Dr. Faustus*, Harmondsworth, 1973, (1947), Penguin.

Marais, Eugene, *The Soul of the White Ant*, Harmondsworth, 1973, (1937), Penguin.

Marcia, J. E., "Development and Validation of Ego Identity Status," *Journal of Personality and Social Psychology*, Vol. 3 (1966), pp.551-558.

Marsh, Clive & Ortiz, Gaye (ed.), *Explorations in Theology and Film*, Oxford, 1997, Blackwell.

Marshall, P. J., (ed.), *The British Discovery of Hinduism in the Eighteenth Century*, Cambridge, 1970, Cambridge University Press.

Martin, Joel W., & Ostwalt, Conrad E. (ed.), *Screening the Sacred: Religion, Myth and Ideology in Popular American Film*, Boulder, 1995, Westview Press.

Martin, Thomas, *Images and the Imageless: A Study in Religious Consciousness and Film*, Lewisberg, 1981, Bucknell University Press .

Marty, Martin E. & R. Scott Appleby (eds), *Fundamentalisms Observed*, Chicago, 1991, University of Chicago Press .

May, John R. (ed.), *Image and Likeness: Religious Visions in American Film Classics*, New York, 1992, Paulist Press.

May, John R., (ed.), *New Image of Religious Film*, Kansas City, 1997, Sheed & Ward.

McClelland, Joseph, "Teacher of Religion: Professor or Guru?" *Studies in Religion/Sciences Religieuses*, Vol. 2 (1972), pp. 226-234.

McCutcheon, Russell T., "The Category 'Religion' in Recent Publications: a Critical Survey," *Numen*, Vol. 42 (1995), pp. 284-309.

McDermott, Robert A., "Religion as an Academic Discipline," *Cross Currents*, Vol. 18 (1968), pp. 11-33.

McFague Teselle, Sallie, *Speaking in Parables: a Study in Metaphor and Theology*, London, 1975, SCM.

McFague, Sallie, *Metaphorical Theology: Models of God in Religious Language*, London, 1982, SCM.

McFague, Sallie, "An Epilogue: the Christian Paradigm," in Peter Hodgson and Robert King (ed.), *Christian Theology: An Introduction to its Traditions and Tasks*, London, 1983, SPCK.

McLuhan, Marshall, *Understanding Media: The Extensions of Man*, London, 1987 (1964), Ark.

Meland, Bernard E., "Theology and the Historians of Religion," *Journal of Religion*, Vol. 41 (1961), pp. 263-276.

Merton, Thomas, *Raids on the Unspeakable*, London, 1977, Burns & Oates.

Milburn, R. Gordon, *The Religious Mysticism of the Upanishads*, London, 1924, Theosophical Publishing House.

Miles, Arthur, (pseudonym of Gervee Baronté), *The Land of the Lingam*, London, 1933, Paternoster Press.

Miles, John, "Bildungsromane and the Pedagogy of Comparative Religion", *Horizons*, Vol. 19 no. 2 (1975), pp 75-86.

Miles, Margaret, *Seeing and Believing: Religion and Values in the Movies*, Boston, 1996, Beacon Press.

Mitchell, Basil, *Neutrality and Commitment*, Oxford, 1968, Clarendon Press (text of an inaugural lecture delivered before the University of Oxford in May 1968).

Mitter, Partha, *Much Maligned Monsters: A History of European Reactions to Indian Art*, Oxford, 1977, Clarendon Press.

Moffat, James, *A Comparative History of Religions*, New York, 1875, 2 Vols, Dodd & Mead.

Mohammadi, Ali (ed.) *International Communication and Globalisation*, London,1997, Sage.

Mohanty, J.N. (ed.), *Religion and Time*, Leiden, 1993, E.J. Brill (Vol LIV in the Studies in the History of Religions series).

Morgan, Daishin, "Choosing Your Way," *The Journal of Throssel Hole Priory*, Vol. X, no. 1, Spring 1983.

Moses, David G., *Religious Truth and the Relation Between Religions*, Madras, 1950, The Christian Literature Society for India, Indian Research Series 5.

Mowlana, Hamid, *Global Communication in Transition: the End of Diversity?* Thousand Oaks, 1996, Sage.

Muir, Edwin, *Selected Poems*, ed. T. S. Eliot, London 1965, Faber.

Müller, Max, *Chips From a German Workshop, Vol. 1: Essays on the Science of Religion*, London, 1867.

Müller, Max, *Thoughts on Life and Religion, An Aftermath from the Writings of Max Müller by his Wife*, London, 1906, (1905), Archibald Constable & Co.

Needleman, Jacob, *The New Religions*, New York, 1977 (1970), E. P. Dutton & Co.

Neill, Stephen, *The Christian Faith and Other Faiths, The Christian Dialogue with Other Religions*, London, 1970 (1961), Oxford University Press.

Newbigin, Lesslie, "Teaching Religion in a Secular Plural Society," in John Hull (ed.), *New Directions in Religious Education*, Lewes, 1982, Falmer Press, pp. 97-107.

Niebuhr, Richard, *The Kingdom of God in America*, New York, 1959, Harper.

Niebuhr, Reinhold, *The Nature and Destiny of man: a Christian Interpretation*, 2 Vols, London, 1941, Nisbet & Co.

Novak, Michael, *Ascent of the Mountain, Flight of the Dove: An Invitation to Religious Studies*, New York, 1978, (1971), Harper & Row.

Nygren, Anders, *Meaning and Method: Prolegomena to a Scientific Philosophy of Religion and a Scientific Theology*, London, 1972, Epworth Press, authorized translation by Philip S. Watson.

O'Brien, Flann, *At Swim Two Birds*, London, 1966 (1939), Hart-Davis, MacGibbon Ltd.

O'Connor, June, "The Epistemological Significance of Feminist Research in Religion," in Ursula King (ed.), *Religion and Gender*, Oxford, 1995, Blackwell, pp. 45-63.

Ong, Walter J., *Orality and Literacy: The Technologising of the Word*, London, 1982, Methuen.

Ortony, Andrew (ed), *Metaphor and Thought*, Cambridge, 1979, Cambridge University Press.

Orwell, George, *Nineteen Eighty Four*, Oxford, 1984 (1949), Clarendon Press.

O'Sullivan, Tim, John Hartley et. al., *Key Concepts in Communication and Cultural Studies*, London, 1994, Routledge.

Otto, Rudolf, *The Idea of the Holy: an Inquiry into the non-Rational Factor in the Idea of the Divine and its Relation to the Rational*, tr. John W. Harvey, Oxford, 1977, (1917) Oxford University Press.

Oxtoby, W.G., "*Religionswissenschaft* Revisited," in Jacob Neusner (ed.), *Religions in Antiquity: Essays in Memory of Erwin Ramsdell Goodenough*, Leiden, 1968, E. J. Brill, pp.590-608.

Paden, William E., *Intrepreting the Sacred: Ways of Viewing Religion*, Boston, 1992, Beacon Press.

Panikkar, Raimundo, *The Intra-Religious Dialogue*, New York, 1978, Paulist Press.

Pannenberg, Wolfhart, *The Apostles' Creed in the Light of Today's Questions*, tr. Margaret Kohl, London, 1972, SCM.

Pascal, Blaise, *Pensées*, tr. A.J. Krailsheimer, Harmondsworth, 1966, Penguin. (This is the first translation into English to follow the order of the *Pensées* as Pascal left them at his death in 1662.)

Pirsig, Robert, *Zen and the Art of Motorcycle Maintenance*, London, 1974, The Bodley Head.

Postman, Neil, *Amusing Ourselves to Death: Public Discourse in the Age of Show Business*, London 1986 (1985), Methuen.

Postman, Neil, *Technopoly: the Surrender of Culture to Technology*, New York, 1992, Knopf.

Prozesky, Martin, *Religion and Ultimate Well-Being: An Explanatory Theory*, London, 1984, Macmillan.

Pruyser, Paul, *Between Belief and Unbelief*, London, 1975, (1974), Sheldon Press.

Race, Alan, *Christians and Religious Pluralism: Patterns in Christian Theology of Religions*, London, 1983, SCM.

Ramsey, I. T., *Models and Mystery*, London, 1964, Oxford University Press.

Reat, Noble Ross, *Buddhism, a History*, Berkeley, 1994, Asian Humanities Press.

Reps, Paul (compiler), *Zen Flesh, Zen Bones*, London 1971 (1957), Penguin.

Richards, I. A., *Mencius on the Mind: Experiments in Multiple Definition*, London, 1932, Kegan Paul.

Robertson, Roland, "Globalisation or Glocalisation?" *Journal of International Communication*, Vol. 1 (1994), pp.33-52.

Robinson, Fiona, "Rethinking Ethics in an Era of Globalisation," *Sussex Papers in International Relations*, no.2, 1996, International Relations & Politics Subject Group, University of Brighton

Rossano, Pietro "Christ's Lordship and Religious Pluralism in Roman Catholic Perspective," in Gerald H. Anderson and Thomas F. Stransky (ed.) *Christ's Lordship and Religious Pluralism*, New York, 1981, Orbis Books.

Rupp, George, *Beyond Existentialism and Zen: Religion in a Pluralistic World*, New York, 1979.

Sacks, Sheldon (ed.), *On Metaphor*, Chicago, 1978, University of Chicago Press.

Said, Edward W., *Beginnings, Intention and Method*, New York, 1975, Basic Books.

Samartha, Stanley, "The Lordship of Jesus Christ and Religious Pluralism," in Gerald H. Anderson and Thomas F. Stransky (ed.), *Christ's Lordship and Religious Pluralism*, New York, 1981, Orbis, pp. 19-36.

Schement, Jorge & Hester Stephenson, "Religion and the Information Society," in Daniel Stout & Judith Buddenbaum (ed.), *Religion and Mass Media: Audiences and Adaptations*, Thousand Oaks, 1996, Sage, pp. 261-289.

Schmid, Georg, *Principals of Integral Science of Religion*, The Hague, 1979, Mouton.

Schnapper, Edith B., *The Inward Odyssey: the Concept of The Way in the Great Religions of the World*, London, 1980, (1965), George Allen & Unwin.

Schultz, Quentin J., "Secular Television as Popular Religion," in R. Abelman & S. Hoover (ed.), *Religious Television: Controversies and Conclusions*, Norwood, 1990, Ablex, pp. 239-248.

Sharpe, Eric J., *Comparative Religion, A History*, London, 1975, Duckworth.

Shibles, Warren A., *Metaphor: an Annotated Bibliography and History*, Wisconsin, 1971, The Language Press.

Smart, Ninian, *A Dialogue of Religions*, London, 1960, SCM.

Smart, Ninian, *Secular Education and the Logic of Religions*, London, 1968, Faber.

Smart, Ninian, *The Science of Religion and the Sociology of Knowledge*, Princeton, 1973, Princeton University Press.

Smart, Ninian, *The Phenomenon of Religion*, New York, 1973, Herder & Herder.

Smart, Ninian, *Beyond Ideology: Religion and the Future of Western Civilization*, London, 1981 (the Gifford Lectures for 1979-1980).

Smart, Ninian, "Religion," in Eric Barnouw (ed.), *International Encyclopedia of Communication*, New York, 1988, OUP.

Smart, Ninian, *The World's Religions: Old Traditions and Modern Transformations*, Cambridge, 1989, Cambridge University Press.

Smart, Ninian, *Choosing a Faith*, London, 1995, Boyars.

Smart, Ninian, *Reflections in the Mirror of Religion* (ed. John P. Burns), London, 1997, Macmillan.

Smith, Huston, *The Purposes of Higher Education*, New York, 1955, Harper & Row.

Smith, Huston, *The Religions of Man*, New York, 1958, Harper & Row (*The World's Religions*, a completely revised and updated edition, appeared in 1991).

Smith, Jonathan Z., *Imagining Religion: From Babylon to Jonestown*, Chicago, 1982, Chicago University Press.

Smith, Wilfred Cantwell, *The Meaning and End of Religion*, London, 1978 (1962), SPCK.

Smith, Wilfred Cantwell, *The Faith of Other Men*, New York, 1972, (1963), Harper & Row.

Smith, Wilfred Cantwell, *Questions of Religious Truth*, London, 1967, Gollancz.

Sontag, Susan, *On Photography*, Harmondsworth, 1978 (1973), Penguin.

Soskice, Janet Martin, *Metaphor and Religious Language*, Oxford, 1985, Clarendon Press.

Spence, Jonathan, *The Memory Palace of Matteo Ricci*, London, 1985, Faber.

Spiegelberg, Herbert, "Amiel's 'New Phenomenology'", *Archiv für Geschichte Der Philosophie*, Vol. 49 (1967), pp. 201-214 .

Stace, W. T., *Mysticism and Philosophy*, London, 1960, Macmillan.

Staudenmaier, John, "The Media: Technique and Culture," in John Coleman and Miklos Tomka (ed.), *Concilium* 1993/6, pp.12-20.

Steiner, George, *After Babel: Aspects of Language and Translation*, London, 1975, OUP.

Steiner, George, *Language and Silence, Essays 1958-1966*, London, 1985, (1967), Faber.

Sterne, Laurence, *The Life and Opinions of Tristram Shandy*, London, 1950, (1760), Rupert Hart Davis, edited by J. A. Work.

Stockhausen, Karlheinz, "*Weltmusik*" in *Texte zur Musik: 1970-1977*, Koln, 1978. English translation by Berhard Radloff, "World Music," in *The Dalhousie Review*, Vol. 69 no. 3 (1989), pp. 318-324.

Strauss, Anselm, *Mirrors and Masks: the Search for Identity*, London, 1977 (1959), Martin Robinson.

Streng, Frederick J., *Emptiness: a Study in Religious Meaning*, New York, 1967, Abingdon.

Streng, Frederick J., "Religious Studies: Process of Transformation," in *The Proceedings of the American Academy of Religion*, Academic Study of Religion Section, 1974, pp. 118-131.

Swami, Shree Purohit, and W. B. Yeats (tr.), *The Ten Principal Upanishads*, London, 1971, (1937), Faber.

Taylor, Mark & Saarinen, Isa, *Imagologies*, London, 1994, Routledge.

Tehranian, Majid & Tehranian, Katharine Kia, "That Recurrent Suspicion: Democratisation in Global Perspective," in Philip Lee (ed.), *The Democratisation of Communication*, Cardiff, 1995, University of Wales Press, pp.38-74.

Thyssen, Johannes, "The Concept of 'Foundering' in Jaspers' Philosophy," pp. 297-235 in Paul Arthur Schilpp (ed.), *The Philosophy of Karl Jaspers*, New York, 1957, Tudor Publishing Co..

Tomlinson, John "Cultural Globalisation and Cultural Imperialism," in Ali Mohammadi (ed.), *International Communication and Globalisation*, London, 1997, Sage.

Toynbee, Arnold, *An Historian's Approach to Religion*, Oxford, 1956, Oxford University Press, (based on Toynbee's Gifford Lectures for 1952-53).

Toynbee, Arnold, *Mankind and Mother Earth*, London, 1976, Oxford University Press.

van Buren, Paul, *The Edges of Language*, London, 1972, SCM.

van der Leeuw, Gerardus, *Religion in Essence and Manifestation: A Study in Phenomenology*, tr. J. E. Turner, London 1938 (1933), George Allen & Unwin.

Waardenburg, J. D. J., "Research on Meaning in Religion," in Th. P. van Baaren and H. J. W. Drijvers (ed.), *Religion, Culture and Methodology*, The Hague, 1973, Mouton.

Wach, Joachim, *Sociology of Religion*, London, 1947, Kegan Paul, Trench, Trubner & Co. Ltd (in the *International Library of Sociology and Social Reconstruction* series, edited by Karl Mannheim).

Warren, Michael, *Communication and Cultural Analysis: a Religious View*, Westport, 1992, Bergin & Garvey.

Welbon, Guy Richard, *The Buddhist Idea of Nirvana and its Western Interpreters*, Chicago, 1968, University of Chicago Press.

Wiggins, James, *In Praise of Religious Diversity*, New York & London, 1996, Routledge.

Wilder, Thornton, *The Eighth Day*, London, 1967, Longmans, Green & Co.

Wisdom, John, "Gods," *Proceedings of the Aristotelian Society*, Vol. 45 (1944-5), pp.185-206.

Wittgenstein, Ludwig, *Notebooks 1914-1916*, Oxford, 1961, Basil Blackwell, edited by G. H. Von Wright and G. E. M. Anscombe, translated by G. E. M. Anscombe.

Woods, G. F., *Theological Explanations: A Study of the Meaning and Means of Explaining in Science, History and Theology*, Welwyn, 1958, James Nisbet & Co. Ltd.

Woods, James, Haughton, *The Value of Religious Facts: A Study of Some Aspects of the Science of Religion*, New York, 1899, Dutton.

Woods, James Haughton, *Practice and Science of Religion: A Study of Method in Comparative Religion*, London, 1906, Longmans, Green & Co.

Woodward, Kenneth, "Religion Observed: the Impact of the Medium on the Message," in John Coleman and Miklos Tomka (ed.), *Concilium* 1993/6, pp.99-110.

Woolf, Virginia, *Jacob's Room*, Harmondsworth, 1971, (1922), Penguin.

Zaehner, R. C. (ed.), *The Concise Encyclopaedia of Living Faiths*, London, 1971, (1959), Hutchinson.

Zaehner, R.C., *Hinduism*, Oxford, 1977, (1962), Oxford University Press.

Zaehner, R.C., *The City Within the Heart*, London, 1980, Unwin.

Zeldin, Theodore, *An Intimate History of Humanity*, London, 1995, Minerva.

Zimmer, Heinrich, *Artistic Form and Yoga in the Sacred Images of India*, Princeton, 1984 (1926), Princeton University Press, tr. Gerald Chapple & James Lawson.

Zimmer, Heinrich, *Philosophies of India*, (ed. Joseph Campbell) New Jersey, 1969 (1951), Princeton University Press.

Name Index

Subject Index

Certain headings in this Subject Index are asterisked. This is to indicate their importance in the text and the impossibility of indexing them exhaustively. Several items have simply been omitted from the index for the same reason ("hall of mirrors" and "pluralism," for example).